Fourth
in Science

Fourth Wave Feminism in Science Fiction and Fantasy

Volume 1. Essays on Film Representations, 2012–2019

Edited by VALERIE ESTELLE FRANKEL

McFarland & Company, Inc., Publishers
Jefferson, North Carolina

The essay "*Black Panther* and *Wonder Woman*: A Study in Feminist Representation" was adapted from the blog post "The Feminism of Black Panther vs. Wonder Woman" (2018) by Shoshana Kessock.

LIBRARY OF CONGRESS CATALOGUING-IN-PUBLICATION DATA

Names: Frankel, Valerie Estelle, 1980– editor of compilation.
Title: Fourth wave feminism in science fiction and fantasy / edited by Valerie Estelle Frankel.
Description: Jefferson : McFarland & Company, Inc., Publishers, 2019 | This work consists of two volumes. | Includes bibliographical references and index. | Contents: v. 1. Essays on film representations, 2012–2019
Identifiers: LCCN 2019040986 | ISBN 9781476677668 (v. 1 ; paperback) | ISBN 9781476677675 (v. 2 ; paperback) | ISBN 9781476637600 (v. 1 ; ebook) | ISBN 9781476638669 (v. 2 ; ebook) (paperback : acid free paper) ∞
Subjects: LCSH: Motion pictures—United States—History—21st century. | Feminism and motion pictures. | Women in motion pictures. | Sex role in motion pictures. | Science fiction, American—History and criticism. | Feminism and literature—United States—History—21st century. | Women in literature. | Women in literature.
Classification: LCC PN1995.9.W6 F6735 2019 | DDC 791.43082—dc23
LC record available at https://lccn.loc.gov/2019040986

BRITISH LIBRARY CATALOGUING DATA ARE AVAILABLE

ISBN (print) 978-1-4766-7766-8
ISBN (ebook) 978-1-4766-3760-0

Front cover: Rinko Kikuchi as Mako Mori in the 2013 film *Pacific Rim* (Warner Bros./Photofest)

Printed in the United States of America

McFarland & Company, Inc., Publishers
Box 611, Jefferson, North Carolina 28640
www.mcfarlandpub.com

Table of Contents

Introduction

What is fourth wave feminism? That's the number one response when I bring up the topic. This, I suppose, is why this collection is needed. Basically, now, in 2019, and indeed, for most of a decade, we've been telling a new type of story.

For those unfamiliar, the first wave in America and Europe was women seeking the vote. The second wave came in the sixties and seventies with demands for equal pay, Title IX, and the sexual revolution. Culture responded with feminist classics like *Diary of a Mad Housewife* (1970), *The Way We Were* (1973), *A Woman Under the Influence* (1974), *Alice Doesn't Live Here Anymore* (1974), *Annie Hall* (1977), *An Unmarried Woman* (1978), *Coming Home* (1978), *Norma Rae* (1979), *9 to 5* (1980), and arguably the Blaxploitation films. Further, in 1975, theorist Laura Mulvey's *Visual Pleasure and Narrative Cinema* emphasized how much films were angled toward men, and a trickle of edgier, female-directed stories began.

Science fiction, as always, pushed the imagery of what was possible. On television, *The Bionic Woman* and *Wonder Woman* showed off their might. On the big screen, Princess Leia drew a blaster and showed science fiction fans everywhere that a woman could be an action hero and not just scream for rescue. Soon enough, Ripley and Sarah Connor were leaping into action. Women could dream of a future of equality, and, by starring in those stories, help to create them. *Born in Flames* (1983), directed by Lizzie Borden, shows off activism in a futuristic New York when Adelaide Norris, a black lesbian feminist and trade unionist, dies in police custody. In comics, Stan Lee's *Fantastic Four*, *Avengers*, and *X-Men* were envisioning women as superheroes not sidekicks, though the big screen *Supergirl* (1984) was rather a flop. Acknowledging a new message, Disney retreated from their saccharine fifties' princess stories to offer more balanced animal tales.

After the pushback of postfeminism, the nineties offered films uncertain where rebellious women could go and what they should fight for, from *Thelma and Louise* (1991) to *Muriel's Wedding* (1994) to *Clueless* (1995), while

1

in fantasy, *Buffy the Vampire Slayer* spun off into a seven-year television show beside *Xena: Warrior Princess*. However, all these women were somehow ridiculous, campy and unrealistic, not meant to be fully respected as they killed vampires with hairspray or obsessed over a Hollywood wedding. This was the third wave, roughly synonymous with "girl power," as young women emphasized assertiveness through attraction and even materialism. In a beloved Disney Renaissance, *The Little Mermaid* (1989), *Beauty and the Beast* (1991) and *Aladdin* (1992) showed clever heroines saving their princes, though also reveling in glittering ball gowns. The Disney Princess line launched in the early 2000s, promoting dolls and costumes with which a generation of American girls could join the franchise.

Meanwhile, glamorous villainesses and girlfriends filled superhero films like *Batman and Robin* (1997), which also starred a miniskirted Batgirl, though she didn't make the title. *X-Men* (2000) with its endearing teen Rogue had stand-out superheroines, but Wolverine had to spectacularly save her as she hung chained over the city. *Lara Croft: Tomb Raider* (2001) encouraged everyone to stare as the camera focused on Angelina Jolie's padded bra. Charlize Theron's eponymous character in *Aeon Flux* (2005) has an open-front, open-back spandex jumpsuit, to say nothing of all the nudity.

The 2000s were problematic for superheroines. In comics, they descended into villainy as the Scarlet Witch wiped out nearly all the mutants and Wonder Woman committed murder. Outfits tightened to the point of mass internet protests. On the big screen, Halle Berry's 2004 *Catwoman* (in which she battles an evil makeup company in her exaggeratedly tight suit) spectacularly flopped. *Elektra* (2005) was painfully slow and serious, like a superhero film without the fun. Though these both suffered from bad writing, they convinced filmmakers to hold off on central superheroines for a full decade. In the bigger franchises, *Batman Begins* and *Spider-Man* relegated women to the role of girlfriend. *Superman Returns* (2006) had the hero ditching a pregnant Lois Lane who spent the film getting back at him for this treatment. *My Super Ex-Girlfriend* (2006) parodied women with powers. Girls, as *The Lego Movie* would later suggest, just ruined boy's stuff when they were allowed to play.

If a new film revealed that women could be strong without being campy, ludicrous, or underdressed, that was *The Hunger Games* (2012). Three film sequels followed (2013–2015) along with the *Divergent* franchise (2014–2016), *The 5th Wave* (2015), and an entire wave of dystopian teen novels. This only opened the gates for capable heroines leading action films: *The Heat* (2013), *Mad Max: Fury Road* (2015), *X-Men: Apocalypse* (2016), *Wonder Woman* (2017), *Ghost in the Shell* (2017), *Logan* (2017), *Atomic Blonde* (2017), *Red Sparrow* (2018), *Ant-Man and the Wasp* (2018), *Annihilation* (2018), *Bumblebee* (2018), *Black Panther* (2018), *Mortal Engines* (2018), *Alita: Battle Angel* (2019),

Men in Black International (2019), and *Captain Marvel* (2019). Echoing this trend, *Tomb Raider* (2018) starring Alicia Vikander, was rebooted from Jolie's version with a far less sexualized heroine.

Amid all these, *Star Wars: The Force Awakens* (2015) delighted fans with its chosen one Rey, accompanied by black and Latino friends. The next *Star Wars* film, *Rogue One* (2016), was also celebrated for its tough action heroine. However, other trends accompanied that one. The 2014 Gamergate movement had toxic fans harassing the creators of feminist computer games that decreased the violence against women. The all-female *Ghostbusters* (2016) launched with infuriated social media pushback from fans angry at "their franchise" being "rewritten." They also pushed back against the feminism of *Star Wars: The Last Jedi* (2017) as the female admiral and general gently taught the hotshot pilot to subsume his desires for the good of the community.

This in itself became a hallmark of the new fourth wave. "Toxic masculinity" and "rape culture" became buzzwords for a new era. After a 2012 rape in Steubenville, Ohio, horrified the public with a sexual assault documented on smart phones and uploaded to social media, this very evidence was used to convict the guilty. It galvanized a national conversation about rape and rape culture. The Facebook Rape Campaign, which went viral in 2013, with 60,000 tweets and 5,000 emails from members of over 100 women's social justice organizations, pushed companies to pull advertising until Facebook improved community standards concerning violence against women. The Bill Cosby sexual assault cases (2014), Isla Vista killings that sparked the #YesAllWomen campaign (2014), and trial of Jian Ghomeshi (2016) likewise galvanized social media. The #MeToo movement began in 2017 emphasized how many women had been assaulted, as survivors shared solidarity online, and the pervasiveness shocked many. The 2017 Women's March, the day after Donald Trump took office, was the largest single-day protest in U.S. history (estimated at four million marchers in the U.S. and seven million in other countries), supporting science, the environment, women's health, minority rights, immigration, and tolerance.

Further, the new internet era was bringing people together worldwide and alerting them to shared issues on sites like *Feministing* and *Everyday Sexism*. By this point, commentators and filmmakers alike had been clued into painful trends in storytelling like the inevitable death that would follow a happy lesbian couple or Gail Simone's "women in refrigerators" in which women, most notably superheroes' girlfriends, were killed or tortured to hurt the hero. The Final Girl of horror, mystical pregnancies, women existing only as background decoration—all came under discussion.

The Bechdel Test, too, was becoming well-known enough that creators would have women talk to each other about something besides a man at least for a few lines to avoid condemnation for sexism. In fact, alternative tests were proposed: comics writer Kelly Sue DeConnick insists in her "Sexy Lamp" test that women be distinguishable from such an object. The Ellen Willis test requires the story to make sense if the genders were flipped, while Jenn Northington's Tauriel test asks that a woman in the film show competence. The Mako Mori test gives a woman her own plot arc. Kate Hagen's test asks whether crowd scenes and bit parts are half women—a shocking number are not. Some suggest looking for female crew, directors, or screenwriters. Other critics look for minorities of different races or orientations to be well-rounded or have plots besides supporting white, straight protagonists.[1]

While this debate didn't make films perfect, it emphasized a new awareness and desire to be more inclusive. Feminist fans could consider these pitfalls as well as bigger story issues as they commented on sites like *The Mary Sue* (in itself a commentary on flat female characters) or *Feminist Frequency*. Sometimes they even changed film content, as protests at the two planned female characters in *Star Wars: The Force Awakens* led creators to fill the screen with a spectrum of competent women. The "strong female character" who was powerful and attractive but devoid of much personality and often just supported the more likeable man (Trinity, Elektra, Black Widow, Gamora, Tauriel, Wyldstyle, and all the women in *X-Men: Apocalypse* and *Suicide Squad*) was gradually replaced by fun-loving but imperfect Shuri, Moana, and Wonder Woman.

Though it certainly suffers from "strong female character" syndrome, *Logan* (2017) showed the death of Wolverine (himself anchoring the X-Men franchise with seven previous films) as he passed the title off to a little girl (mirroring her status as Wolverine in the comics). Marvel comics themselves were doing plenty of popular race- and/or gender-flipped legacy characters like Miles Morales' Spider-Man, Kate Bishop's Hawkeye, Kamala Kahn's Ms. Marvel, Gwenpool, Moon Girl, Lady Thor, and Iron Heart—Iron Man's teen African American prodigy successor. Women and people of color were emphasizing that the world of superheroes should be shared by all.

Other films race-lifted iconic characters, famously casting Aquaman as Hawaiian actor Jason Momoa in *Justice League* (2017) and the rest of the DC Extended Universe. *A Wrinkle in Time* (2018) made Meg Murray mixed-race, while the breakout play *Harry Potter and the Cursed Child* (2016) cast a black actress as Hermione. *Thor: Ragnarok* (2017) made multiracial Latina actress Tessa Thompson a truly mighty Valkyrie and partner for Thor. Admittedly, *Doctor Strange* (2016), *Marvel's Iron Fist* (2017–2018) and *Ghost in the Shell* (2017) were all criticized for casting white characters in Asian storylines, emphasizing that the trend was still imperfect.

Wonder Woman broke ground as Patty Jenkins became the first female director to helm a major superhero film as well as a film that pulled in more than $100 million in its opening weekend. Though still rare in Hollywood, female directors were triumphing in *Frozen, A Wrinkle in Time, Cloud Atlas, Jupiter Ascending, Kung Fu Panda 2, Bend It Like Beckham, Bride & Prejudice, Deep Impact, The Kids Are All Right, Belle, The Virgin Suicides, Persepolis, Selma, The Hurt Locker,* and *Lost in Translation.* Likewise, female scriptwriters brought their work to audiences with *Fifty Shades of Grey, Guardians of the Galaxy, Captain Marvel, Alice in Wonderland* (2010), *Maleficent, Divergent, Tomb Raider* (2018), *Nanny McPhee, The Danish Girl, Kick-Ass, Miss Peregrine's Home for Peculiar Children, King Kong, The Lord of the Rings, The Hobbit,* and all the *Twilight* films.

A few more disabled characters arrived beyond Professor X in the *X-Men* franchise, in *Mad Max: Fury Road, Finding Dory, The Notebook, The Vow, In Darkness,* and *Me Before You. The Good Doctor, Sherlock,* and *Fantastic Beasts* starred characters on the autistic spectrum. Older powerful heroines began taking more significantly central roles in films and shows like *Star Wars: The Last Jedi, Wonder Woman, Ocean's 8, How to Get Away with Murder, Star Trek Discovery, Orphan Black, Harry Potter and the Cursed Child, Doctor Strange, Thor: Ragnarok, Suicide Squad,* and *A Wrinkle in Time.*

Trans characters, too, began appearing much more frequently. There were a cluster of films like *Boy Meets Girl* (2014), *Tangerine* (2015), *3 Generations* (2015), *The Danish Girl* (2015), *Just Charlie* (2017), and *A Fantastic Woman* (2017). Beyond this, however, trans main characters arrived in the shows *Supergirl, Orange Is the New Black, Pose, Sense 8,* and *Glee.* The year 2018 brought the teen fantasy film *Every Day* in which the protagonist inhabits a different body daily. Respected gay central characters made progress as well, as they finally broke into the biggest television franchises—*Star Trek, Doctor Who,* and the DC Arrowverse. Even Disney's *Beauty and the Beast* (2017) slipped in a gay Lefou, though Lando in *Solo* (2018), Albus and Scorpius in *Cursed Child,* and Dumbledore in *Fantastic Beasts: The Crimes of Grindelwald* (2018) were what fans describe as "queerbaiting"—suggestively open to a homosexual pairing but not explicitly gay.

Disney, once the proponent of the most traditional romances and fairytale plots, began to subvert and challenge their previous messages as Tiana insists on earning her dream through hard work and Kristoff lectures Anna on the ridiculousness of love at first sight. *Maleficent* (2014) deconstructs the Sleeping Beauty fairytale and Disney's 1959 treatment of it, enquiring what patriarchal cruelty has made her into a villainess. In this collection, Melissa Wehler considers the film's new messages about self-love and the mother-daughter bond.

Pixar's beloved *Finding Nemo* (2003) gender-flipped to *Finding Dory* (2016). Meanwhile, *Inside Out* (2015) delves into the psychology of the post-millennial girl, emphasizing the angst of an environmentally and financially uncertain world even while encouraging all children to embrace their emotions. Disney's *Ralph Breaks the Internet* (2018) let Sarah Silverman's spunky racer girl Vanellope von Schweetz deconstruct all the princesses. She also fully carries half the adventure while combatting, of all things, Ralph's smothering neediness. The princesses of *Brave* (2012), *Frozen* (2013), and *Moana* (2016) choose not to marry at all, with a new feminist message explored in this collection by Lisann Anders, who decides these single princesses (along with those in *The Princess and the Frog* and *Tangled*) are offering a new, more independent message and coming-of-age adventure. Ananya Chatterjee and Nisarga Bhattacharjee consider Elsa and Merida beside *Finding Dory,* considering how Dory's marginalization can generate discourses of empowerment for the millennial audience. In all these films, female relationships claim center stage, in a genre that previously had emphasized traditional romance and friendships with mostly male sidekicks.

The new cartoon heroines are so strong that little boys sing "Let It Go" on the playground and wear Elsa costumes as they play with new, tougher Leia and Rey action figures from the *Forces of Destiny* line. Even as Disney's new heroines appeal to both genders, some male heroes are embarking on a traditionally feminine path. When these appear in children's or teen films, they model alternate routes to power besides slashing with a sword. In her own essay, filmmaker Patti McCarthy considers Dreamworks' *Rise of the Guardians* (2012) such a story, in which Jack Frost succeeds through traditionally marginalized trickster powers and ancient moon magic as well as a gleeful childishness.

While all this strength and diversity is certainly celebrated in recent non-genre films (*Hidden Figures, Ocean's 8, Dear White People, Beatriz at Dinner, Crazy Rich Asians, Disobedience, Battle of the Sexes, Girls Trip*) as well as other mediums from comic books to video games, this collection specifically is limited to science fiction and fantasy films. These emphasize a world uncircumscribed by reality in which women can either turn invisible or reboot the universe in pointed cultural commentary. Film, meanwhile, is the great threshold—the most conventional of mediums as it is the costliest to create. What books, comics, computer games, and even television have done for some time makes the greatest splash on the big screen. An essay collection on fourth wave science fiction and fantasy television is nonetheless lined up as a companion book to this one, covering this trend in *Star Trek, Doctor Who, Supergirl,* and so on.

While the second and third waves were criticized for featuring middle-class white women's struggles, the fourth wave showed a much more fiercely inclusive model. Aamir Aziz and Farwa Javed consider how social media campaigns have reached out to the marginalized and created a community of women demanding respect in real life and in fiction. Films have become increasingly multicultural like *Pacific Rim* (2013), whose heroine was so strong that she inspired a "Mako Mori Test" as an option for judging the feminism of stories. Here, Tim Posada considers the test in the context of the film and its strengths.

Black Panther (2018) blew viewers away with its celebration of an uncolonized Africa filled with blazingly competent women. Shoshana Kessock explores how these are more feminist than *Wonder Woman* in her own film, as Shuri, Okoye, and Nakia work beside the superhero as well-respected equals. My own essay weighs *Black Panther*'s celebration of competent women against the gender battles seen in *Ghostbusters* and *Star Wars: The Last Jedi*, while considering online responses to the feminist modeling in each.

Carol Zitzer-Comfort and José I. Rodríguez consider what Wonder Woman's groundbreaking 2017 film has brought to the canon through the lens of invitational rhetoric as a path to social change in "Riding the Waves of Feminism in *Wonder Woman*: A Shock Heard 'Round the World." Meanwhile, Christian Jimenez considers the film in context of the original Golden Age comics with their differing perspectives and messages. Of course, other superheroines are taking the big screen beside the longest-lasting feminist icon among them. Don Tresca looks at the evolution of Ant-Man and the Wasp, from Silver Age comics to their treatment in the MCU films.

The establishment of new rules and deconstruction of traditional genres continues. Martin Ricksand examines the complex gender balance needed to form the heroine of *Mad Max: Fury Road*. Fernando Gabriel Pagnoni Berns, Canela Ailén Rodriguez Fontao and Mariana S. Zárate consider the flipping of horror tropes like the Final Girl in subversive films *The Final Girls* and *Happy Death Day*. In "Katniss, the Naive Virgin: Fourth Wave Heroines Recentering Neoconservative Values," Paula Talero Álvarez weighs how *The Hunger Games* saga weakens feminist ideals as Katniss is often more asexual than empowered by her womanly side. On the other side of the curve, Alexis Brooks de Vita tackles *Annihilation* as an example of the "New Weird" with its fantastically gendered symbolism as well as an example of millennials' and post-millennials' view of the new era.

The fourth wave has decidedly arrived, establishing that all main characters can be gay, trans, or nonwhite instead of playing Falcon or Black Widow beside Captain America. Utopias like *Black Panther* celebrate non–European alternate paths. Disney princesses reject the old patterns. Dystopian heroines lead uprisings against the gloating force of the patriarchy. Now women can be Ghostbusters or Jedi, captain Stormtroopers or even dispense advice like Yoda. There's pushback, but progress keeps coming. Most of all, Wonder Woman can be well-rounded, funny and heroic without being campy or laughable. More superheroines like Wasp and Captain Marvel take to the screen—modestly dressed at last. One thing is clear—this new wave of storytelling will create a bright, caring generation of children … those who understand that the future can be female.

NOTE

1. http://geekfeminism.wikia.com/wiki/Media_test offers a long list of options. Likewise, https://projects.fivethirtyeight.com/next-bechdel applies many tests to a list of films.

Section I
NEW RULES

Passing the Mako Mori Test

Female Agency in Men's Science Fiction and Fantasy Cinema

TIM POSADA

When *Pacific Rim* (2013) premiered, critics praised its approach to multiculturalism in a futuristic setting, *The Daily Beast*'s Marlow Stern lauding it as a "refreshing" departure from the Eurocentric norm of most big-budget franchises. Even though the primary protagonist is white, he resides in a pluralistic culture where ethnic and racial groups maintain their identities unfettered by the myth of a post-racial future that often becomes a pseudonym for a one culture's dominance. Still, amidst this utopian future, very few women fill important positions in the military program charged with global defense against skyscraper-sized aliens. *Vulture*'s Kyle Buchanan criticized the film for this, noting that of the fifty-six credited actors, only three women receive speaking parts.

While *Pacific Rim* succeeds in one respect, it flounders in another, also failing the Bechdel test, developed from a feminist comic strip creator, which asks for bare minimum female representation built into three simple criteria: "One, [the film] has to have at least two women in it, who, two, talk to each other about, three, something besides a man" (Bechdel 22). However, in a post on Tumblr, user spider-xan chastised "white women" for boycotting the film because it failed the Bechdel test. As an Asian woman, she had a different perspective on a key character in the film, Mako Mori:

> someone like Mako—a well-written Japanese woman who is informed by her culture without being solely defined by it, without being a racial stereotype, and gets to carry the film and have character development—almost NEVER comes along in mainstream Western media. And honestly—someone like her will probably not appear again for a very long time.

In response, fellow Tumblr user chaila proposed another tool to complement the Bechdel test, the Mako Mori test, which requires that a film include "a) at least one female character; b) who gets her own narrative arc; c) that is not about supporting a man's story" (Romano). The test has since been added to *Geek Feminism*'s digital archive and one user on social media site Letterboxd continues to compile a list of films that pass the test, finding just over 470 that pass, dating back to 1928's *The Passion of Joan of Arc* (Brittany). Moreover, since *Pacific Rim* premiered in July 2013, more than 150 films have passed.[1]

While the Mako Mori test applies to female-lead films, the goal here is to examine instances where heroes are surrounded by heroines in science fiction and fantasy films (SFF), mimicking the premise of *Pacific Rim*, a film with a male lead *and* a fully realized female character. This analysis tests Jeffrey A. Brown's claim that a heroine's presence on "a predominantly male team or partnered with a male" can result in "a possibility for strong female characters," subsequently bringing "the topic of gender roles and sexuality to the forefront" (*Beyond Bombshells* 55). In particular, SFF cinema can rupture gender expectations in ways unavailable to other genres; SFF can "imagine empowering social and political roles for marginalized people" (Allen 20). At its greatest heights, SFF cinema provides women a unique platform as stories "boldly go where no one has gone before," borrowing *Star Trek: The Next Generation*'s gender-inclusive tagline.

Of the less than two hundred films since *Pacific Rim* premiered, if the Letterboxd list is partially accurate, only fifteen SFF films with male leads—normally named after male titular characters—pass, or come close to passing:

1. *The Wolverine* (July 2013)
2. *Ex Machina* (April 2014)
3. *Mad Max: Fury Road* (May 2015)
4. *The Martian* (September 2015)
5. *Batman v Superman: Dawn of Justice* (March 2016)
6. *The Huntsman: Winter's War* (April 2016)
7. *Captain America: Civil War* (May 2016)
8. *Doctor Strange* (November 2016)
9. *Logan* (March 2017)
10. *Spider-Man: Homecoming* (July 2017)
11. *Thor: Ragnarok* (November 2017)
12. *Black Panther* (February 2018)
13. *Pacific Rim: Uprising* (March 2018)
14. *Deadpool 2* (May 2018)
15. *Solo: A Star Wars Story* (May 2018)

In these films, three depictions of female characters occur to varying degrees. First, female characters move beyond romantic interests, from overt subversion (*Ex Machina, Fury Road*) to more positive displays of romantic entan-glement (*Black Panther*). Second, even as supporting characters, or sidekicks, in men's stories, they are still afforded more agency on screen, especially in superhero films (*Batman v Superman, Ragnarok*). When this occurs, fandom tends to favor these performances over the male leads. Third, female char-acters move from margin to center as powerful characters, no longer damsels in distress or objects of desire (*Doctor Strange, Winter's War*). This is not an exhaustive list but an overview of popular feature films often with budgets north of $100 million, in which producers are less likely to take risks (and women in prominent positions carry that label, especially in foreign markets resistant to egalitarian messages on screen), making the presence of Mako Mori characters noteworthy, even if they are not entirely successful.

Passing the Test

Pacific Rim clearly focuses on a white male protagonist, Raleigh Becket, but the partner most suited for him to "drift," the pseudo-science explanation for "sharing the neural load" required to operate a skyscraper-high jaeger machine, is Mako Mori, played by Rinko Kikuchi. The two remain close, but their relationship is never romantic. Further, when they drift for the first time, an overwhelming experience for rookie Mako, she loses focus and *drifts* into a traumatic memory. As she relives the moment she lost her family, Raleigh cannot help. He tries to snap her out of the memory, entering it to do so, but her trauma is too great. Only deactivating the jaeger shakes her free. Mako does not improve with aid from a male character; she confronts her trauma alone. Finally, when she must drift for combat, she defeats a skyscraper-high kaiju following her declaration in Japanese, "For my family!" Surrounded by men, her thoughts are not of them but loved ones she seeks to avenge.

The Mako Mori test refers to any female character who moves her own story forward unrestrained by, or in this case alongside, male narratives. Like the Bechdel test, this is not meant to be the only measure of a film's use of female representation, but it does fill in gaps. For example, *Gravity* (2013) fails the Bechdel test because the film's female astronaut stranded in space never speaks to another woman. As a high-profile film featuring a female lead, *Gravity* is worth consideration beyond the confines of one barometer, and the Mako Mori test fills in such a gap. That said, films primarily about men create a challenge. What qualifies as "not about supporting a man's story," as the test requires?

While more than fifteen SFF films might pass the Mako Mori test, they do so in minimal ways, and including them here both muddies this analysis and confuses what the test seeks to accomplish: highlighting women's note-worthy character arcs, something that does not occur in these films. Elle in *Godzilla* (2014) earns points for staying in San Francisco to provide medical aid when Godzilla and two other monsters approach, but, subverting this independence, her choice occurs to keep her nearby, making the reunion with her husband, the film's primary hero, more satisfactory. Similarly, Mason Weaver in *Kong: Skull Island* (2017) goes through part of an arc, transitioning from jaded war photographer to Kong sympathizer, but all these realizations occur alongside a male character and then in service of the Kong himself as a damsel to be saved. Finally, *Edge of Tomorrow* (2014) includes a very notable female character in elite soldier Rita, but since the film revolves around a day resetting with each death of William Cage, only he can receive a complete story arc by narrative design.

In a more detailed example, *Avengers: Infinity War* (2018) passes the Bechdel test but is considered as a problematic Mako Mori recruit. The film includes several female characters, but their arcs only minimally branch into Mako Mori territory. As *The Mary Sue* claims, the film mostly "fails" its female characters (Baugher). This occurs by marking them more as romantic inter-ests (Gamora, Scarlet Witch), placing them in the background (Mantis, Black Widow), displaying their suffering more than others (Nebula), or in one case, through the act of "fridging," defined in fannish parlance as killing a female character to move a male character's story forward (Griffin 126). Gamora comes closest to fulfilling the Mako Mori criteria, but when she is fridged, her arc's conclusion serves as a defining moment for Thanos, her killer, and vengeful motivation for her lover, Star Lord. In minimal ways, however, *Infin-ity War* does pass. Nebula, a "daughter" of Thanos, exerts independence from her aggressor's patriarchal upbringing (beginning in 2014's *Guardians of the Galaxy*) by gradually planning his demise. Her plan fails, but she remains one of the only characters in the entire film to traverse a galactic landscape on her own, joining the fight against Thanos in the final act of her own voli-tion. Though her revenge is directed toward a male character, this motivation aligns with Mako's own desire to defeat the monsters who killed her family. Further, Wakandan scientist Shuri, sister of the Black Panther, is the only tech genius with a clear mission who performs her task without direct help from men. On the battlefield, Scarlet Witch, prompted to join the fight despite boyfriend Vision's vulnerable state in Shuri's care, teams up with Black Widow and Okoye to take on villain Proxima Midnight, three women fighting a fourth. This moment is brief, however, in a 149-minute film, serving as one of the few breaks from men's stories as the central male characters deal with their inner and interpersonal conflicts while battling the male supervillain. The result is a film with many powerful women, but few notable Mako Mori candidates.

Subverted Desire

Popular cinema often features an active male protagonist and passive female characters, a common dilemma Laura Mulvey, the predominant writer on the sexist gaze, claims characterizes most, if not all, Hollywood films (20). The female romantic interest normally falls prey to this depiction as a direct object of desire in *Homecoming, Doctor Strange, Civil War, Batman v Superman*, and *Deadpool 2*, the latter even fridges that love interest throughout most of the film. Across these films, if a female character functions as a romantic interest, her story likely is intertwined with the male protagonist, meaning her chances of passing the Mako Mori test greatly dwindle. Still, passing is possible. Amidst all the films analyzed here, three feature agentive women whom are love interests: *Huntsman, Black Panther*, and *Solo*, while two others confront male-female relations in a different way.

Fury Road and *Ex Machina* confront love's perverse forms. In *Fury Road*, the Five Wives seek to escape their patriarchal arrangement with Immortan Joe, who sends all his War Boys after them. The visual of hundreds of men chasing after the Five Wives in muscle cars addresses patriarchy head on, while *Ex Machina* transforms men into "victims" thanks to a reliance on "heterosexual stereotyping" (Mackinnon 606). Here, two men often discuss romance and gender dynamics directly, one falling in love with robot Ava, programmed to mimic a heterosexual woman. By the film's end, Caleb, the primary protagonist, plans to liberate Ava and run away with her, but he is a patsy, used and discarded. Ava desires to be free of the glass cage she inhabits, but her identity is not rooted in male intimacy promised upon her freedom; she resides beyond "the male circuit of power/knowledge" (Jelača 396). The male characters read gender into her character, one seeing her as a damsel in distress and the other as a literal object. Ultimately, however, Ava is a "femme fatale" who violently resists "masculinity's imagined superiority" (615). Ava and the women of *Fury Road* confront (toxic) masculinity, ultimately killing or banishing those who both oppress and/or underestimate them. Still, this is not the only depiction of heterosexual coupling in Mako Mori films; both *Black Panther* and *Solo* present very different perspectives.

As Délice Williams notes, *Black Panther*, as a film that imagines an African utopia untouched by colonialism, is not about the Black experience as understood through the African diaspora: characters like Nakia "want to help suffering people, but not necessarily because they believe that those people are like them" (27). The citizens of the fictional nation of Wakanda remain in isolation, attempting to preserve their way of life, hiding their progress from outsiders. T'Challa/Black Panther might care about the surrounding world, but he remains more involved in state and family affairs as the newly minted king. In contrast, his ex, Nakia, aware of her privileged position, is first introduced passing as a victim of a mass kidnapping in a neighboring region. She is a heroic figure independent of her relationship with T'Challa, actually ending their courtship to continue her work. She still cares for him but resists becoming a queen, continually identifying more as a "spy," trying to open Wakanda's borders. While her story is integrated into T'Challa's, she does not become subservient. Only when he changes, accepts Wakanda's responsibility to the world, as Nakia champions, working beside her instead of insisting on her retirement, does she decide to stay by his side.

Okoye serves as another example of a love interest without subservience baggage. To start, fan criticism occurred surrounding the alleged removal of an implicate lesbian moment between Okoye and another member of the all-female warrior guard the Dora Milaje (Robinson). Instead, Okoye is married to a man, W'Kabi, though her story does not merely complement his. She functions as a general, navigating loyalties to her country. As T'Challa's body-guard, her story is partially bound to his, but she remains a powerful character, making her own choices and taking pride in her heritage, a point that taps into the Tumblr user's original intent for the Mako Mori test when she praises a character for being "informed by her culture but without being solely defined by it." This is obvious when Okoye fights in a South Korean nightclub, donning a wig as a disguise which she excitedly removes during combat, resisting "the idea of trying to fit into the outside world's normative, Eurocentric beauty ideals" (Allen 21). While she is informed by her own cultural identity, in a later scene, she also proves she is not "solely" controlled by it when she finally turns on villain Killmonger, who has won her sworn loyalty by taking the throne from T'Challa in ritual combat. Her husband leads an attack in support of Killmonger, while Okoye breaks with tradition to fight a leader she believes does not deserve the throne. She even comically disarms her husband when his charging rhinoceros breaks its attack to lick her in greeting. In this moment, their relationship becomes a weapon she can use to win the day as much as her fighting prowess.

The most problematic example of a love interest occurs in *Solo*, which passes the Mako Mori test with a disclaimer. Qi'ra is clearly Han Solo's love interest, but she rejects him to follow her own path in her final scene. Throughout the film, she is the object of Han's gaze, and she seems to recip-rocate until the enemy is defeated and she abandons plans to run away with Han. Instead, she contacts the head of the criminal underworld to which she reports, directly communicating with the once Sith Lord, Darth Maul. While this scene can be interpreted as a choice to leave one man for another, the novelization of the film provides more context. In it, "Qi'ra had no idea who was on the end of that call when she made it" (Whitbrook). Her choice is not one man over another but ambition to run a criminal empire over a relationship with Han. Her story may end in tragedy, but in this moment, she chooses not to be a damsel swooped away.

Beyond Sidekicks

Contemporary superhero films pepper their plots and subplots with women, finally doing so with less female undressing and damsel scenarios (though they are still commonplace). In *Ragnarok*, for example, Valkyrie is a fully realized, fully clothed character. Introduced as a once great warrior now drowning her regrets in alcohol, she is unmoved by Thor's many pleas to help him escape captivity on the planet Sakaar and aid in his battle against a foe she once failed to defeat. Only time and the right circumstances change her mind, not any one piece of dialogue exchanged between hero and heroine. Following her decision to finally help Thor, the two discuss her change of heart, Thor commenting on her excessive drinking, which is not her actual problem:

> VALKYRIE: I've spent years in a haze trying to forget my past. Sakaar seemed like the best place to drink, and to forget, and to die, one day.
> THOR: Well, I was thinking that you drink too much, and it was probably gonna kill you.
> VALKYRIE: I don't plan to stop drinking. But I don't wanna forget. I can't turn away anymore. So, if I'm gonna die, well, it might as well be driving my sword through the heart of that murderous hag.

The Mary Sue's Kaila Hale-Stern notes the film fails the Bechdel test, but she cannot entirely condemn the film, in part, because of Valkyrie, described as "a fully fleshed-out, fully nuanced woman warrior, unsympathetic when you meet her, totally uncompromising, brash and flawed and resilient." She even claims the film passes "the Kaila test," but her praise for both Valkyrie and the film's female villain, Hela, align well with the Mako Mori test.

While Valkyrie moves the story forward on her own, her prominent role serves a greater purpose in the Marvel Cinematic Universe; she will be back in some capacity, big or small. A cinematic universe obliges individual films to expand their scope, construct stories that both survive independently and keep an eye on the next entry. Wonder Woman's presence in *Batman v Superman* meets this criteria much like Black Widow's introduction in *Iron Man 2* (2010). In the film, though her presence distracts from the central conflict between Batman and Superman and adds more to a bloated story, critics considered her the film's standout. Starting in the Marvel Cinematic Universe, audiences often meet new characters in other superheroes' films. To consider Wonder Woman—from her introduction at Lex Luthor's mansion in search of hidden documents to her decision to stay and fight—a Mako Mori victory—is only part of the full story as the photo she seeks teases the plot of *Wonder Woman* and her team-up prepares for her character arc in *Justice League* (2017). Of course, the idea that she needed an introduction prior to her film also reveals concern about a cold introduction in *Wonder Woman* (2017), unnecessary anxieties considering the film's popularity as well as worldwide box office gross of $821,847,012, more than any other superhero origin film at the time.

The role of women evolves across two Wolverine films, *The Wolverine* and *Logan*. In *The Wolverine*, Wolverine/Logan engages in a relationship with one woman, Mariko, while he copes with the ghost of a woman he both loved and had to kill in *X-Men: The Last Stand* (2006), Jean Grey. However, his relationship with Yukio (Rila Fukushima), a sword-wielding mutant with the ability to see people's deaths, is different. While she enters his life out of obligation to a male employer, she remains in it once the events of the film conclude, a sign of Logan's evolution "from a narcissistic masculinity to a more 'dialogic masculinity'" (Miczo 143). While this alone does not make Yukio a fully realized character (that occurs through her independent investigation throughout the film), it does set the stage for Wolvey's final journey in *Logan* when he encounters Laura, a mutant clone created from his DNA.

For *Vulture*'s Emily Yoshida, Laura is primarily defined by "the silent, deadly little girl" trope, including characters like *Firefly*'s River Tam, *Stranger Things*' Eleven, and Hit-Girl from *Kick-Ass* (2010), though she serves a foul-mouthed revision of this type. Yoshida goes so far as to say, "Laura and her ilk aren't characters," despite praise from others that Laura has been described as "kick-ass" and "a little badass." While debate continues regarding the function of this convention, particularly when male writers employ it, Laura, or X-23, enjoys her own arc throughout the film. Though she is introduced as a child Logan must protect, she is, in fact, "badass," with duel claws similar to her (clone) father's. At one point, she leaves Logan, seeking safety with a group of young mutants on the run from seedy mercenaries. When Logan dies, the final moments of the film belong to her as she embarks on a new life, not merely bidding farewell to her a father figure but reflecting on the X-Men's legacy, in a scene when she tilts a cross on his buried body sideways to resemble an X instead. As *The Washington Post*'s Alyssa Rosenberg says:

> though Logan is able to tell Laura "Don't be what they made you" before his own death, it's not remotely clear that his affection for her and the brief protection he provided her will be enough to make up for the circumstances of her birth and upbringing, or the lingering psychological effects of violence she inflicted on others as she fought for her freedom.

As a sidekick, Laura does help Logan learn a final lesson about the importance of family, but the film ends like *Ex Machina* with her story left unresolved, and with rumors of her own spinoff perhaps to come (Couch). This is a clear passing of the torch from aging male to assertive female, mirroring a similar transition in the comics.

Other superhero films provide minor examples of female character arcs that barely break Mako Mori territory. Black Widow decides for herself whether to support Iron Man and later Captain America in the superhero standoff in *Civil War*. While the both sides of the argument—superheroes regulated by governments versus superheroes dictating their own actions—are embodied in male characters, she turns the tide of their major battle by switching sides and eventually goes into hiding when she must deal with the consequences of her choice. In *Deadpool 2*, which fridges an important female character from the first film, Domino (a mostly white superheroine with black spots in the comics but here played by Black actress Zazie Beetz), teams up with the titular character because her mutant power, luck, guides her to the "merc with a mouth," as he is called. She later encounters the facility where she was raised and liberates the children in it, leaving the other male characters involved in a separate fight. Further, *Homecoming*'s most notable female character, Michelle (Zendaya), rarely interacts with Spider-Man/Peter Parker, spending most of the film on her own. She eventually opens up to classmates, revealing her nickname M.J.—the same nickname of Spidey's love interest Mary Jane in the comics—but no clear romantic attraction is established. These examples remain minor victories that barely pass the test, but they are often praised for providing unique and refreshing elements to otherwise entirely masculine narratives.

The Power

Mako Mori films approach power in unique ways. Even when Thor uncovers the god of thunder within, fighting without his beloved hammer, he still cannot defeat his much more powerful sister Hela; only a joint attack with Valkyrie can stall Hela long enough until brother Loki summons an ancient foe to finally defeat her. Elsewhere in *Solo*, the titular character's combat abilities pale compared to Qi'ra's, as she saves him from the highly trained crime lord, Dryden Vos. In many cases, power is shared, easily seen in *The Huntsman* as titular huntsmen Eric and Sara fight together, equal in ability and egalitarian in their relationship. In more than half these films, power is no longer understood as masculine but something equally distributed or, in some instances, female dominant.

When casting was announced for *Doctor Strange*, media outlets chastised

Marvel Studio's omission of a central Asian character, a move familiar to films like *Ghost in the Shell* (2017), "criticized for centering EuroAmerican agency through whitewashing, yellowface, and plots that valorize the white savior complex" (Ho 591). In *Doctor Strange*, the Ancient One, a centuries-old Tibetan man in the comics, would be played by Tilda Swinton, a white woman, a move that "[suggests] a strategic whitewashing of Hollywood films, one that avoids casting Chinese people as unlikable villains or drawing attention to hot-button political issues like Tibet" all in favor of the global box office (Kokas 35). For the film's director, Scott Derrickson, this was an attempt to avoid stereotyping. "We weren't going to have the Ancient One as the Fu Manchu magical Asian on the hill being the mentor to the white hero," Derrickson told *The Daily Beast*, later adding that an Asian female character would result in "a straight-up Dragon Lady" (Yamato).

While *Beast* reporter Jen Yamato concludes such attempts to remain "one kind of woke" result in something "most unfortunately unwoke," she does praise Swinton's interpretation of the character, who "has far more to do, and more on her mind, than just help Strange realize his super-powered potential—although yes, she also does that. She battles, she leads, she ponders the mystery of life and beyond with a complexity that belies the sparse details of her background." *Doctor Strange* functions in a unique way alongside the Mako Mori test. As Yamato points out, the Ancient One is the most powerful sorcerer on Earth, she teaches a man the mystic arts, and her story does not merely accent protagonist Stephen Strange's. Even when she dies, an inciting incident borrowed from the comics, her final moments revolve around her current circumstance, not his. "Death is what gives life meaning, to know your days are numbered, your time is short," she says. "You'd think after all this time, I'd be ready. But look at me, stretching one moment out into a thousand just so that I can watch the snow."

Fury Road creates equal power between Max and Furiosa, who is actually the "heroic agent" of the film (Yates 360). Their first encounter is a fair fight, and when they work together, they share the burden of protecting the Five Wives equally in their firearms proficiency (though Furiosa is a better shot with a sniper rifle). Certain feminist critics argued Furiosa's plan to reach the Green Place, what she believes is the last fertile refuge still run by women, invokes "the long-standing association between women and nature" which trends to "depict women as docile, unintellectual and ruled by their physicality" (Yates 354). Still, *Fury Road*'s "Edenic" hero is not male but female; Furiosa is the one who puts all the film's events into motion and personally defeats Immortan Joe, an act that allows to her become the new leader of Joe's kingdom (360). Further, as the women in the film "ascend to agency," Max is not "reduced," but he "still represents hegemonic white masculinity," hence the film concludes with his decision to leave, allowing Furiosa to lead divorced from patriarchy (Yates 360–361).

The assumed thesis of this analysis is that most Mako Mori films present more positive depictions of women on screen. If that is generally the case, *Winter's War* is the exception. For a film with three high-profile and powerful women—one a skilled warrior and two endowed with supernatural abilities—their stories remain troublesome. To start, *Winter's War* has been declared a victory for women's pay in Hollywood following the 2014 Sony hack. *Winter's War* star Chris Hemsworth was originally paid substantially more than Charlize Theron, even though both reprised roles in the sequel to *Snow White and the Huntsman* (2012). Because of the hack's forced transparency, Theron negotiated "a deal worth more than $10 million, the same as Hemsworth" (Smith).

However, her star-power does not transfer as effectively into the film itself. As *Bustle* notes, what should be "a game-changer for feminism in fairy-tales" is "a frustrating step back for women on-screen" (Funk). To start, Queen Fraya hardens her heart following the death of her baby girl at the hands of her lover and becomes a rigid ruler who requires her huntsmen to remain chaste. Along with Fraya, *Bustle*'s Allie Funk says, the other female characters suffer a similar problem. "Although the women *appear* to act of their own will and volition," she writes, "their decisions are actually reactions to situations involving relationships with male characters, all of whom are in positions of power." Within the context of the film, the women technically "act of their own will and volition," passing both the Bechdel and Mako Mori tests, which do "not necessarily say anything about gender depiction" (Maureira and Rombout 546).

Other Mako Mori films include similar baggage. For example, *Fury Road* provides a violent resistance to patriarchy, but it does feature predominately white women, and the three non-white actors "are light-skinned," which "masks the way that capitalist patriarchy has disproportionately exploited women of colour's sexuality and reproduction" (Yates 368). Such criticisms remain important, but, as the Mako Mori test rhetorically stresses, complete dismissal ignores the glimmers of hope possibly at work in an imperfect film industry. Therefore, even though *Black Panther* revises a lesbian character's backstory, it still succeeds in other ways: a majority Black cast, including strong and agentive female characters, in a film directed by a Black man entrusted with a budget of more than $200 million. *The Martian's* portrayal of a female Navy commander leading a Mars mission celebrates STEM representation. Even though young mutant Laura begins *Logan* as a silent, violent killer, she is also a strong Latinx character, who even defeats the Wolverine clone, X-24, that Logan could not.

R.I.P. Mako

Strengthening Mako Mori's place in the *Pacific Rim* universe, Cait Coker says Mako's presence in "a few panels" of 2013's *Pacific Rim: Tales from Year Zero* prequel comic establishes her presence within the broader *Pacific Rim* canon as something that "cannot be erased" (214). That might be true, but she can die. Almost five years after *Pacific Rim*'s premiere, *Uprising* brought the franchise back to the big screen, with more supporting female characters, who talk to each other about topics unrelated to men; two women are even attached as screenwriters. While the film passes the Mako Mori test, to a degree, it fails Mako Mori's character, killing her off in the first act to advance a male character's story. While a new slate of younger characters narratively move freely, Kikuchi's character, played by an actor in her mid-thirties, lost her relevancy when Charlie Hunnam, the actor who played Raleigh Becket, decided not to reprise his role in the sequel. Without Hunnam's Raleigh, Mako is not a character worth exploring, according to *Uprising*.

The Mako Mori test is beneficial for analyzing female characters in a changing cinematic landscape, but it also reveals how fragile representation agentive female characters are, especially in films with male leads. Just as *Uprising* fails Mako, the *Furiosa* prequel comic by Vertigo fails the Five Wives, according to *The Mary Sue*: "this was a chance to show a narrative that discussed rape on women's terms, in women's voices, rather than just splaying their legs all over the page as if a woman truly is the object that her rapist would reduce her to" (Mardoll). Beyond further entries that undo important Mako Mori moments, some films analyzed here barely pass the test (*Homecoming*, *The Martian*, *Civil War*), while others only pass with explanation (*Solo*). This is not the original intent of the test.

Even more troubling, of all fifteen films analyzed, all directors are male and only two non-white, while *Uprising* features the only female writing credits. Still, while the Mako Mori test does not require a female character to be non-white, the origin of the test based on *Pacific Rim*, started as a criticism to viewers far too willing to a condemn a film for one reason without noting other positive contributions. Similarly, condemnation of *Deadpool 2*'s fridging could omit the positive inclusion of Domino, a comics character "traditionally portrayed with ice-white skin," which even prompted actor Zazie Beetz to fear "backlash" from fans (Armitage). Non-white characters are often whitewashed, so any inverted examples are important.

The Mako Mori test, like the Bechdel test, is not a perfect formula, but it provides a unique perspective for an evolving film industry that owes much to Laura Mulvey's concerns regarding the male gaze but also faces new challenges as well. Amidst the many positive and troubling examples noted here, one truth remains clear, in large part thanks to the Mako Mori test. The 1990s are riddled with examples of "action [heroines] … enacting masculinity rather than providing legitimate examples of female heroism" (Brown, "Gender, Sexuality" 47–48). In contrast, when a more modern character like Valkyrie gets drunk or fights—previously male coded behavior—she does so as a fully realized female, not a masculine substitute. Instead, many of the female characters depicted here, to paraphrase spider-xan, are *informed by gender without being solely defined by it.* Science fiction and fantasy films remain a promising discursive space for emerging female representation, but like the great unknown in the stars, that remains only a partially explored frontier.

NOTES

1. The user-made list on Letterboxd is not all-inclusive, and some films analyzed here do not appear on the list. Still, it remains important to note the cultural impact of the Mako Mori test.

WORKS CITED

Allen, Marlene D. "If You Can't See It, You Can Be It: *Black Panther*'s Black Woman Magic." *Africology: The Journal of Pan African Studies*, vol. 11, no. 9, 2018, pp. 20–22.

Armitage, Hugh. "*Deadpool 2*'s Zazie Beetz Was 'Worried' About Backlash Over Domino's Race." *Digital Spy*, 12 May 2018, http://www.digitalspy.com/movies/deadpool/news/a856887/deadpool-2-zazie-beetz-domino-race. Accessed on 25 October 2018.

Baugher, Lacy. "How *Avengers: Infinity War* Fails Its Women." *The Mary Sue*, 7 May 2018, https://www.themarysue.com/avengers-infinity-war-fails-women. Accessed 25 May 2018.

Brittany. "The Mako Mori Test," Letterboxd, https://letterboxd.com/waltgoggins/list/the-mako-mori-test. Accessed 25 September 2018.

Brown, Jeffrey A. *Beyond Bombshells: The New Action Heroine in Popular Culture.* University Press of Mississippi, 2015.

_____. "Gender, Sexuality, and Toughness." *Action Chicks: New Images of Tough Women in Popular Culture*, edited by Sherrie A. Inness, Palgrave Macmillan, 2004, pp. 47–74.

Buchanan, Kyle. "There Isn't Much Room for Women in the Future of *Pacific Rim*." *Vulture*, 15 July 2013, http://www.vulture.com/2013/07/does-pacific-rim-have-a-woman-problem.html. Accessed 13 October 2018.

Bechdel, Alison. *Dykes to Watch Out for #1.* Firebrand Books, 1986.

Coker, Cait. "The Mako Mori Fan Club: *Pacific Rim* Fandom Online." *Dis-Orienting Planets: Racial Representations of Asia in Science Fiction*, edited by Isiah Lavender, University of Mississippi Press, 2017, pp. 204–217.

Couch, Aaron. "'Logan' Team on Dreaming Up a 'Laura' Spinoff and Finding the Drama in Wolverine's Goodbye." *The Hollywood Reporter*, 24 October 2017, https://www.hollywoodreporter.com/heat-vision/logan-hugh-jackman-laura-movie-recasting-wolverine-1051147. Accessed 30 October 2017.

Funk, Allie. "The Big Problem with How *The Huntsman: Winter's War* Handles Its Female Characters." *Bustle*, 22 April 2016, https://www.bustle.com/articles/155616-the-big-problem-with-how-the-huntsman-winters-war-handles-its-female-characters. Accessed 9 October 2018.

Griffin, Penny. *Popular Culture, Political Economy and the Death of Feminism: Why Women Are in Refrigerators and Other Stories.* Routledge, 2015.

Hale-Stern, Kaila. "Should It Matter if *Thor: Ragnarok* Passes the Bechdel Test?" *The Mary Sue*, 31 October 2017, https://www.themarysue.com/thor-ragnarok-bechdel. Accessed 4 Jan. 2018.

Ho, Tamara C. "Articulating Asia in SF." Review of *Techno-Orientalism: Imagining Asia in*

Speculative Fiction, History, and Media, edited by David S. Roh, Betsy Haung, and Greta A. Niu. *Science Fiction Studies*, vol. 44, no. 3, 2017, pp. 587–591.

Jelača, Dijana. "Alien Feminism and Cinema's Posthuman Women." *Signs: Journal of Women in Culture and Society*, vol. 43, no. 2, 2018, pp. 379–400.

Kokas, Aynne. *Hollywood Made in China*. University of California Press, 2017.

Mackinnon, Lee. "Artificial Stupidity and the End of Men." *Third Text*, vol. 31, nos. 5–6, 2017, pp. 603–617.

"The Mako Mori Test." *Geek Feminism*, http://geekfeminism.wikia.com/wiki/Mako_Mori_test. Accessed 20 July 2018.

Mardoll, Ana. "Review: We Need to Talk About the Furiosa Comic." *The Mary Sue*, 20 June 2015, https://www.themarysue.com/furiosa-comic-review. Accessed 23 June 2015.

Maureira, Marcello A. Gómez, and Lisa E. Rombout. "The Vocal Range of Movies—Sonifying Gender Representation in Film." *Entertainment Computing—ICEC 2015: International Conference, ICEC 2015 Trondheim, Norway, September 29–October 2, 2015 Proceedings*, edited by Konstantinos Chorianopoulos, Monica Divitini, Jannicke Baalsrud Hauge, Letizia Jaccheri, and Rainer Malaka, Springer, 2015, pp. 545–552.

Miczo, Nathan. "Wolverine in Transition: Shifting Portrayals of Masculinity and Identity." *The X-Men Films: A Cultural Analysis*, edited by Claudia Bucciferro, Rowman & Littlefield Publishers, 2014, pp. 137–150.

Mulvey, Laura. *Visual and Other Pleasures*, 2nd ed. Palgrave Macmillan, 1989.

Robinson, Joanna. "*Black Panther* Footage Reveals the Ferocious Female Warriors of Wakanda [Updated]." *Vanity Fair*, 18 April 2018, https://www.vanityfair.com/hollywood/2017/04/black-panther-gay-danai-gurira. Accessed 30 November 2018.

Romano, Aja. "The Mako Mori Test: *Pacific Rim* Inspires a Bechdel Test Alternative." *The Daily Dot*, 18 August 2013, https://www.dailydot.com/parsec/fandom/mako-mori-test-bechdel-pacific-rim. Accessed 20 July 2018.

Rosenberg, Alyssa. "After *Logan* and *Arrival,* Can We Stop Pretending 'Genre' Movies Are Unserious?" *The Washington Post*, 9 March 2017, https://www.washingtonpost.com/news/act-four/wp/2017/03/09/after-logan-and-arrival-can-we-stop-pretending-genre-movies-are-unserious/?utm_term=.f2f6bf26c5b0. Accessed 23 October 2018.

Smith, Emily. "Charlize Gets More Than $10M Deal After Fighting for Equal Pay." *Page Six*, 7 Jan. 2015, https://pagesix.com/2015/01/07/charlize-hemsworths-earning-10m-for-huntsman-and-so-should-i. Accessed 21 Jan. 2015.

spider-xan. *The Amazing Spider-Xan*, 15 August 2013, http://spider-xan.tumblr.com/post/58305944138/also-i-was-thinking-more-about-why-white-women. Accessed 20 July 2018.

Stern, Marlow. "Guillermo Del Toro's *Pacific Rim* Is a Total Blast." *The Daily Beast*, 9 July 2013, https://www.thedailybeast.com/guillermo-del-toros-pacific-rim-is-a-total-blast. Accessed 13 October 2018.

Yamato, Jen. "*Doctor Strange* Director Owns Up to Whitewashing Controversy." *The Daily Beast*, 2 November 2016, https://www.thedailybeast.com/doctor-strange-director-owns-up-to-whitewashing-controversy?ref=scroll. Accessed 3 November 2016.

Yates, Michelle. "Re-Casting Nature as Feminist Space in *Mad Max: Fury Road*." *Science Fiction Film and Television*, vol. 10, no. 3, 2017, pp. 353–370.

Whitbrook, James. "The *Solo: A Star Wars* Novel Adds an Interesting Twist to That Major Cameo." *io9*, 27 August 2018, https://io9.gizmodo.com/the-solo-a-star-wars-novel-adds-an-interesting-twist-t-1828628622. Accessed 30 August 2018.

Williams, Délice. "Three Theses About *Black Panther*." *Africology: The Journal of Pan African Studies*, vol. 11, no. 9, 2018, pp. 27–30.

Blockbusters for a New Age

Sisterhood Defeats Angry Young Men in Black Panther, Captain Marvel, Last Jedi *and* Ghostbusters

VALERIE ESTELLE FRANKEL

Powerful lone heroes or even heroines are being phased out in today's new type of storytelling. Emphasis is going to teams—and finally, these teams are made of minorities and women with different skills to offer. The mighty *Avengers* film, with a significantly less mighty seductress in her Black Widow catsuit, is giving way to new stories. Katherine Wright explains in *The New Heroines* that the twenty-first century sees a new kind of narrative: "The monomyth, the emphasis on 'mono' as the 'only, one, or single' myth, transforms into a collaborative process by a number of significant others linked together in their stories through the transmission of affect. New heroism, is, at its core, polymythic" (72).

Of course, much backlash is greeting these stories, with a particular anger at stories that dismiss the men entirely (*Ghostbusters*) or show macho ideals as bad traits (*Last Jedi*) or show women destroying the patriarchal system entirely. Even in a world of protests against comics' female Wolverine and Lady Thor, the film *Black Panther* fared better with less online trolling. Perhaps this was because it was the best made and most enjoyable of the four films, as many fans would argue. Further, Black Panther and his Dora Milaje have been canon in Marvel Comics for decades, preemptively sidelining those fans vocal about a new *Ghostbusters* and *Star Wars* "ruining" the old ones of their childhoods. Most of all, however, *Black Panther*'s feminism offers well-developed characters without preaching or emasculating the men. Instead, it features egalitarian respect and a varied skillset from all the heroes. Certainly, fandom is changing, welcoming a spectrum of characters into the white boys' club. Some patterns, however, are far more accepted by the masses than others.

"Great, another broken white boy for me to fix. This is going to be fun!"

Black Panther was the eighteenth film in the massive Marvel Cinematic Universe (MCU) and the first one directed and co-written by a Black filmmaker—Ryan Coogler, known for *Creed* (2015) and *Fruitvale Station* (2013). At the same time, it truly broke ground, not just with its world of Afro-Futurism, but with his brilliant female characters.

Lupita Nyong'o adds, "Women are allowed to realize their full potential and that's what Ryan [Coogler] wanted to show and he committed to having that number of women around him" (Brockington). "Aside from the black power movement of the film, women were also a stand out feature. The women of Wakanda held positions of strength without detracting from the strength of the men. This spoke volumes in an era of black empowerment and feminine solidarity" (Campbell-Reid). As the superhero and king, T'Challa (Chadwick Boseman) is never rude, disrespectful, or condescending to any of the women in his inner circle. Instead he listens to their desires and helps them achieve their character arcs, though he is the starring superhero.

Nakia (Lupita Nyong'o), Black Panther's ex-girlfriend, is a field operative using her freedom to change the world outside Wakanda. Far more than a love interest in the story, her presence is subversive. When the audience meets her, Nakia is working alone and undercover in Nigeria, pursuing female liberation in a nod to the Boko Haram kidnaping of women and girls. Her presence there functions as a critique against their oppression; it's likely she has come to overthrow the entire government. When T'Challa arrives, she defies him to protect a young soldier, insisting, "This one's just a boy. He got kidnapped as well." With this, she tackles the abuse of child soldiers in a quick social critique tinged with compassion and discerning justice.

While a skilled fighter, Nakia solves problems through feminine empathy and compassion blended with fierce independence and warrior skills. She challenges the isolationist policies of Wakanda and insists they intervene in justice's name. As Jonathan Gray writes in *The New Republic*, "As it is, Nakia's approach recalls the new generation of female activists rising in Africa, like the Nobel Peace Laureate Leymah Gbowee, who has promoted the cultivation of soft power to diffuse war" (Tillet). With this, the film carries its characters beyond the standard tropes of black male political leadership to grassroots social justice.

Though happy to return for T'Challa's coronation, she insists she cares more about defending Wakanda than being its queen. T'Challa tells her, "If you were not so stubborn, you would make a great queen." She shoots back: "I would make a great queen *because* I am stubborn—*if* that's what I wanted."

Both are clear that it's her choice, not his. Turning her back on a pat Hollywood royal wedding—and even the love and power accompanying it—she insists on intervening globally, which means far more to her.

> She shows a willingness to violate the Wakandan Prime Directive, a policy that prevents Wakanda citizens from sharing her country's advanced technologies with and intervening into the politics of other nations. Nakia, on the other hand, embodies a global black feminism in which she both recognizes and resists the ways in which European colonialism and contemporary American foreign policy harm Africa's development. She assumes that her fate is not simply tied to those who live under the veil of Wakanda's vast wealth but also tethered to those who live throughout the continent and the African Diaspora. Though she, as a Dora Milaje, practices armed self-defense, it is her desire to share peacefully rather than withhold the technological innovations and political freedoms of Wakanda with others that initially puts her at odds with T'Challa and makes her a viable alternative to the violent rhetoric of Killmonger (Michael B. Jordan) [Tillet].

T'Challa sighs over her choice but realizes that coercing her is the wrong path. Instead, his persuasion is heartfelt and gentle. More than that, he changes his political beliefs and the country's oldest law in the end, both to win her and because he's been persuaded she is right. At film's end, he tells her, "I think I know a way you can still fulfill your calling. Please stay." With this, he offers to join her in solving the world's humanitarian crises. Here and elsewhere in the film, he realizes her independence and understands that she is a force of her own, not a docile extension of himself. This of course teaches young viewers respect for others. Critic Sesali Bowen decides, "The route towards realizing our maximum potential and freedom in the real world does not require a toll of reverting back towards romanticized ideas about Black male supremacy. In this fight, Black women are the equals of Black men and should be treated as such."

By contrast, the film's villain, Eric Killmonger (Michael B. Jordan), treats his forgettable love interest as a subordinate, then callously allows her to be shot. He is framed as a product not only of American macho values but of abandonment by the Wakandans—their memorable great failure to choose compassion and brotherhood. While his schemes of world domination are framed as misguided, he comes off as sincere and sympathetic—presumably because he makes good points about the unfairness of the world. He demands accountability and an end to the secret utopia of Wakanda. In many ways he and Nakia seek the same path—raising up their fellows rather than hiding in safety. Like Nakia, Killmonger finds his fiery speeches affect the open-minded young king. T'Challa's outreach mission, launched in his defeated cousin's home of Oakland, salutes his rival's dream and emphasizes compromise—a willingness to take the best lessons even from one's enemy.

Even T'Challa's bodyguard captain, Okoye (Danai Gurira) and her fellow warriors like Ayo (Florence Kasumba) choose their definition of duty over obedience. They also share a friendly, teasing, even chiding relationship with their king, emphasizing that their respect and loyalty is two-way and given by choice. On their first mission of the film beside T'Challa, seeking Nakia, Okoye reminds him, "Just don't freeze when you see her," while Ayo later amusedly reports to his family that he froze "Like an antelope in headlights."

The Dora Milaje are framed as basically unbeatable, merging technological expertise with close combat skills. They also project intimidation, to the point at which King T'Chaka's younger brother cringes at their presence, introducing them with a simple, "They won't knock again." Still, their likeability comes from more than strength but like Nakia's, from the nuance and personality of characters with a higher calling and independent thought.

Okoye is more than just soldier—she's feminized by her loving relationship with W'Kabi (Daniel Kaluuya), Wakanda's chief of national security. Like Nakia, she finds growth through her conflict in the story—her personal loyalty to T'Challa versus the laws of Wakanda. Regretfully, she chooses the latter. "Nakia! I'm not a spy who can come and go as they so choose! I am loyal to that throne, no matter who sits upon it," she says, demonstrating the difference between an independent agent and a soldier. She is sworn to her country's laws and reluctantly obeys them. Only when their new king Killmonger ignores the laws can she turn against him, though this also means battling her lover. At her mercy on the battlefield, W'Kabi asks her, "Would you kill me, my love?" and she responds simply, "For Wakanda? Without a question!" This, like Nakia's choosing her mission over marriage, emphasizes the women's lack of obligation to subsume their goals and principles for their men.

> It's a question that conjures a conundrum that Black women have been forced to inherit: to abandon what is right for ourselves, our children, and our communities or act out an undying loyalty to Black men for the sake of upholding their place as patriarchs? Okoye's answer, "For Wakanda? No question," is the call to rethink our centering of masculinity, not just for Black women, but for all of us. Aware of both her honorable allegiance to her country, and her ability to actually end him, W'Kabi drops his own weapon and kneels before her. At that moment, he trusts her leadership more than his own. It's a role-reversal we need to normalize [Bowen].

Another independent thinker, and many viewers' favorite, is Princess Shuri (Letitia Wright). Described by director Ryan Coogler as the smartest person in the Marvel Cinematic Universe, Shuri charms as adorable princess, spunky kid sister, and warrior-heroine, but all these must give way to her role as brilliant scientist and prodigy. Her interests in STEM make her a wonderful role model for young viewers. She hilariously "steals every scene she is in" and offers some of the best lines in the film (Spencer). Teasing in sibling fashion, she protests T'Challa's sandals in her lab and videos him getting knocked on his rear. Most films would make her the comic relief or elegant princess or technology-supplying support staff, but Shuri gets a huge boost from her role as all these and more. She even accompanies her brother to war, insisting, "The Black Panther Lives. And when he fights for the fate of Wakanda, I will be right there beside him."

This is not the only way she defends Wakanda. She is Q the inventor for her brother, but also for Wakanda's infrastructure and even for herself, as she has invented amazing firing gauntlets for combat. "She masterminds everything from T'Challa's fight strategy to the high-speed train system that will frame T'Challa and Killmonger's battle to the death. Her centrality and power is evident in the scene where she coaches Everett Ross (Martin Freeman) through his mission to short circuit Killmonger's plan while simultaneously fighting for her country, family and life" (Spencer).

She represents the spirit of young Black innovation—a symbol, like Wakanda, of unlimited potential. Her scientific and technological genius not only give the Black Panther his agility, strength and resilience, but her expertise includes medical interventions that saves the white "colonizer" from the UN. In this moment, and later, when Wakanda becomes the last bastion of protection for the final infinity stone, Wakanda establishes itself as savior of the world, a political ruler as well as technological. "What if the countries in Africa had never been colonised? What if places of marvel and great wealth and opportunity existed in our home continent? In a place where we are the majority and not the minority. Somewhere where being black isn't a threat to anyone. What would the stories of those in the diaspora be then?" Campbell-Reid wonders. Lupita Nyong'o explains, "Wakanda offers us a glimpse into the world as it could be—self-determined and developed on their own terms without the interruption of colonialism. [It] has figured out how to make the most of all its citizens" (Brockington).

The gender equality in Wakanda, derived from African traditions of Dahomey warriors and ancient matriarchies, likewise shows an alternate history without Eurocentric influence, along with potential for the future. Queen Mother Ramonda (Angela Bassett) plays a bigger role than most fictional queens, to say nothing of superheroes' mothers. She is always dignified and controlled but also frequently onstage, presiding over ceremonies. She also clearly knows how to operate behind the scenes as she leads her small family to the ape people and attempts a coup. Mirroring her strength, the entire political court carries an obvious balance between female and male elders, a small detail that the film wisely presents without comment. Gender equality is a simple fact of life in Wakanda. Bassett says the women's roles are a reflection of how they are viewed in African nations. "[T'Challa] can't do it without them," she says, adding that there can't be a king without a queen (Brockington).

In the story, the women are decisive, brave, and fully, brilliantly capable alone. By contrast, T'Challa spends a surprising amount of the film unconscious and at other times appears indecisive and overwhelmed. Even without him, the women work in concert to drive the narrative forward in a way unusual in film. *Refinery29*'s Anne Cohen found the movie a call-out of a sexist film industry. "*Black Panther* is basically the poster child for intersectionality, a public shaming of a Hollywood industry that has long defended its male-centric projects by claiming that audiences could only handle rooting for one group, and then only in one movie, at a time. There are no token female sidekicks here" (Bowen). Even with so many women, romance barely appears as the film instead highlights bonds of family but also friendship and professional respect. The few disagreements are solved with civility and reason.

"Why are you pretending to capture ghosts?"

The female-flipped *Ghostbusters* team of 2016 (a film written by Paul Feig and Katie Dippold, who also wrote *The Heat*) is far from perfect—many felt the comedians were underutilized with a script that tried too much for cameos and not enough for really funny jokes. Still, this film too showcases very different women in contrasting roles.

Erin Gilbert (Kristen Wiig) is awfully neurotic. Erin kicks off the film lecturing at Columbia in an awkward plaid suit … only for the camera to pan to the empty room—she's been practicing, not teaching. All this emphasizes her compulsive desperation for control and her awful outfit, which the tenure chair can't quite bring himself to blatantly criticize. He's discovered her dark secret—she once wrote a book about the paranormal that's selling on Amazon, ruining her professional credibility. Off she goes to find her co-writer and high school friend Abby Yates (Melissa McCarthy) and ask her to take it down.

Abby appears in her lab wearing a wacky helmet she's invented herself, making a silly entrance. Abby promptly makes fart noises and tells Erin she has enough "stuffed up her butt." She's also obsessed with the bad delivery food and how few wontons and shrimp they put in the soup. Despite her humor, Melissa McCarthy comes across as underutilized without the nuances the character might have had. She has no growth, no plot arc, nothing really at stake. Unlike Erin, who wants tenure, respect, and a hot guy, Abby's entire life appears ghost hunting and possibly soup. Even when talking down the supervillain, Abby protests: "There's so many terrific things out there. I mean, wonderful things that are worth living for. I mean, you got soup, and, you know, that first…. You know when…. Oh, God. I can only think of soup." Her story ends anticlimactically over the credits with her getting a soup container of all wontons.

Of course, the problem with *Ghostbusters* being imperfect is that it offers an excuse to avoid making these films in future and stick women with classic gender roles. Anita Sarkeesian, founder of *Feminist Frequency* and the *Tropes vs. Women in Video Games* series, and a victim of targeted misogyny campaigns, explains:

> Even as female-led comedies continue to make and break box office records, there is still an overarching sense that they just aren't good or won't be successful, and that if they aren't successful, it's somehow a commentary on women as a group, and what kinds of roles they should or shouldn't play. While these illogical sentiments continue, there is a tremendous amount of undue pressure put on comedies that star women to be masterpieces. In a better world, there would be plenty of comedies starring women, some great, some forgettable, and it wouldn't be a big deal. But this is the world we live in, and the outrage directed at the very existence of the new *Ghostbusters* indicated that it is, indeed, a very big deal.

The next team member did much to redeem the film. "Come here often?" Jillian Holtzmann (Kate McKinnon) asks provocatively from her perch in Abby's lab. She specializes in nuclear engineering and builds all their gadgets. In her jeans jacket and sloppy overalls with platinum hair and giant clunky necklace and goggles, her look makes a clear statement. She's clearly Abby's new partner, an upgrade on pompous Erin.

Holtzmann's deliberate goofiness contrasts Erin's at every turn. She uses their video camera on their first case together to interview Erin about her tiny bow tie, adding, "Can you tell us what it's like to walk around in those shoes all day?" She cuts the tension of their first ghost by crunching potato chips, continuing to chew, mesmerized, as it appears. When they find new headquarters, Holtzmann starts the lip-syncing and dancing, complete with Bunsen Burners spouting fire as Erin fusses.

> McKinnon is this film's secret weapon, and it's worth seeing the 2016 *Ghostbusters* just for her. She's goofy, nerdy, and aggressively weird. She's an instant idol for smart, dorky women who feel a little out of place, but don't feel particularly bad about that. She steals scenes from the main cast just with her facial expressions when she's lurking in the background, and when she takes the foreground to dance to DeBarge's "Rhythm of the Night" or enthuse about her latest crackpot invention, she comes across like the world's most upbeat Batman villain [Robinson].

She paints and drives the Ghostbusters vehicle and proposes interesting uses for a corpse if there's one in the back. She greets ghosts with a delighted smile. When they capture one at the concert, she encourages the crowd's cheers and even smashes a guitar. As the inventor and comic relief, she's self-sustaining without any character change. In the final battle, she gives her self-designed guns a big lick. "Forgot about my new toys. Let's go." She takes down swarms of ghosts in spectacular fashion, ending with a giant one. "You just got Holtzmanned, baby!" It's a delightful moment.

Hilariously, she gets the other women to test her equipment instead of trying it out herself. On the job, she suddenly remembers to supplement Erin's weapon with a grounding wire "so you don't die." Meanwhile, Erin, as the butt of various jokes and the uncool member, gets slimed on their first and second encounter, especially obvious in her light-colored outfits. Together, they make a team of contrasts.

Their fourth member, Patty Tolan (Leslie Jones), first appears at her subway station job, greeting oblivious passerby with cheery optimism. She pops into their office and greets the three Ghostbusters with fun facts about the city—mostly grim, criminal facts delivered in her cheerful monologue. "Also, I saw a ghost," she adds, and they're off. However, she keeps coming back. "I'm joining the club," she announces. "I know New York." She's well-read in nonfiction and proactive, borrowing a hearse to transport their equipment. Showing a practical side, she also brings them the coveralls.

Some critics deplored Leslie Jones's getting the stereotyped blue-collar worker job, much as the only Black Ghostbuster had had a generation before. "Like Ernie Hudson's Winston Zeddemore in the original films, she's presented as the 'working-class' member of the team, leaving her job at the MTA to join up, while the other three come from highly educated, scientific backgrounds," protests Anita Sarkeesian. At the concert, Patty launches herself into the crowd and no one catches her. "I don't know if this is a race thing or a lady thing, but I'm mad as hell," she insists from the floor. Patty's loud, brash personality, and especially this moment of getting dropped echo the sort of simplistic race writing avoided in *Black Panther*. Nonetheless, she's a likeable, mighty character with quite a bit of fun to offer. In one memorable scene, she fights off a possessed Abby even while hauling Holtzmann one-handed out of the window. Still, she too has no real stakes—she joins the team for fun and that's it.

While the other three basically stay as they are, uptight Erin has a character arc. "Ghosts are real! I believe in ghosts!" Erin crows after their first encounter. Moments later, she's fired for their ghostbusting and accompanying online video and must walk out of Columbia University carrying the contents of her desk. After they've captured their first ghost, the camera cuts to their office, and the dancer isn't Holtzmann but Erin. As she eagerly kisses their ghost-holding canister, she's thrown herself into their triumph. The story suggests that tenure wasn't her real goal, but this is, her passion project with this loving group of friends. Of course, she's still insecure. When the famed ghost debunker Martin Heiss (Bill Murray) needles them, like the previous franchise challenging their validity, she's so desperate to impress that she opens the canister and releases the ghost. It kills Heiss.

Despite this symbolic triumph over the establishment, she fails to get professional respect. As the climax approaches, she bursts in on the mayor's lunch (hilariously unable to find the door) and shrieks and babbles hysterically, "Get out of the city! They're coming! Don't you understand? These ghosts kill people!" His security guards haul her away and everyone dismisses her. Still, she's far from incapable. Erin is the one to save the team from a Staypuft balloon that's crushing them all. "Proton guns are all well and good, but sometimes you need the Swiss Army," she says, standing powerful and armed against the increasingly occult skyline. She dives into an otherworldly portal to save Abby at the film's climax, telling her friend, "I wasn't gonna leave you twice." Both are prematurely aged, again suggesting character maturity and new wisdom.

Member five, Kevin (Chris Hemsworth), is hilariously the male bimbo. Emphasizing why they're hiring him. Erin can't take her eyes off him and instantly offers him the job. "On its own, this would be frustrating, but again, because *Ghostbusters* gives us a range of women with notably different personality types, no one character is holding all the weight for womankind, so the film has more freedom to explore comedic territory without reinforcing negative stereotypes" (Sarkeesian). As the women ask whether he's seeing anyone and ask him to whip out his drawings, they're committing sexual harassment. Erin caps this off by insisting they keep him around "to look at." Kevin trips on everything and garbles the phone messages, hanging up whenever anyone tells him anything too complicated. He shows the women shirtless headshots of himself (playing saxophone versus listening to a saxophone). He even stops to grab a sandwich in the middle of the action. In one memorable moment, he makes a plan, saying, "Okay, I got it. We need to form a group and build something to fight these damn ghosts." Abby must retort, "That's exactly what we already do here." His male advice plainly isn't helping.

Some of the people most determined to hate the 2016 *Ghostbusters* are already griping that it makes women look smart and men look dumb and useless. (Welcome to how women felt about virtually every action film made in the 1980s, guys.) And they're particularly pointing to the *Thor* star as the proof of Feig's bottomless determination to be PC (or feminist, or an SJW, or reverse-sexist, or misandrist, or whatever the coded defensive-dude swear word of the day is). They're missing the part where Hemsworth (a) is hilarious, (b) gets to play a much wider range than the blindingly incompetent but decorative secretary he starts off as, and (c) gets about half the movie's biggest laugh moments. Hemsworth is having a lot of fun playing with his image in this role. The film's willingness to objectify him feels a little subversive, but letting him play a really silly part half the time, and swagger the rest, doesn't make him the butt of the jokes, it lets him control and focus them [Robinson].

Kevin is "a male subversion of the old stereotype of the female secretary who is kept around more for her looks than for her skills. Kevin is as inept as he is attractive, and his sheer obliviousness about how to even do the most basic things like answer the phone properly leads to a number of funny moments throughout the film" (Sarkeesian). Abby announces on the verge of the climax, "All right, let's go save this city and get our terrible receptionist back. We're not gonna find another one that pretty." In fact, the women do rescue his helpless, possessed handsome body, as they yell, "Nobody hurts Kevin!" With this, he's positively become the damsel. All in all, the film is not groundbreakingly brilliant but the women (and Chris Hemsworth) have a good time defending the city, nodding to the original films and flipping stereotypes.

Of course, the controversy surrounding the film suggested something far different. "Ever since it was announced, though, the primary question surrounding it hasn't been 'Is it better than the original version?' or 'Is it funny?' It's been 'Why do we need this movie? What's the point of remaking a beloved comedy classic with women?'" (Robinson). Before the film had come out, reviewers trashed it with one-star ratings. This sort of purposeful trashing of feminism online is a concentrated movement appearing in this era. As Prudence Chamberlain writes in *The Feminist Fourth Wave: Affective Temporality*:

> The fourth wave of the social movement has been married to an environment of abuse, fear, and a sense of invasion, in which it is almost impossible to withdraw from the far-reaching Internet. This has created a whole new, and still developing, set of dangers for women. Ranging from very basic Twitter trolling, to the publication of women's addresses online, to the explosion of revenge porn, the Internet has created a forum in which misogyny can expand and develop. The difficulty is that the Internet allows for anonymity, which can be empowering for women looking to move beyond their sex and gender, but also enables trolls to continue campaigns of abuse without any chance of retribution [165].

Unlike Faludi's model of eighties' era postfeminism appearing a decade or two after women left the home, the internet is enabling simultaneous feminist wave and backlash in the form of trolling—all at an accelerated rate. "This chronology of wave and backlash seems to have changed in this specific moment, in part on account of the technology, but also in part because the dialogue between feminists and their opposition is sustaining the energy of this movement" (Chamberlain 134). Much of the backlash was launched in racist comments toward Leslie Jones. Hackers filled her Twitter with what appeared to be naked photos as well as truly disturbing racism. Jones sadly left Twitter for a time, but also implored the company to reform their policies on harassment and hate speech—which they did. This case emphasizes how the personal becomes political because the personal can so quickly escalate online. Of course, the trolls involved saw her as the icon of societal change. The leader of an alt-right group insisted after, "I'm sick and tired of men being portrayed as idiots. There was a time we ruled society and I want to see that again. That is why I voted for Donald Trump" (Bradley and Matthews).

Then there are the Ghostbros, the noisiest if not most numerous contingent, for whom reviving the franchise with women in the leading roles is the ultimate desecration. It would have been one thing to pass the torch, as Ivan Reitman had originally planned, with a sequel in which the classic quartet trained a newer, spryer group in the finer points of busting ghosts. But effectively redoing the original movie with the genders flipped smacks of political correctness and revisionist history. Or at least, that seemed to be the argument, insofar as one could extract a series of propositions and conclusions from the wailing and gnashing of teeth. It's tempting to dismiss the objections to the *Ghostbusters* reboot as manbaby hissyfits. Take the video in which James Rolfe, who bills himself as the Angry Video Game Nerd, announced that he wouldn't review the movie, or even see it, because "If you already know you're going to hate it, why give them your money?" [Adams].

This trolling campaign is actually reflected in the villains of the film. "We have a hundred comments already and they're not all crazies!" Abby crows, and then accidentally pulls up a web comment from a troll who doesn't want to see a female ghostbusting team: "Ain't no bitches gonna bust no ghosts." In another scene, Abby encourages her friends to ignore all the crazies on the web. Meanwhile, Bill Murray's ghost debunker ridicules the female team, and Homeland Security condescends to them. The image-obsessed mayor (Andy Garcia) and his pushy aide Jennifer Lynch (Cecily Strong) launch a propaganda campaign against them, even while privately admitting they're right (and there's gender relations in a nutshell). After having their car towed, Lynch takes the patriarchy's side, painfully dismissing the Ghostbusters: "It was just another publicity stunt by these incredibly sad and lonely women. It's like they read *Eat, Pray, Love* and just ran with it," she tells the press. However, the team are vindicated in the end when the aide returns and asks them to keep saving the city, "fully funded" and rents the overpriced firehouse for their new base. As Sarkeesian concludes, "It's great to see a funny, entertaining film in which women triumph in spite of the sexist attitudes they encounter, and it's made all the more sweet by the fact that this film also represents something of a triumph against legions of entitled men in the real world who felt so threatened by the simple idea of women busting ghosts."

Beyond this, of course, the main villain is an angry incel. Like Kylo Ren or Killgrave of Netflix's *Jessica Jones,* or Loki from the *Avengers* franchise, he thinks he should be ruling the world. Janitor Rowan North (Neil Casey) bursts out at Abby that he wants to destroy New York. "You must've been afforded the basic dignity and respect of a human being, which I have been denied," he insists, oblivious to the irony. Sarkeesian explains:

When he's confronted by the Ghostbusters, he gives them a spiel about how hard it has been to be so brilliant and never get the respect he deserves. Abby, of course, knows exactly what it feels like to not be treated with respect, just as any woman who has had to struggle against the boys' club mentality of scientific circles would, and she says as much. The camera cuts to Patty (Leslie Jones), who no doubt could teach

Roland a thing or two about what it's like to not be respected by society, and she doesn't need to say a word; her look says it all.

Rowan, still oblivious to others' pain, insists, "I am a genius. I see things that no one else does. And for it, I am rewarded with nothing but scorn and mockery. Luckily, I am not the only one seeking revenge. Behind these are millions of souls, souls which have been cast aside. Souls who see the world as it truly is, as garbage. Garbage that needs to be cleaned up." Thus, he unleashes ghosts on New York. Further, he hurls sexist insults for the rest of the film, from calling women "always late" to snarking, "You shoot like girls." Their triumphant battle against him suggests a crusade against all the trolls of the web. When he's banished to the underworld, there's clearly a wish-fulfillment attitude.

"This is not going to go the way you think"

Star Wars: The Last Jedi also was met with aggressive trolling. Before *The Force Awakens,* the presence of a Black stormtrooper in the trailers sparked outrage. The hashtag #BoycottStarWarsVII shot to the top of Twitter's trending topics, perpetuated by "a handful—as in, fewer than a dozen—of people creating their own echo chamber of racial discontent" (Koski). As *Vox Magazine* adds, the cry for #BoycottStarWarsVII was led by people offended "that *The Force Awakens'* cast features not one, but *multiple* people of color, a situation a small but vocal minority sees as evidence of a 'white genocide' in the *Star Wars* universe, perpetuated by Abrams, a white-hating Hollywood Jew. Yes, it's ridiculous and disgusting on many, many levels" (Koski). Boyega's response was a dignified but forthright Instagram message: "Get used to it" (Dowd). "It was unnecessary," he says of the negativity. "I'm in the movie, what are you going to do about it? You either enjoy it or you don't. I'm not saying get used to the future, but what is already happening. People of color and women are increasingly being shown on-screen. For things to be white-washed just doesn't make sense" (Dowd).

Of course, feminists filled the internet too: There were campaigns, upon seeing Rey and Leia introduced as the new franchise's only female characters, to get more added. The angry article "Hey Star Wars—Where the Hell Are the Women?" blasted it: "There is only one new female character being added to what is arguably the world's most beloved mythic series. It's as if 51 percent of the population cried out in pain and was suddenly silenced" (Newitz). The studio listened to this criticism, and accordingly gender-flipped Captain Phasma and Maz Kanata before the story's start. "Whether it is a single tweet of protest, or hundreds of activists on the street, there is a sense that the fourth wave focuses strongly on exposure and response, using the anger and disbelief to fuel action, which embodies those strong and infectious affects" (Chamberlain 118).

Despite the pre-publication clamor, *Force Awakens* was very popular—both girls and boys appreciated Rey's strength and heroism in the very traditional, even derivative *Star Wars* plot. The simultaneous backlash, however, continued, sometimes aimed at every positive review on a feminist blog. "These messages are intended specifically to shame and frighten women out of engaging online, in this new and increasingly important public sphere," notes journalist Laurie Penny in *Cybersexism: Sex, Gender and Power on The Internet* (284–285). Penny describes having an opinion online as "the short skirt of the internet" (loc. 247), in which expression in a public forum means a woman is allegedly "asking for" threats of sexual violence and bodily harm. In 2016, Daisy Ridley (Rey), posted on Instagram deploring gun violence. "As I sat in the audience yesterday tears were streaming down my face at the tribute to those that have been lost to gun violence…. We must #stoptheviolence" (qtd. in Pantozzi). So many hateful responses appeared that she quietly deleted her account. Jill Pantozzi, who broke the story, comments, "And well, because she, a celebrity, dared to share an opinion about something other than *Star Wars* on her own page, fans took the opportunity to tell her how wrong she was and that she should just never talk about politics at all. Like they own her or something." Many requested she stop making liberal statements, presumably because they had enjoyed *Star Wars* and wanted to admire the actress as the Rey they visualized, not an actual woman with her own opinions (though of course, anyone who believes Rey would have no opinion about the deaths of teenage civilians missed some massive *Star Wars* themes).

Laurie Penny herself was the target of misogynist death threats on the internet and also doxing and real-life bomb threats, much like Anita Sarkeesian, Caroline Criado-Perez, Hadley Freeman, Grace Dent, Catherine Mayer and Mary Beard (Chamberlain 136). Penny addresses this online abuse, arguing that the Internet is not separate from our reality, but instead engaging with and creating the outside world. She adds that our increased interaction online, both socially and for work, means that "violence online is real violence … reaching epidemic levels and it's time to end the pretense that it's either acceptable or inevitable" (loc. 278).

As *Last Jedi* released a more deconstructive story, setting aside the hero's journey to instead condemn lone heroes and epic battles, the gamergate set lashed out, insisting that the "social justice" agenda had ruined the film. While critics almost universally enjoyed *Last Jedi*, leaving it with a 93 percent on Rotten Tomatoes and an 86 on Metacritic (Jasper), an alt-right group flooded Rotten Tomatoes, bringing its score down to a 54 percent user score with bots (Bradley and Matthews). "The self-identified member of the 'alt-right' claimed that Poe Dameron (played by Oscar Isaac) is a 'victim of the anti-mansplaining movement,' that Poe and Luke Skywalker (Mark Hamill) are in danger of being 'turn[ed]' gay, and that men should be reinstated as rulers of 'society'" (Bradley and Matthews). Further, over 10,000 people signed a Change.org petition urging Disney to remove *The Last Jedi* from canon. Reasons for signing include "You ruined Luke Skywalker," "I am 42 yrs old this is not the Star Wars I have grown up watching!" and "This movie is an abomination and an SJW wet dream Kill it" (Jasper). There was also a vicious campaign against the Vietnamese American actress playing Rose. She, like Daisy Ridley, gave up social media in disgust.

It's true that recent films have produced some notably gentle male protagonists. *The Hunger Games* features Katniss choosing Peeta the self-deprecating baker, while *Fantastic Beasts and Where to Find Them* stars another baker, beside Eddie Redmayne's gentle creature-tender Newt Scamander. In *Frozen,* Kristoff sweetly asks permission to kiss Anna, while the plot emphasizes how princes are no longer needed. *X-Men Apocalypse* sees Professor X beaten half to a pulp, and then pleading with his protégé Jean Grey to trounce the villain in his place. These have escaped the systemic campaigns against *Ghostbusters, Star Wars,* and similarly protested franchises like the gender-flipped *Star Trek* and *Doctor Who.* Is it because these films are marketed to a teen audience or because they're new franchises unrooted in reimagining the past?

Returning to *Last Jedi,* the plot may be controversial, but the characters are a delightful addition to the universe. As with *Black Panther, Last Jedi* emphasizes different paths to power—as an engineer, an admiral, or a wise old woman. And unlike Leia in the first films or Padmé in the second set, these women aren't objectified. In fact, Captain Phasma gains an aura of mystery by keeping her full armor for two films. Her onstage parts are very short, but she's revealed as competent and even vicious. Adding nuance to the story, she's a villain, basically the first female one of the film franchise, though nothing in her role or costume insists on femininity.

In contrast with the previous two eras, the sequel films show many women and minorities throughout the galaxy. In small roles, there are many female officers including the ground logistics officer Koo Millham and pilots Cova Nell, Jess Pava, and Pammich Nerro Goode. Korr Sella, emissary to the New Republic and Leia's assistant, dies in *Force Awakens.* Lieutenant Kaydel Connix is delightfully played by Billie Lourd, Carrie Fisher's real-life daughter. Older women (a rarity in action and science fiction) appear in Commander D'acy and Dr. Harter Kalonia, who tends Chewbacca's wounds. Hux's female bridge officer is played by Kate Dickie, while Amira Ghazalla is Captain Canady's First Order commander. In *Last Jedi,* there's also an entire island of female Caretakers in wimples.

It's delightful to see diversity in this top franchise, with the computer-generated Maz Kanata portrayed by Lupita Nyong'o. However, as with Nien Nunb, Jar-Jar, and Darth Vader himself, Maz's voice appears but her real features are concealed, letting her only partway into the franchise. As critic Chauncey DeVega sorrowfully writes in *Salon Magazine*, "This is a carryover from classic 'golden age' American science fiction where racial erasure was accomplished by turning non-whites into robots and aliens for the purposes of either well-intentioned allegory about the social evils of racism and prejudice or just plain old fashioned, ugly white supremacy." Despite this complication, the elderly alien is a delight—teasing and wise, ruler of a substantial castle.

Kelly Marie Tran plays Rose Tico and becomes the first *Star Wars* woman of color not concealed by CGI. This representation is essential. "It's something that I think about a lot," Tran said. "I just remember growing up and not seeing anyone that looked like me in movies" (Flaherty). She takes over a major part of *Last Jedi*, all in a bulky olive jumpsuit even more concealing than Rey's rags and just as unglamorous. While Finn wanders about in a clear bacta suit over his boxers and Kylo Ren stands shirtless in a towel, *Last Jedi*'s heroines do nothing of the sort.

A second Asian American woman appears in her sister Paige. In the Expanded Universe, the pair have several sister adventures together in novels and comics. Onscreen, Paige's short scene onboard a bomber marks her as a soldier, as she's told "It's all up to you. Drop the payload, now!" and releases the bombs in a desperate struggle, only to die alone on her ship. It's striking. *The Mary Sue*'s Laura Jernigan observes, "Paige Tico (Veronica Ngo), Rose's sister, is an unknown in her last moments as she deploys the bombs to destroy a Siege Dreadnought, and yet we watch her struggle, and we connect with her fight. In the first twenty minutes of a major franchise movie, an Asian woman is our hero, and though she dies, it's not so focus can shift to only white characters."

Rose, in mourning but determined to save what remains of the Resistance, spends the film as a well-rounded character with lots of quirks. Director Rian Johnson calls her "Genuinely a nerd. Like someone I would've hung out with in high school. She felt like someone who didn't belong in the *Star Wars* universe, and that genuinely appealed to me" ("The Director and the Jedi"). She and Finn fly off together, both specifically not chosen ones or royalty, emphasizing that anyone can share in the franchise. "Notions of giftedness are tied into exclusionary ideologies that use genetic intelligence to mask social and racial inequalities" (Wright 44). By featuring diverse ordinary soldiers as characters, the show invites all people into its franchise. Further, Rose demonstrates her technical competency and firm morality. Finn respects her as a matter of course and no one expresses surprise.

When they reach the casino planet of Canto Bight, Rose reveals her social justice drives. "The one-percenters on Canto Bright achieved their wealth by selling weapons to the First Order. They're war profiteers; their money is blood money. To Rose, and to those watching through her eyes, their way of life isn't beautiful, it's evil—and deserving of destruction," notes Ngela Watercutter in "*Star Wars: The Last Jedi* Will Bother Some People. Good." She is the Millennial activist, fighting the one-percenters whose strip-mining killed her parents. Further, Rose visits the oppressed stablehand children there, reveals herself as Resistance member, and frees the racing animals. At the film's climax, she stops Finn's suicide run, insisting, "I saved you, dummy. That's how we're gonna win. Not fighting what we hate—saving what we love." She's the one to initiate their romance by kissing him, as well as dismantling the lone hero myth.

> Certainly, her iconic line is an inspiring message, one that fits her role in the story—she stirs the wider universe and emphasizes the ordinary people the Resistance must save. Once again, the imagery reflects an America torn by prejudice and partisanship, in which many gloat about the other party's pain or support increased hardship for everyone if it takes down those on the opposite side. Rose thus comments directly on American politics as she encourages everyone to stop focusing on anger at the other and instead fight to preserve the best parts of their civilization [Frankel 197].

The movie's final scene has one of the young stablehands (played by Temirlan Blaev) wielding his broom like a lightsaber and calling it to his hand with the Force. He is the next generation, who will soon take up the cause. This reaches out to all the young viewers, acknowledging them as the real hope of the future. Jernigan explains, "The story of the rebellion is being heralded by a young Black child—and if that didn't strike a chord with you, you haven't been paying attention to the world recently.... There is hope for the future, and that hope comes in the form of people who are too often forgotten."

In the previous film, *Force Awakens,* Rey (Daisy Ridley) is the true standout. She grows up scavenging in the junkyards, forced to live on the scraps the previous generation has left her, much like millennials in the post–Boomer generation. Still, she has hope of fixing the galaxy. Through her compassion and moral sense, she's determined to fight beside the heroes of the last era and defend her friends. This culminates in a great lightsaber battle with Kylo Ren. His own perspective is chillingly recognizable:

> Now, in early 21st century America, the villain is an unstable young white man who had every privilege in life yet feels like the world has wronged him. Unbeknownst to his family, he finds and communicates with a faraway mentor who radicalizes him with a horrific, authoritarian ideology. By the time his family finds out, it's too late, and now this unstable young white man has this horrific ideology, access to far too many weapons, and the desperate desire to demolish anything that he perceives as a threat—or is told to perceive as a threat [Hillman].

He is another incel or alt-right villain, an entitled millennial prepared to burn down the world, who tries to recruit Rey but also chillingly comments with rape overtones, "You know I can do whatever I want," while she lies strapped to a torture chair. As Kayti Burt notes in "Toxic Masculinity Is the True Villain of *Star Wars: The Last Jedi*," Kylo Ren may be laughable with his tantrums, but with his army, he can't be dismissed. "He is scary because he reminds us of the real-world men whose anger and frustration and sadness have curdled into something ugly inside of them, causing them to lash out at those they perceive to have robbed them of what they deserve." Rey defiantly rescues herself and leaves him far behind.

In the second film, mirroring *Empire*, she seeks training with a hidden master. The story sets her up to spend the film learning from Luke and battling Kylo and Snoke, perpetuating the traditions of the previous generation. However, Luke rejects her offer of his old lightsaber, disdainfully flinging it away in a moment that alerts viewers this will be a different kind of film. Rian Johnson, the writer-director, explains, "Luke's slamming a door in her face seemed like the most obvious thing in the world … there are folks in your life that you expect to fulfill a certain thing, and as we grow up, we realize that that doesn't always happen" ("The Director and the Jedi"). Luke insists he'll only teach her why the Jedi "must end."

Unlike her amazing skillset in the first film in everything from fighting to languages to repairing the Millennium Falcon, this time Rey makes mistakes. She keeps destroying bits of the island, to the misery of the caretakers. And she gets the Force wrong—she defines it as "a power that Jedi have that lets them control people and … make things float" only to be the target of Luke's sarcastic "Impressive. Every word in that sentence was wrong."

> While he insists he wants the Jedi to end, Luke also teaches her that the Force and Force wielders will continue without Jedi training. It's an important lesson echoed in the film's final scene with a young stablehand calling a broom to himself. Through the course of the story, Rey seems to accept that she can wield the Force without thousands of years of patriarchal teachings. This works as a metaphor for old attitudes towards women, minorities, LGBT, traditional governments, corporate power, and more—it's time to evolve [Frankel 180].

Kylo serves Supreme Leader Snoke—his own patriarchal force as he belittles Kylo for being bested by "a girl who had never held a lightsaber." However, Kylo bisects Snoke at his moment of triumph, emphasizing an end to the system. Kylo takes over, but his own gigantic war force fails against Luke Skywalker's mocking shadowy presence. Luke sacrifices himself to cover the Resistance's escape, emphasizing once again the fading of the old ways and the futility of macho warfare. Instead, Kylo ends looking foolish on a beach with the Resistance fleeing to light the spark of revolution among ordinary people.

A third plot likewise dismantles the patriarchy. General Leia Organa (Carrie Fisher) arrives at the head of the Resistance, saving the day in *Force Awakens*. She begins the second film similarly leading her people in battle.

Her costume, with pewter coat over a grey silk gown, suggests business attire, a place in the male hierarchy. While flashy, heroic Poe Dameron (Oscar Isaac) is her protégé, she dismisses his reckless plans. When lives are lost, she censures him. In battle, General Leia has a truly transcendent moment (dismissed by some fans as a far-fetched or silly "Space Poppins" scene) as she floats through space in a protective bubble and survives, though in a coma. After this, her replacement must take charge.

Laura Dern's Vice Admiral Amilyn Holdo tears down the "one woman in the galaxy" pattern with a second female authority figure and friend for Leia. As "a tall thin woman in late middle age, wearing a draped floor-length dress that leaves every curve and angle of her body visible; a woman with dyed-purple hair in a style that requires at the very least a great many pins and more likely a curling iron in addition" she looks more frivolously feminine than mighty, as Arkady Martine of *Tor.com* notes. Poe says incredulously to another pilot: "That's Admiral Holdo? Battle of Chyron Belt Admiral Holdo? Not what I was expecting." While General Leia is commanding, Holdo is softer-sounding. She proclaims, "We are the spark that will light the fire that will restart the resistance," and insists on retreating and spreading their message throughout the galaxy—recruitment, not combat. Her glamor and flirtatiousness along with self-deprecation make her very easy for male characters and audience to dismiss or distrust her. "Women who look like Holdo— femme fatales, even in their middle age, women who look like women who do politics rather than fight, who like frivolous things, jewels and bright hair and makeup even in the darkest moments—we are primed to read women like that as women who will betray. This is an old trope" (Martine).

Still, she cuts Poe down to size, calling him one of the "trigger happy flyboys" and ordering him, "so stick to your post and follow my orders." Further, she refuses to share her plans with him. Watercutter notes: "In a franchise where the heroes have historically succeeded by being cocky and often reckless, placing cooler heads at the helm feels like a pointed demotion for the stuckup, half-witted, scruffy-looking nerf herders." Clearly, the balance is shifting.

In most stories, the hero would disobey orders, go off on his own, and manage to save the day. However, Poe's skirting the chain of command is a disaster. Kayti Burt explains: "Poe's rogue heroics—sending Rose and Finn to Canto Bight, for example—not only don't work, they lead to the near-quashing of the entire Resistance force. Hundreds of people die, and it's at least partially because Poe had visions of glory." Poe continues to defy Holdo, even staging a mutiny until General Leia rises from her sickbed to blast open the doors. She sides with Holdo, shocking the self-righteous Poe.

> Still Leia and Holdo don't dismiss Poe but take the time to explain the larger plan and the need to all work together to achieve it. Instead of glorifying the lone male cowboy, the film emphasizes women's roles as teachers and insists men should con-

sider their effects on the larger society and work as part of it. This subverts the concept of the hero male and emphasizes the silent, enduring power of the women who must suffer as he leaves them behind to clean up [Frankel 212].

Holdo's final plan is to draw enemy fire while letting smaller ships escape under cloak, and finally sacrificing herself. The admiral and general, friends and teammates rather than competitors, bid each other a touching "May the force be with you, always." After, Leia tells Poe about Holdo's sacrifice, "She cared more about protecting the light than seeming like a hero," which, as Burt says, is "subverting the tired narrative trend of the alpha male hero as the only viable or best leadership choice."

> Leia doesn't need to use the Force; she already has a superpower. From Leia's quashing of Poe's ill-advised mutiny to Rose's quashing of Finn's suicidal run for glory, *The Last Jedi* is filled with women trying to explain to men that their actions have consequences outside of their own hero's journey, that glory and pride and victory are never the most important thing—at least not for the larger cause. That the decision that is best for the group is the one made by the group and its chosen leaders, not by the alpha male hero who thinks he knows best [Burt].

Reactions to the film ranged from admiration at its originality to disappointment at its lack of epic story. The trolls got their licks in, and the film was followed by the much more traditionally gendered *Solo* (2018). Unlike in *Ghostbusters*, *Last Jedi*'s preachiness was essential to the plot, but like it, many fans considered the gender-themed message awfully heavy-handed.

"I'm not going to fight your war. I'm going to end it"

At last, Marvel's long-promised superheroine film arrived, as the twenty-first in the MCU lineup (by contrast with *Wonder Woman* two years previous, the fourth film in the DC schedule). Like *Ghostbusters*, *Captain Marvel* incurred plenty of hatred before release. Much of it centered on lead actress Brie Larson's interview comments to *Marie Claire*. Her interviewer, a disabled journalist, commented on how rare it was for her to be sought out. Larson responded that she'd noticed movie reviewers were "overwhelmingly white male." As she added:

> I spoke to Dr. Stacy Smith at the USC Annenberg Inclusion Initiative, who put together a study to confirm that. Moving forward, I decided to make sure my press days were more inclusive. After speaking with you, the film critic Valerie Complex and a few other women of colour, it sounded like across the board they weren't getting the same opportunities as others. When I talked to the facilities that weren't providing it, they all had different excuses.

Thereupon, she resolved to pursue inclusion within the industry. Honored at the Crystal + Lucy Awards, the signature fundraiser for women in film, she made a similar speech: "Am I saying I hate white dudes?" Larson asked. "No, I'm not ... [but if] you make the movie that is a love letter to women of color, there is an insanely low chance a woman of color will have a chance to see your movie and review your movie" (Marotta). Larson continued: "[Audiences] are not allowed enough chances to read public discourse on these films by the people that the films were made for. I do not need a 40-year-old white dude to tell me what didn't work for him about *Wrinkle in Time*. It wasn't made for him. I want to know what it meant to women of color, to biracial women, to *teen* women of color, to *teens* that are biracial" (Marotta).

The previously discussed trolls were incensed over Larson's decision to include more nonwhite reporters. Misquotes of her *Marie Claire* interview demonized her and emphasized her alleged hatred of white men.

> The quote was picked up by film sites last month and regurgitated under headlines that emphasized the words "white" and "male" rather than "inclusive," priming men's rights activists and so-called "incels" to mobilize online over an imagined slight. To them, a call for expanded access to opportunities for women and people of color in a space traditionally dominated by white men (like a Marvel film's press junket) is not only an insult—it amounts to a threat to take away what they consider theirs. And at this point, five years after Gamergate established the playbook for how online harassment campaigns target those who advocate for diversity, websites and content creators have caught on, to their benefit.
>
> Hence the page after page of search results for "Brie Larson" on YouTube, as journalists Matthew Yglesias and Ben Collins noted on Twitter, with titles like "Brie Larson is Ruining Marvel!" (eleven minutes long, 786,000 views) and "How Brie Larson Cost Marvel One Hundred Million Dollars" (20 minutes long, 1.6 million views, extremely faulty math). The latter calls Larson "the demise of entertainment," a "loudmouth blonde-haired narcissist," and "confused." The former argues that one could actually mute a clip of Larson entirely and still glean her pure hatred toward white men: it's in "that little head jerk" of hers, the video maintains. Tweets parroting this point abound. (Leon)

The audience reviews page for *Captain Marvel* on Rotten Tomatoes was flooded with negative, angry "reviews" of the film, most expressing anger about *Captain Marvel*'s starring a female hero. The commenters also criticized star Brie Larson's backing of sending underprivileged girls to see *Captain Marvel* and complained that the film would be a "social justice warrior" film or would ruin the franchise like *Last Jedi*. Many criticized her for not smiling enough in the posters and trailer—so she responded by posting pictures on Instagram of the other Avengers with fake smiles pasted on to show how silly this would look.

All in all, *Captain Marvel*'s audience score was dragged down to a 44 percent audience rating before the film launched thanks to systematized review-bombing campaigns. This was only continuing the attack on all films of this nature, it seemed. The year before, *Black Panther* had seen similar nastiness, as the group "Down With Disney's Treatment of Franchises and its Fanboys" organized an event to start review-bombing *Black Panther* called "Give Black Panther a Rotten Audience Score on Rotten Tomatoes." It drew 3,700 participants. By the time of *Captain Marvel*, the group had been deactivated, but now the attacks were increasingly coordinated. After this, Rotten Tomatoes finally changed how fans could review upcoming films, which included blocking users from leaving a comment or review prior to a movie's theater release. It also purged over 50,000 user reviews from their website. This helped the score better reflect the actual response to the film. "Still, angry men seized the occasion to cry censorship and post screenshots of themselves canceling ticket orders" (Leon).

At last, the film premiered on International Women's Day, March 8, 2019. With an estimated $153 million, *Captain Marvel* proved a massive success, as the third highest March opening of all-time. Exit polls show the opening weekend crowd as 55 percent male and 45 percent female, "which, along with *Black Panther* and *Ant-Man and the Wasp*, is the smallest gender divide among films in the MCU, but nowhere near the 52 percent female crowd *Wonder Woman* played to back in June 2017. Additionally, 64 percent of the film's opening weekend crowd was aged 25 or older, which ranks as one of the older audiences for an MCU film" (Brevet). Internationally, *Captain Marvel* delivered an estimated $302 million, making it the fifth highest international opening weekend of all-time and the sixth largest worldwide debut ever.

Online, however, responses were very polarized. Many women were thrilled at seeing the tough heroine walk around in sloppy clothes, cockily stealing a motorcycle from the guy who tells her to smile. Other viewers were bewildered by the barrage of alien locations and agendas, set against a heroine with little revealed backstory. *USA Today*'s Brian Truitt protested, "Carol's personality, caught between stoic alien warrior and need-for-speed maverick, never gets a chance to fully burst forth as much as her sparkling fists. We spend a lot of time seeing her overcome obstacles and only fitfully glimpse her enjoying life, but never really get to know *her*." However, as Helen O'Hara of *Empire Online* snarkily comments, "Some people will find it disorientating to watch. *Captain Marvel* offers zero concessions to ease anyone in or win them over to Carol Danvers' point of view. If that makes it hard for some viewers to relate to her, she'll deal." True, the movie could have spent longer on Carol's character. However, Truitt points out that many films share this problem—and even get a pass for doing so. As he adds, "It took three *Thor* films for Chris Hemsworth's thunder god to find his groove. Although Larson's heroine is still a work in progress, *Captain Marvel* lays a solid foundation to follow her wherever she flies next." The pre-release harassment emphasizes how much it's not getting the same benefit of the doubt.

While Carol dominates the screen, there are delightful women sharing the story. Carol begins to recollect her memories of earth when Fury helps her find her mentor Wendy Lawson's files, but she truly reclaims herself joking with her old friend Maria Rambeau in Louisiana. "They have a really sisterly, free and sarcastic human friendship," her actress Lashana Lynch says. "A lot of what Carol feels in the first part of the movie is brought about by Maria reminding her of who she is, reminding her of what her power is—as a woman, not a superhero" (McIntyre and Sullivan 43). Defending her home against the alien intruder Talos, Maria gets a memorable zinger in when she announces, "Call me young lady again and I'll put my foot in a place it's not supposed to be." Her daughter, Carol's beloved "Lieutenant Trouble" (Akira Akbar), redesigns Carol's uniform and encourages her mother to set out on the ultimate epic space battle. "You have the chance to fly on the coolest mission of all missions…. I just think you oughta consider what kind of example you're setting for your daughter," little Monica supplies helpfully. More amusingly, comic book fans recognize Monica Rambeau as the second Captain Marvel, a future superhero in her own right. As the first wave of heroes pass beyond their contracts, a new wave of younger ones will rise to take their place.

Further, Maria remarks that "the Air Force still wasn't letting women fly combat" in 1989, so Wendy Lawson made a way for both her and Carol to go on true missions. Gender-flipping the original Kree Mar-Vell (alias Walter Lawson) into a woman gives Carol both a mentor and a lineage of feminist power. Nick Fury and the hilarious alien cat round out her entourage. Both provide the humor and tough support on Carol's journey to discover who she is. However, the youthful Fury must let her take charge, since Carol can battle the aliens he never suspected existed. Physically, she's also more capable. This is demonstrated when he uses clever spycraft to get through a door by lifting a fingerprint. Carol blasts the next door easily. "You watched me sit there and play with tape?" Fury protests.

"I didn't want to steal your thunder," she quips, with shared humor that nonetheless emphasizes that she can manage fine without him. The origin story is played in reverse, starting her off as a competent soldier, already with superpowers. As her team leader Yon-Rogg (Jude Law) insists, "Your life began the day it nearly ended. We found you with no memory. We made you one of us, so you could live longer, stronger, superior. You were reborn." However, "Vers," as she's called, must rediscover her entire self as Carol Danvers and fight off the lies that have confined her. When she finally does, she discovers her powers truly have no limits.

Certainly, the film had many jobs to do, enough that some fans felt overwhelmed. The film introduced the Skrulls (and then threw out all of the heroine's and comic book audience's expectations of them in a surprise twist). It supplied more backstory on the Kree. As a prequel, it established how Fury and Coulson began the Avengers Initiative even as it also bridged into *Avengers: Endgame* (while, many speculate, setting up a *Secret Invasion* conflict in future). It also had to provide a fresh new origin story in a superhero franchise getting tired of the formula. It sought to inspire young girls and older women while entertaining the boys as well. Mock the nineties for young fans and nostalgically visit them for older ones. Keep its heroine likeable but also incredibly tough. Beyond all this, of course, it had to earn enough money to prove female superheroes could excel.

It's no surprise the film had no time for a love interest. Angry without apology, Carol is battling all the oppression in the galaxy and fighting for herself and a better tomorrow. "She scoffs at authority, drives herself to extremes and sometimes loses her temper. She's Marvel's first solo female lead, and she is not here to play" (O'Hara). While her female anger wasn't specifically a big criticism, many fans seemed at least confused by their trouble connecting with the film. Comments like "she just seemed so wooden and distant" or "I just liked Wonder Woman better" emphasized the contrast between storytelling styles. While *Wonder Woman* tries not to zoom in on the heroine's curves (unlike *Justice League*), its heroine wears several decidedly skimpy outfits and also dons a ballgown to distract and entice the enemy. She has a conventional romance. Further, Diana tries persuading the World War I brass in Britain to see her side, and when she's dismissed as a hysterical woman, she is forced to sneak off to the front. In all these ways, Diana conforms, despite her strength. She never even raises women up—the other females of "man's world" are Steve's tough but obedient secretary and wicked General Ludendorff's subordinate Doctor Poison, who ends the film cringing and sobbing on the ground. Diana is presented as a magical exception who mostly conceals herself, even to the point of playing Steve's secretary. The status quo remains.

Carol never plays Fury's subordinate—infiltrating the P.E.G.A.S.U.S. base, she's a fellow agent and, thanks to her blaster, clearly doesn't need him. She never dresses to please others or smiles to put them at ease. Her scenes with Maria, Mar-Vell, and the Supreme Intelligence emphasize that major areas of her life don't involve men at all. While Wonder Woman makes mistakes in "man's world" and welcomes a guide, Captain Marvel is so capable that she doesn't need anyone … and that made some viewers uncomfortable. Director Anna Boden comments: "She has a lot of swagger and a real sense of humor. She's a fighter pilot in the Air Force, so she has that kind of Top Gun/Maverick attitude. Part of that comes from a deep-seated need to prove herself, which comes from having some self-doubt and fear. Does she become humble? Dies she end the movie with any less swagger than she began it with?" (*Official Movie Special* 10). Clearly, she doesn't.

As the climax approaches, Carol discovers that determined women can topple all aspects of the patriarchy. First, she banishes the Supreme Intelligence's control over her and rips off its inhibitor. "I've been fighting with one arm tied behind my back. But what happens when I'm finally set free?" She glows with new powers. The 1995 hit "Just a Girl" plays while she handily defeats her former team. By no longer seeking approval or obeying, she tears apart the entire system, fighting for her desires instead of the goals of others. "*Captain Marvel* says that, when we stop looking for approval, we can become literally godlike. This is not another cheap girl-power cliché; it's an explicitly feminist apotheosis" (O'Hara).

After this, she flies on her own, saves earth from a barrage of Kree missiles, decimates an enemy space fleet, and makes the all-powerful fanatic Ronan the Accuser withdraw in disgrace. With this, she returns to earth to beat up her former mentor Yon-Rogg, who once insisted her giving up her emotions would make her the "best version" of herself. He proposes they fight hand to hand so he can remind her that she's still too emotional. With this, he tries to frame the combat to suit his macho outlook. Instead, she blasts him across the wasteland and then towers over him. "I have nothing to prove to you." As he lies defeated, she drags him to his plane and straps him with a message to relay. "Tell the Supreme Intelligence I'm coming to end it. The war, the lies, all of it." She will spend the next decades tearing apart the entire system, beginning with those who convinced her she was weak. No wonder some men cringed at the film.

Additionally, some watchers felt they had no point of view character. If in 2017 they hadn't wanted to empathize with Diana (despite her sword-fighting action and willingness to join the boys' club), there was Steve Trevor, manly all-American hero who gets the girl and finally sacrifices himself to save the world. Watchers of *Captain Marvel,* however, had trouble connecting to Fury, as he played rather a goofball and cooed devotedly over a pet cat. With no one filling the tough-guy job, many macho fans felt cast adrift. "Everyone wants to identify, to aspire up," said Kelly Sue DeConnick, who reinvented the comics heroine from 1977's underdressed Ms. Marvel to the tough, modestly-dressed captain in 2012, and faced backlash in the process (McIntyre and Sullivan 42). "So if you are female and therefore lower status in terms of your cultural power, it's much more comfortable to identify up with a male hero than it is for men to identify down to a lower status [character]" (McIntyre and Sullivan 42).

In the end, this film felt written for women and not for men—the majority of fans were fine with that, though a significant minority filled the web with complaints. In light of this, Brie Larson has become more aware of how much girls need these films: "'It's so interesting, as it's not something I thought about until I was in the cinema watching *Wonder Woman*. About two minutes in, I was sobbing …It was seeing all of these warrior women who were so self-sufficient. That wasn't something I identified with growing up—my hero was Indiana Jones. To have the chance to be one example of this is powerful and exciting" (Brown). At the same time, it seems clear that making them will continue the pushback.

Conclusion

Clearly, there are many angles possible in a female empowerment film. Most writers agree that the key is offering different women, of different backgrounds, and celebrating different paths to power—Maz or Rose is as legitimate a type of hero as Rey. Beyond this, there are different types of structure. One can flip a story to contain female leads, like *Ghostbusters, The Heat,* Jodie Whittaker's *Doctor Who* or *Ocean's 8*. One can set heroines against the patriarchy, from an all-powerful male leader like Katniss's President Snow to tantrum-filled Kylo Ren. One can create an island of all women, where everyone is a celebrated hero, as in *Wonder Woman,* or show that any woman can tear down the system like *Captain Marvel.* Increasingly in television and film, a man encourages a woman to step out of the shadows and be a central figure or take over the story (*Justice League, The Hunger Games, Star Trek Discovery, Moana, X-Men Apocalypse, Logan, A Wrinkle in Time, Class, Agents of S.H.I.E.L.D.*). However, this risks the woman, as in *X-Men: Apocalypse* or *Logan,* appearing more killing machine than person, while leaving her male mentor with the agency.

Further, these very direct, often exaggerated models don't teach the most balanced approach to true partnership. It's found in *Black Panther* or *Thor: Ragnarok* or *Into the Spiderverse,* or *Deadpool,* in which women may technically be sidekicks but they're also respected as equals and emerge with fully formed personalities. Female-led action films are a tougher balancing act, as there are so few, but *Hunger Games* and *Divergent* as well as *Wonder Woman, Ant-Man and the Wasp, A Wrinkle in Time, Mortal Engines, Moana,* and *Frozen* succeeded with female saviors partnered with very competent male leads. Instead of humiliating the men and showing them to be painfully wrong as with misguided Poe in *Last Jedi* or doofus Kevin in *Ghostbusters,* leaving out the trolls entirely sends a better message—when the heroes of both genders band together to create a better world. Still, it's awfully satisfying to see Carol Danvers flatten them all.

Works Cited

Adams, Sam. "Why the *Ghostbusters* Backlash Is a Sexist Control Issue." *Indie Wire,* 14 July 2016. https://www.indiewire.com/2016/07/ghostbusters-reboot-backlash-1201705555/.
Black Panther. Directed by Ryan Coogler, Disney, 2018.
Bowen, Sesali. "Black Panther Has a Message for Black Men: Trust Black Women." *Refinery*

29, 16 February 2018. https://www.refinery29.com/en-us/2018/02/191093/black-panther-ending-women-wakanda-feminist-message.

Bradley, Bill, and Matthew Jacobs. "Surprise, Surprise: The 'Alt-Right' Claims Credit for Last Jedi Backlash." *Huffington Post,* 20 December 2017. https://www.huffingtonpost.com/entry/rotten-tomatoes-last-jedi-ratings-bots_us_5a38cb78e4b0860bf4aab5b1.

Brevet, Brad. "*Captain Marvel* Delivers a Massive $153M Domestic Opening and $455M Worldwide." *Box Office Mojo,* 10 Mar 2019. https://www.boxofficemojo.com/news/?id=4493&p=.htm.

Brockington, Ariana. "Why the Women of Wakanda Rule *Black Panther.*" *Variety,* 14 February 2018. https://variety.com/2018/film/news/black-panther-women-marvel-wakanda-angela-1202695899.

Brown, Keah. "Brie Larson on Superheroes, Success and her Hollywood Sisterhood." *Marie Claire,* 7 Feb 7 2019. https://www.marieclaire.co.uk/entertainment/tv-and-film/brie-larson-64175.

Burt, Kayti. "Toxic Masculinity Is the True Villain of *Star Wars: The Last Jedi.*" *Den of Geek,* 15 December 2017. http://www.denofgeek.com/us/movies/star-wars/269657/toxic-masculinity-is-the-true-villain-of-star-wars-the-last-jedi.

Campbell-Reid, Natalie. "Wakanda For-never?" *Medium,* 2 March 2018 https://medium.com/@nataliecampbellreid/wakanda-for-never-7c438d02c507.

Captain Marvel The Official Movie Special. Titan, 2019.

Chamberlain, Prudence. *The Feminist Fourth Wave: Affective Temporality.* Palgrave Macmillan, 2017.

DeVega, Chauncey. "Our New Post-Obama Star Wars: Race, the Force and the Dark Side in Modern America." *Salon,* 19 December 2015. https://www.salon.com/2015/12/19/our_new_post_obama_star_wars_race_the_force_and_the_dark_side_in_modern_america.

Dowd, Kathy Ehrich. "Star Wars Director J.J. Abrams Addresses Black Stormtrooper Casting Controversy: People Complaining 'Probably Have Bigger Problems.'" *People,* 1 December 2015. http://people.com/celebrity/star-wars-director-j-j-abrams-addresses-black-stormtrooper-casting.

Faludi, Susan. *Backlash: The Undeclared War Against Women.* Vintage, 1991.

Flaherty, Keely. "The Rise of Rose." *BuzzFeed,* 14 November 2017. https://www.buzzfeed.com/keelyflaherty/the-rise-of-rose.

Frankel, Valerie Estelle. *Star Wars Meets the Eras of Feminism: Weighing All the Galaxy's Women Great and Small.* Lexington Press, 2018.

Ghostbusters. Directed by Paul Feig, Village Roadshow Pictures, 2016.

Hillman, Melissa. "'This Is Not Going to Go the Way You Think': *The Last Jedi* is as Subversive AF and I Am Here for It." *Bitter Gertrude,* 20 December 2017. https://bittergertrude.com/2017/12/20/this-is-not-going-to-go-the-way-you-think-the-last-jedi-is-subversive-af-and-i-am-here-for-it.

Jasper, Marykate. "Good Grief, Now There's a Petition to Remove *The Last Jedi* from *Star Wars* Canon." *The Mary Sue,* 19 December 2017 https://www.themarysue.com/last-jedi-petition-remove-canon.

Jernigan, Lauren. "*Star Wars: The Last Jedi* Ushers in the Future of Storytelling." *The Mary Sue,* 22 December 2017. https://www.themarysue.com/last-jedi-future-of-storytelling.

Johnson, Rian. "The Director and the Jedi." *Star Wars: The Last Jedi.* Disney, 2018. Blu-ray.

Koski, Genevieve. "How 2 Racist Trolls Got a Ridiculous *Star Wars* Boycott Trending on Twitter." *Vox Magazine,* 19 October 2015. https://www.vox.com/2015/10/19/9571309/star-wars-boycott.

Leon, Melissa. "How Brie Larson's *Captain Marvel* Made Angry White Men Lose Their Damn Minds." *The Daily Beast,* 6 Mar 2019. https://www.thedailybeast.com/how-brie-larsons-captain-marvel-made-angry-white-men-lose-their-damn-minds.

Marotta, Jenna. "Brie Larson Promises 'I Do Not Hate White Dudes,' but Laments Lack of Inclusion among Film Critics." *IndieWire,* 14 June 2018. https://www.indiewire.com/2018/06/brie-larsons-i-do-not-hate-white-dudes-lack-of-inclusion-film-critics-1201974617.

Martine, Arkady. "*Star Wars'* Vice-Admiral Holdo and Our Expectations for Female Military

Power." *Tor*, 21 December 2017. https://www.tor.com/2017/12/21/star-wars-vice-admiral-holdo-and-our-expectations-for-female-military-power.

McIntyre, Gina and Kevin P. Sullivan. "They're Only Human." *EW: The Ultimate Guide to Captain Marvel*. March 2019, pp. 40–43.

O'Hara, Helen. "Captain Marvel Review." *Empire Online*, 5 Mar 2019. https://www.empireonline.com/movies/captain-marvel/review.

Pantozzi, Jill. "Daisy Ridley Deleted Her Instagram." *The Nerdy Bird*, 2 August 2016. http://thenerdybird.com/daisy-ridley-harassed-off-instagram-political-opinion.

Penny, Laurie. *Cybersexism: Sex, Gender and Power on the Internet*. Bloomsbury Publishing, 2013.

Robinson, Tasha. "*Ghostbusters* Review: A Crowd-pleaser That More Than Justifies Its Existence." *The Verge*, 13 July 2016. https://www.theverge.com/2016/7/13/12173084/ghostbusters-movie-review-paul-feig-kate-mckinnon.

Sarkeesian, Anita. "*Ghostbusters* (2016) Review." *Feminist Frequency*, 18 July 2016. https://feministfrequency.com/2016/07/18/ghostbusters-2016-review/.

Spencer, Robyn C. "Black Feminist Meditations on the Women of Wakanda (Spoiler Alert)." *Medium*, 21 February 2018. https://medium.com/@robyncspencer/black-feminist-meditations-on-the-women-of-wakanda-5cc79751d9cd.

Star Wars Episode VIII—The Last Jedi. Directed by Rian Johnson, Walt Disney Studios, 2018.

Tillet, Salamishah "*Black Panther*: Why Not Queen Shuri? (Guest Column)." *Hollywood Reporter*, 19 February 2018. https://www.hollywoodreporter.com/heat-vision/black-panther-why-not-queen-shuri-guest-column-1086012.

Truitt, Brian. "Review: *Captain Marvel* Sparkles as intro to Brie Larson's Work-in-progress Warrior." *USA Today*, 5 Mar 2019. https://www.usatoday.com/story/life/movies/2019/03/05/review-captain-marvel-sparkles-as-brie-larsons-superhero-intro/3057153002.

Watercutter, Ngela. "*Star Wars: The Last Jedi* Will Bother Some People. Good." *Wired*, 15 December 2017. https://www.wired.com/story/star-wars-last-jedi-inclusion.

Wright, Katherine. *The New Heroines*. ABC-CLIO, 2016.

Sci-Fi/Fantasy Movies
for Identity Politics
in Fourth Wave Feminism

AAMIR AZIZ *and* FARWA JAVED

Feminism is a revolutionary phenomenon, not just as a literary theory but as a practical movement in history too. Until recently, we have been studying it in books and in modern critical theory texts but in this age of pronounced social media relevance when anything can go viral in public within a time span of seconds, and when new issues regarding socio-economics, politics, literary arts and many other public institutions are usually trending every other day, feminism is also a very widely talked about phenomenon, not just in literary circles but also in the common social circles, in general. Women are no longer considered a biologically weak or inferior gender. They speak loudly for themselves. Public feminism is not a new issue but because of the fact that more women are giving voice to their problems by including themselves in the movements like "me too" and "women's marches," this term has gained much significance in recent years. There are special media platforms to address and to attempt to resolve this kind of issue.

Feminism is not just a literary theory anymore. It has become a socially urgent subject in which its supporters demand equal rights and opportunities for both men and women. They want to see even representation of both these genders in every walk of life be it education, politics, business, or sports. Feminists are using new media platforms and venues as tools to express themselves and they are going out of their way to give voice to these problems. These new media platforms include the social media websites like Facebook, Twitter, and Instagram.

Feminism might have been a little perplexing for a lay man to fully comprehend during its early days, but, afterward, it gained enormous acclaim and popularity among the concerned population because of the print and electronic media. If we go through world literatures, we can see some radical characters outlined by brilliant authors over the course of literary history who have used art as a vehicle to address problems that were primarily the outcome of patriarchy and its excesses. These characters are polemical in the sense that they were way ahead of their times but at the same time, feminists call them radicals. From a theoretical standpoint, feminism urges women to create their own language and tools of creating art from their own perspectives. The feminist literary theorists did not come up with absolutely new insights; rather, the pioneer theorists just presented the opposite ideas of whatever disrespectful comment was said against them by avowedly patriarchal theorists like Freud or Lacan. Feminism is a voice box for women that makes men of the society realize what it is like to be a woman in a male-dominated society. Feminist literature supports the feminist thinking of shaping, developing and defending equal civil, political and socio-economic rights for women.

Mary Klages explained this theory in her book *Literary Theory: A Guide for the Perplexed*. She explains how women are being treated in patriarchal societies and how they are pushed back upon pretext of men's claim that all the great professions are for them. Many feminists like Virginia Woolf, Gilbert and Gubar, Cixous, Irigary, etc., reacted to what Freud and Lacan meant by writing only revolving around men. They said that whoever has a male sexual organ can write and others can't, whereas all the feminist theorists said that women have more powerful sexual organs than men and in fact men need women for jouissance; therefore, females are an equally significant part of society. The most prominent contribution to this utopian experimentalist ideology came from French feminism by the works of Kristeva, Cixous and Irigaray after inspiration from Barthes, Derrida and Lacan. This idea gained enormous popularity during the 1970s and 80s as it related jouissance and the sexual difference (Dekoven 1691).

This stance is being proved in this age of fourth wave of feminism, though the third wave definitely gave it a push. Most people agree that the fourth wave started in 2012 with many of the strong female sci-fi characters depicting a feminism we had never seen or talked about before. For example, as more of a traditionally third wave feminist character, Pepper Potts from the first *Iron Man* movie is more than the superhero's girlfriend or rescue object. Tony Stark (the protagonist) admits at the end of the movie that he loves her and needs her to run his business. Her strength speaks for itself. This is one of the few characters that became inspiration for the fourth wave characters.

Contemporary feminists like Judith K. Brown propose fourth wave feminism as the answer to the misappropriation of the term feminism, associated with the third wave (1073). To better understand contemporary feminist issues, it is essential that we understand how the previous waves of feminism saw gender and how this affected the purpose and approach of each movement. First and second wavers did not show a special concern with theorizing and understanding gender. However, they did share a common idea of what gender was, which shaped their approach.

First wave and second wave feminists both acted on the belief that male and female were separate and distinct categories. They operated under the understanding that gender was binary. They also assumed gender was biologically determined by sex. This understanding of gender translated to view the society where male domination and oppression formed a patriarchal structure. It was this belief that, perhaps erroneously, had them focus on women's rights, without considering in depth what the term "women" delineated. The need to understand gender emerged in the third wave as a reaction to a perceived misrepresentation of women in the previous waves. Because of an increased interest in understanding what "women" constituted, with the aim of being an inclusive movement, which represented all women, many theoretical feminists became increasingly invested in understanding the complexities of sex, gender and sexuality.

In attempting to challenge binary categorizations, feminists became involved in sociological experiments which sought to understand how, if at all, Biology or Sociology affected and predisposed biologically "considered" female or male persons to the culturally associated attributes of femininity and masculinity. This concern third wavers had for theoretical understandings of the complexities of womanhood initiated debates around gender fluidity and intersectionality, a term coined by Crenshaw in 1989. Intersectionality is: "The view that women experience oppression in varying configurations and in varying degrees of intensity. Cultural patterns of oppression are not only interrelated, but are bound together and influenced by the intersectional systems of society. Examples of this include race, gender, class, ability, and ethnicity" (Vidal).

The idea is that women's identities are composed of many multi-layered aspects, which present their own difficulties that must be dealt with, and hence, a "one-size-fits-all approach" does not benefit feminism. Intersectionality is a relatively new concept for the public, and yet the ideology behind it is surely one that any feminist could relate to: be inclusive of all types of women within the movement, take into account different types of life experience, show respect for these varying identities and include all women in the debate. Fourth wave attempts to put these ideas, initially sparked by third wave thinking, into practice. It takes a step back from the idea of male and female opposition and extends the concern for true representation to all on the gender spectrum. However, fourth wave is defined by intersectionality;

it accepts that there can be many other factors pertaining to one's identity, which lead to inequality, which can act in relation to gender. With this, gender alone cannot be and should not be spoken for as a sole defining constituent for inequality. It is this idea of intersectionality that has sparked concerns for cultural appropriation within feminism. In third wave, we saw a growing practice of media analysis, a deconstruction of text and image, which sought to understand the differences in how men and women were marketed to and represented in the media. Third wave acknowledged the importance of representation, both within the movement and in the media and looked at the current media texts as well as historical ones to fully understand the process of representation that women had undergone.

Adequate representation is important because it affects the way we see ourselves within the wider context of society. The media provides role models; it is important that these attempt to represent everybody, since inadequate representation can marginalize or stigmatize members of society. Third wave showed special concern with how misrepresentation, underrepresentation, objectification and hyper-sexualization of women in the media created stereotypes. They challenged media portrayals pertaining to gender, because they believed these stereotypes encouraged self-fulfilling prophecies (Gill) and hence limited the advancement of women. Media portrayals of women particularly in second wave advertising encouraged female domesticity and maintained an oppositional relationship between men and women, where women were shown as the more vulnerable "second sex" (Beauvoir). The transition from radio to TV as the main household appliance for receiving information shifted visual representation from print to screen.

The film industry no longer lived in the cinema; films now had a wider audience and so these, and television programs played a significant part in representation (Briggs and Burke). Though developments had been made by the time third wave was born, there were still many concerns for how influential representation was, and how women in particular were portrayed in the media. As Cochrane states:

> Many of those at the forefront are in their teens and 20s, and had their outlook formed during decades in which attitudes to women were particularly confusing. They grew up being told the world was post-feminist, that sexism and misogyny were over, and feminists should pack up their placards. At the same time, women in the public eye but often either sidelined or sexualized, represented in exactly the same way as they had been in the 70s, albeit beneath a thin veil of irony [Cochrane].

In recent years, not only has there been a high rise of women hating men, but a rise of women hating other women as well. The fourth wave is a judgment free zone and encourages all women of different body types, appearances, and personalities to do whatever makes them feel most comfortable and confident: No more telling women what to do, when to do it, and how to do it. What does the world need less of? Body shaming. What does the world need more of? Body positivity and positivity, in general.

"Fem" might be in feminism, but that doesn't mean men can't be a part of the action, too. Male feminists are very common now. The fourth wave suppresses misandry and actually acknowledges those men who fight for equality. For example, what do Ryan Gosling and Tony Goldwyn have in common? They're both men and feminists. The fourth wave helps us recognize that inequality needs to be resolved with efforts from both or, rather, all genders. The fourth wave brings genders together, instead of dividing against one another.

Since this is the age of sci-fi and fantasy fiction, the live-action fairytale has also seen a Hollywood renaissance in recent years, marked by films ranging from the Oscar-winning *Mirror Mirror* to the newest addition to the live-action fairytale family *Cinderella*, as well as the wildly popular television series, *Once Upon a Time*. The trend shows no sign of slowing down. Disney's recent release of a live-action version of *Beauty and the Beast* with Emma Watson broke box office records. The actress is also a UN ambassador of the "He for She" campaign and she is becoming a popular figure of fourth wave. Her character in the movie is a strong young female who knows what she wants, known for her intellect, beauty and strong personality. She does not allow her poor circumstances to be obstacles, but rather she accepts what she has and makes the best out of it. When she is caught in the castle of the Beast, she is not depicted as a scared teenager but as a woman of compassion and strong willpower. She represents the women of this age. Despite being a young village girl, she is passionate for her dreams and becomes an inspiration and an icon of bravery and courage for even the Beast.

This is what fourth wave of feminism represents and teaches. This adaptation tells that the beastly Prince will need Belle more than Belle needs him ever, and that is a big step in fantasy films. It also proves the idea that women don't need men as much as men need women. From the theoretical approach, it is feminists' stance that men need women for jouissance, but women can do whatever they want and they don't need men. Belle and Beast's relationship also proves this stance from a different angle. Belle is condemned by the villagers for wanting "more than this provincial life," but refuses to be bullied into marriage even when her father's life is threatened, and it's difficult to think of a better embodiment of sexual menace than Gaston. *Beauty and the Beast* is less about dreams coming true and more about overcoming dire circumstances. It possesses a certain darkness that, if properly tapped into, could speak to gender inequality in society rather than making incomplete albeit well intentioned attempts to co-opt feminism into fairy tales.

Comments that Watson made during her International Women's Day Facebook chat on March 9, 2017 (McKenzie and Parke), denounced once and for all the Tall-Tale-As-Old-As-Time that chivalry and feminism can't coexist. Instead, Watson's public persona has perfectly embodied the idea of embracing the inherently traditional while standing firm in a gender-equality ideology. This has been reflected in several recent fairytale adaptations, which, if similarly championed, may eventually provide a brilliant insight that may help the fifth wave feminists. In other words, we may soon see the day when it is impossible to make a fairytale adaptation without a feminist slant.

Maleficent in the movie *Maleficent,* whom critics felt was the savior of an otherwise unwarranted reimagining, is also an advocate of fourth wave feminism. The film received substantial positive commentary on its exploration of abuse and victimhood through the character of Maleficent who, in the film, was portrayed as a fairy driven to vengeance after being stripped of her wings by Aurora's father in his ambition to rule her kingdom. In fairytales, women are typically either the damsel or the villain, and allowing Maleficent to tell her story, let alone one that mirrored rape culture, defied this stereotype. Maleficent also ultimately upheld the notion that the relationships between strong women are more powerful than romance, by making the spell-breaking "true love's kiss" a maternal act of love on the part of the title character.

Similarly, in television's *Once Upon a Time*, Snow White's daughter Emma saves her son Henry after selflessly collaborating with his ill-intentioned adoptive mother (the Evil Queen) and giving him a kiss on the forehead, once again emphasizing the strength of maternal love, but also indirectly emphasizing sisterly love.

Disney's recent animated princess adventure, *Frozen*, received widespread praise not only for its chart-topping soundtrack and quality as family entertainment, but also for establishing a new paradigm in Disney's princess genre by making the kingdom-thawing "true love" the bond between the two royal sisters, rather than involving any male counterpart. *Frozen* depicted a woman of passion in the character of Elsa who does not want to ruin her sister's life and for that, she sacrifices her own comfort and royalty and starts to live far away from her sister to protect her. From this movie, we get the idea that even though she has an evil power that can destroy an entire kingdom and the huge castle in seconds, if she learns to embrace her magic instead of fearing it, she can make it a force for good.

On the other hand, her sister Anna longs for a perfect wedding, but she cannot bear her sister's separation. Over the course of the film she comes to realize that a handsome prince cannot solve all her problems. Anna is the younger sister, but she is the one who makes her elder sister realize that goodness outweighs all other qualities. Fourth wave feminism depicted from movies like these suggests that women can do wonders in even little acts. They have the courage and compassion to sacrifice their own life and comfort for someone else and for a righteous cause; they can be one's worst nightmare too.

The Last Jedi is a brilliant *Star Wars* film for women. Most obviously, there are women there at every level, from high-ranking military to lowly technicians in sloppy coveralls. New character Rose, played by Kelly Marie Tran (the first Asian actress in the film franchise), has a taser and a brain and isn't afraid to use either. In an early scene, John Boyega's Finn stands in front of her, mansplaining, until she loudly interrupts him. There are no lone heroes in *The Last Jedi*; everything is a team effort, but what heroics there are truly belong to the ladies, from the very early bombing scene to the final rocky rescue. General Leia leads the rebellion, eventually replaced by Laura Dern's Admiral Holdo after a bit of Force flying. Powerful older women are showing up in fourth wave more than ever, with this film deliberately offering two.

Rey's rejection of Kylo's romantic overtures and offer of shared power is a feminist triumph. Unlike Leia, who earns her credentials as general but originally was adopted into royalty and born into her Skywalker family destiny, Rey is revealed to be absolutely nobody. This made people cheer and cry. The previous film, *The Force Awakens,* was desperately trying to hint that Rey's parentage was Luke-and-Leia special and the internet was agog with speculation for months, but *The Last Jedi* threw that old trope into a trash compactor where it belongs. Rey is herself, with no resources inherited or bought, self-made with no help from anyone, not even Luke, really. His rejection of her request for training and the entire obsolete Jedi tradition itself cause Rey to reinvent the Force on her own terms. Clearly, the Master/Padawan relationship belongs to the failed patriarchy of the old films. New *Star Wars* belongs to a new generation, and this time it's women.

Harry Potter and the Cursed Child, a theatrical sequel to the Harry Potter series, got published in July 2016. Though it is a boy-oriented play starring Scorpius Malfoy and Albus Severus Potter, the character of Hermione Granger is a huge inspiration for the readers. She is depicted as the Minister of Magic, which is justified as she was the brightest witch of her age. This is the first time in Harry Potter series that we are shown a female Minister of Magic. People have seen Hermione being a sassy and intellectual girl in the original Harry Potter books and movies franchise, though she was always stigmatized for coming from a Muggle family. Now, older Hermione is flipped to a Black actress for new levels of representation. Her character emphasizes that her ideal qualities led to her achieving the highest post of the wizarding world. There, she chastises Harry Potter the great hero and makes plans that even the adult Draco Malfoy follows.

Mad Max: Fury Road delivers a lot of strong messages and perspectives of how women can actually replace men in the battlefield and better the situation even when they are the objects of sexual abuse. When it comes to defending their loved ones, gender is not something to think about. Most of them just do it for the sake of their safety because women and men are both fundamentally human beings wrapped by feelings and strong wills too. This then leads to the questions of women's roles in everyday life and how some of their socially assigned roles are only pushing them to develop as competitors to men. Another feminist perspective depicted in the movie is how the female character proves to the world that the successful ending of this movie is primarily because of the role played by its women. Furiosa, for instance, is represented as an equal of Max with as many if not more skills. The film also depicts destruction of this society due to the ancient form of patriarchy (Barrett 5).

This movie addresses the issue of gender inequality that the fourth wave of feminism seeks to negate. We find many occasions when the women face inequality and struggle to meet their needs in the movie. Furthermore, the equality in the *Mad Max: Fury Road* movie is seen from the male's perspective. Max, the main male character, agrees to let the heroine Furiosa do what she needs to do because he knows she's capable. One of the ways to reach equality toward women is by reaching out with men's perspectives about it. Once one man believes the same thoughts as women, that women have equal rights and opportunities, then gender equality can be realized easily. The fourth wave of feminism is more humanistic than the previous ones. It teaches that anyone, independent of his gender, facing injustice or inequality is a victim. That is why the fourth wave supports anyone who is being suppressed.

Another recent sci-fi movie is *Wonder Woman*. As the name suggests, it is the perfect wonder of fourth wave feminism. The protagonist is a female who knows that the world is in danger and she decides to fight the evil. Although her loved ones tell her not to go, she is a rebel in this sense. She goes beyond the odds to break this stereotype that women can't fight, as she battles to protect innocents. The fourth wave of feminism advocates that whatever a person wants to do, she can do and he or she should not be judged for those goals.

Last but not the least, Katniss Everdeen from the *Hunger Games* series is the ultimate character who comes to mind in fourth wave feminism. In many Hollywood action films, such as *Lara Croft: Tomb Raider* or *Catwoman*, the heroine is often sexualized and objectified; however, Katniss Everdeen is not. After Katniss' father has died, the patriarchy has clearly failed and as a result, Katniss is forced to step in as the provider for the household, a male position, developing her skills at hunting and archery. To allow an audience to empathize with the protagonist, male orientated language and themes like arson, violence and gore must be employed to the point that if Katniss were a male, the basic storyline would not be that much different. This is an example of how a writer using a female protagonist is faced with the issue of *écriture feminine,* or women's writing. Even if the novel and screenplay author Suzanne Collins had wanted to avoid stereotyped roles, to be able to tell a story the audience can relate to, she needs to conform to the male model of the world.

Katniss also acts as the protector for her younger sister, Primrose Everdeen, again fulfilling the role of the father. She claims this role to the extent of volunteering to compete in the Hunger Games in lieu of her sister. As provider and protector of the household, she feels responsible for the family. When Katniss is taken away, she is isolated in a room and given three minutes to speak with her family and friends. When she is talking to her mother about caring for Primrose, she speaks very emphatically. Her tone and language are not consistent with a conversation between daughter and mother. Cixous et al. claim that it is our sexuality that is directly tied to how we communicate in society. Katniss' manner of speaking is more consistent with a conversation between husband and wife; as head of the household, she is telling her mother to look after Primrose, "No matter what you feel, you have to be there for her, do you understand? Don't cry. Don't." She presents a new model of leader rather than damsel.

Conclusion

The fourth wave of feminism, especially with the reference to sci-fi and fantasy movies, proves that women are an equal gender to men. In fact, this wave is actually more humanistic, so its stance is that every human being is equally important, independent of his gender. The major focus of this movement is on women, so the characters discussed above are all female. The characters from different movies describe and depict practically what it means to be a woman, particularly a woman of strength. Whether one is a village girl or a princess, a witch or a fighter, these characters tell a story that every woman faces challenges that she can overcome just like men. All she needs is willpower, courage and a vision.

Works Cited

Barrett, Kyle. "*Mad Max: Fury Road*—Challenging Narrative and Gender Representation in the Action Genre." *Media Education Journal,* vol. 3, Winter 17–18, pp. 3–6.
Brown, Judith K. "A Note on the Division of Labour by Sex." *American Anthropologist* vol. 72 no. 5, 1970, pp. 1073–78.
Cixous, Hélène, Keith Cohen, and Paula Cohen. "The Laugh of the Medusa." *Signs,* vol. 1, no. 4, Summer 1976, pp. 875–893.
Cochrane, Kira. "The Fourth Wave of Feminism: Meet the Rebel Women." *The Guardian,* 10 December 2013. https://www.theguardian.com/world/2013/dec/10/fourth-wave-feminism-rebel-women.
de Beauvoir, Simone. *The Second Sex.* Translated and edited by H.M. Parshley. Vintage Books, 1989.

Dekoven, Marianne. "Jouissance, Cyborgs, and Companion Species: Feminist Experiment." *PMLA* vol. 121, no. 5, 2006, pp. 1690–1696.

Gill, Rosalind. "Post-Postfeminism? New Feminist Visibilities in Postfeminist Times." *Feminist Media Studies,* vol. 16, no. 4, 2016, pp. 610–630.

Klages, Mary. "Feminism." *Literary Theory: A Guide for the Perplexed.* Bloomsbury Publishing, 2007.

McKenzie, Sheena, and Phoebe Parke. "Emma Watson: Don't Let Anyone Tell You What You Can or Cannot Achieve." *CNN,* 9 Mar 2015. https://www.cnn.com/2015/03/06/europe/emma-watson-he-for-she-international-womens-day/index.html.

Vidal, Ava. "'Intersectional Feminism.' What the Hell Is It? (And Why You Should Care)." *The Telegraph* 15, 2014.

Imperator Furiosa, Fury Broad

Gender in Mad Max: Fury Road

MARTIN RICKSAND

Introduction

Mad Max: Fury Road received much attention at its release, to some extent because of its depiction of women. The movie was seen as a feminist triumph, but was simultaneously the object of critique, labeled by men's rights activists as feminist propaganda. At first glance the movie may appear to be an unequivocal treatment of female liberation, at least judging by the critics' reactions: Kyle Smith of the *New York Post* calls it "the rare action blockbuster that fully acknowledges the importance of women"; Sarah Stewart, writer at *Indie Wire*, says that the movie "is an unambiguously and unapologetically feminist, Bechdel test-passing sci-fi blockbuster." This essay examines *Mad Max: Fury Road* and its purportedly feminist discourses, showing that although the movie does appear to advocate feminist values with its strong, independent female character fighting for the emancipation of women, the treatment of gender discourses is more complex than critics make it out to be. A close reading of the film, more specifically of the female lead character Imperator Furiosa, reveals that the purported female emancipation may not be as central as critics have argued. A more mitigated interpretation of the movie is necessary, as the film's treatment of questions pertaining to sex and gender cannot be reduced to something as simple as pro/against, but rather a step in a new direction.

A Brave New Post-Apocalyptic World

Mad Max: Fury Road takes place in a dystopian future in a desolate wasteland. In the beginning of the film, Max is captured and brought to one of few remaining cities, the Citadel, ruled by the dictator Immortan Joe. One day, a load of breast milk (a precious commodity) is to be transported in a large trailer truck (or "war rig") by one of Joe's high-ranked officers, Imperator Furiosa, to a nearby city. It turns out that Furiosa has secretly rescued Joe's five wives from captivity, and once they get out of the city, she sets her course for her former home (from which she was taken at a young age), a haven inhabited only by women. Joe dispatches his entire army—along with those of the neighboring cities—to capture Furiosa and bring back his wives and the 18-wheel truck. Max is brought along but manages to free himself and teams up with Furiosa and the wives. They eventually manage to get to their destination, only to find that Furiosa's home is gone. The Vuvalini, the amazonian tribe from which Furiosa originates, has only five women left alive. Max convinces the women to face Joe, and they successfully defeat him and return to the Citadel, now liberated from its dictator.

What a Dame! What a Lovely Dame!

Initially, Furiosa seems like one of the toughest women ever depicted on the silver screen: she is a fierce warrior, a resourceful mechanic and skilled driver, possessing qualities usually expected from a male action hero. When compared to other post-apocalyptic heroines, however, her uniqueness diminishes. Firstly, the setting may be a reason why she is "allowed" be as strong as she is. Sherrie Inness explains that women are freer to be independent and tough in post-apocalyptic settings because those are worlds where the normal order of things has been turned upside-down (*Tough Girls* 123). Yvonne Tasker does not discuss post-apocalyptic heroines in particular but does note that it was common in the 1970s to reassert a heroine's femininity by "explaining away" her actions (*Spectacular Bodies* 20). The post-apocalyptic setting, a context where normal laws no longer apply and women are allowed to act unconventionally, could be such an "explanation" that defuses the threat posed by the subversion of gender roles. Furiosa's toughness is perhaps portrayed as something as unnatural as other factors in this fictitious world.

On the other hand, one could criticize Inness' disparaging evaluation of the post-apocalyptic setting by seeing it as the kind of speculative depiction that the genre of science fiction is so apt at providing, where a new order can be conceived whilst retaining credibility. In a contemporary setting, Furiosa might have come off as less plausible, breaking too much with established conventions, but thanks to the different temporal setting new structures can be created. One may concede that the world is "topsy turvy" (as Inness puts it), but this need not be pejorative; it simply means that this world is different, but a world where women are allowed and/or encouraged to display their strength would appear as different *irrespective* of its temporal setting. The very purpose of the post-apocalyptic dimension is to emphasize Furiosa's prowess, which is not a devaluation thereof. In that case, the world of Mad Max can function as a synecdoche of our own, a simplified image of our society where certain aspects are crystallized and possible alternations can be explored.

With that said, action heroines cannot be analyzed as a homogeneous group; there are diverse subcategories, some of which fit the heroines of the eighties and nineties better than Furiosa, in spite of her similarities with them. Among action heroine categories mentioned by Tasker, Furiosa shares some traits with "the tomboy," i.e., a girl resembling men in terms of physique (e.g., muscles) or clothes (Tasker, *Working Girls* 81). Masculinity need not be perceived as an essential trait permeating her very being; masculine apparel can be presented as a disguise hiding the "real" figure of the woman. Tasker links the tomboy's ambiguous sexual identity to a refusal of an Oedipalization, resulting from an immature identification with her father which functions as an explanatory framework for her masculinization. Unlike other heroines, the tomboy acts only as undeveloped protagonist, not romantic interest (Tasker, *Working Girls* 81–84).

In spite of the similarities, Furiosa does not conform to Tasker's definition, as the crucial aspect of Oedipalization is absent. Tasker stresses the importance of the tomboy's identity because of her relationship to her father, but with Furiosa the *opposite* seems to be the case: the Vuvalini are also called The Many Mothers, so the *maternal* relation compels Furiosa to adopt a masculine identity: she wants to be reunited with her symbolic *mothers*. Furthermore, the activity of action heroines has often been compensated by stressing their sexuality, and an emphasis on sexuality and/or femininity can serve to limit the threat posed by a tough woman (Tasker, *Spectacular Bodies* 19; Inness, *Tough Girls* 89–90). Furiosa's sexuality is never emphasized, so she cannot be reproached for disavowing her activity in favor of a disempowering femininity.

However, this need not be to Furiosa's advantage. Jeffrey Brown explains that a common criticism against action heroines is that they are actually "men in drag," their demeanor being identical to that of *male* action heroes (*Beyond Bombshells* 21). While there is a transgressive dimension to performance of the gender of the opposite sex, this performance entails reinscription of gendered traits as the norm, as the traits are depicted as mutually exclusive (Brown, *Beyond Bombshells* 60). Rikke Schubart provides a concrete example of this: Ellen Ripley was criticized for her behavior in *Aliens*, as masculinity was appropriated at the expense of relations between women, and because of her use of masculine violence and her lack of feminine signifiers (183). Such arguments are directed at the idea that power can only be accessed by women transformed into men. In that case, Immortan Joe still "wins" on an ideological level, as his positive evaluation of masculinity is adopted indiscriminately by Furiosa; she beats him only because she becomes more like him, reinscribing traits as gendered. By contrast, some critics thought that Ripley could be seen as *androgynous,* contrasted with the much more butch woman Vasquez (Schubart 179). This criticism, however, only confirms the former, in the sense that Ripley is *still* empowered through downplaying feminine qualities. Likewise, Furiosa is empowered insofar as she exerts herself not to be a woman, and in this sense she is almost identical to Ripley. Taken on her own, Furiosa does not seem radically different from older generations of heroines. However, Furiosa's uniqueness becomes more apparent when she is studied in context, for instance in relation to the other women of the film.

Furiosa and Other Women

Furiosa lacks typically feminine traits, and her "otherness" becomes all the more tangible in juxtaposition with the women she rescues. Clothes, among other things, set a heroine apart, as they remind viewers that she has distanced herself from femininity (Inness, *Tough Girls* 25). The wives are clad in translucent dresses reminiscent of ball gowns, emphasizing their femininity and enhancing their beauty, whereas Furiosa wears a worn-out tank-top and pants, functional but hardly embellishing, enhancing her masculine appearance. Inness mentions two functions of revealing clothes: they either render the woman more sexually appealing, reminding the spectator of her femininity, or they reveal her muscles, another factor increasing the heroine's toughness (which is clearly the function of Furiosa's clothes) (*Tough Girls* 24, 107). Furiosa's appearance signals her belonging to the macho world of Immortan Joe's male soldiers, the War Boys, rather than the feminine sphere of the wives.

Furiosa seems even more like an anomaly when they reach her real home and she is contrasted with the Vuvalini, who retain more of their femininity than Furiosa. One factor indicating this is their hairstyles. The Vuvalini and the wives all have long hair while Furiosa's is cropped. Hair is a recurrent signifier among other action heroines, and one can see some similarities with Demi Moore's character Jordan O'Neil in *G.I. Jane*. Brown thinks that the message of *G.I. Jane* is that women are able to enter the most masculine military service, provided that they relinquish their femininity ("Gender, Sexuality, and Toughness" 55). In O'Neil's case, this means, among other things, getting rid of her long hair.

Similarly to how O'Neil is aligned with her fellow soldiers by adopting their hairstyle, the short fuzz on the top of Furiosa's head makes her visually reminiscent of the bald War Boys, blending her in with their macho culture. O'Neil is not the only woman whose hair metonymically represents her femininity; another woman to lose hers is Samantha/Charly in *The Long Kiss Goodnight*. Samantha is a nice, seemingly innocent schoolteacher suffering from amnesia, living with her family in the suburbs. She learns that she used to be a professional assassin, and as she regains her memory she turns back to her former self. One part of this process of empowerment consists of dyeing her hair blond and cutting it short (Brown, "Gender, Sexuality, and Toughness" 54). Similarly, in *Alien 3*, Ripley must shave her head and subsequently resembles the male inmates on the planet she has reached (Schubart 187).

Here it may be objected that Furiosa retains some of her femininity through her use of improvised make-up: she moistens her fingers with leaking motor oil and smears it on the upper part of her face. However, one part of Samantha's transformation into Charly consists of harsher makeup in combination with a leather jacket replacing a wooly sweater (Brown, "Gender, Sexuality, and Toughness" 54). Against Furiosa's masculine clothes the motor oil looks less like makeup and more like war paint, adding threat, not glamour. Her use of oil also emphasizes her role as a driver, reminding the spectator of her close relation to technology rather than maternity.

The oil also sets her apart from the other women of the Citadel in its capacity as a liquid. Some of the Citadel's women are perpetually drained of their breast milk, the same liquid that subsequently nourishes the wives' offspring and is sold to neighboring cities. Furiosa is never connected to mother's milk, producing neither it nor children in need of it; she fits better in the world of warriors and mechanics than in kindergartens and rooms of delivery. Hence, the movie may give the impression that it portrays masculine values as superior, with a woman's path to emancipation relying on a renunciation of her femininity. This trope was popular in the eighties (and carried over to some extent to the nineties), but it would be misleading to focus on that trope alone in *Fury Road*, as the movie presents a more complex image of women's relation to masculinity. Furiosa's empowerment *does* derive from her becoming more masculine, and in that case, she is almost identical to Ripley, O'Neil, and Samantha/Charly, but what sets *Fury Road* apart is its *depiction* of its women: Furiosa may resemble earlier action heroines to some extent, but the *evaluation* of her gender qualities is not as simple as that of older movies.

Before discussing the movie's evaluation of gender traits, it is important to note that the paradoxical consequence of the reasoning above is that women are criticized for being "men in drag" when thoroughly tough, and for being too weak when they display feminine characteristics. Brown defends feminine heroines, pointing out that such arguments make it impossible for action heroines to be considered as genuinely tough (*Dangerous Curves* 33). He argues that it is, on the contrary, to their advantage that they can encompass *both* masculine and feminine traits. For instance, Kathryn Hill argues that *Buffy the Vampire Slayer* shows how empowerment and femininity can go hand in hand (728). Furiosa displays little femininity, but the principle of the argument is still crucial: depreciation of both masculinity and femininity in women makes it impossible for action heroines to be genuinely empowered. Furiosa may adopt masculine traits but is not reproached for doing so.

It is the more dynamic and complex conception of women's relation to gendered traits that sets *Fury Road* apart from older depictions of action heroines. Brown's line of reasoning is reconcilable with the broad image of the gender spectrum in *Fury Road*, with the important difference that diverse gender traits are not embodied in a *singular* woman, as it was sometimes in older heroines: Ripley and Samantha/Charlie are both tough when necessary but retain their maternal instincts and therefore their femininity. In *Fury Road*, a similarly complex image of gender properties cannot be found in one individual, but is illustrated through the juxtaposition of *all* of the female characters: women encompass feminine and masculine traits to varying extents without being disparaged for doing so, and this is overlooked if Furiosa is studied out of context. The wives cannot defend themselves, but manage and reload weapons when the others fight, and successfully distract a soldier with their charms, allowing Furiosa to sneak onto his vehicle. The Vuvalini find themselves somewhere in the middle in terms of gender qualities: they are more feminine than Furiosa but less so than the wives. Furiosa displays very little femininity compared to the Vuvalini and the wives, but thanks to her juxtaposition with them it is apparent that she is not portrayed as an anomaly, which is not as obvious in cases like Samantha/Charly and O'Neil. *Fury Road* is a clear step away from older depictions of women, as no woman has to fully embody either masculine or feminine qualities, nor embody both masculinity and femininity in perfect balance; the film depicts different types of womanhood that all contribute in different but ever so important ways. Eve Ensler—writer of *The Vagina Monologues*—was consulted during the production of the movie, and she indirectly confirms this in an interview: "All the women in the film maintain their inherent womanness. They're tender and loving and still fierce. They get to be all those things" (Dockterman). They retain their woman-ness, even if to different extents, but more importantly, *together* they form a heterogeneous spectrum of what it can mean to be a woman, in which all of them encompass femininity to varying degrees without being punished for doing so. Ultimately, this means that sex becomes less important, as the movie provides an image of women that is neither homogeneous, nor prescriptive.

Furiosa and Max

So much for Imperator Furiosa studied separately and with other women; how does she work together with Max? Coupling a woman with a man enables women to be included in the action, but in more stereotypical and traditional depictions of heroines it can also function as a strategy to neutralize any threat posed to ideal manly heroism. Sometimes this diminishes the woman's role, but the dynamics between the characters may also grant her the possibility to challenge traditional gender roles (Brown, *Beyond Bombshells* 54–55). One example of how a woman's part in the action may be reduced is when a woman in a male team can be allotted the task of seducing a villain whilst a male team member acts; the man's role is action, hers is distraction (Brown, *Beyond Bombshells* 58–59). Furiosa, however, does not become an attractive decoy, as she never so much as *attempts* to defeat her enemies by resorting to her looks. As mentioned in the previous section, it is *the wives* who act as a distraction, with Furiosa being the one acting whilst they do so.

A common conception among critics seems to be that Furiosa's strength is not diminished to Max's advantage, or even that she is the *real* protagonist, with Max as supporting character (Coning 175; Smith). This interpretation is understandable: Max is an outsider ending up in the Citadel by chance. He is originally not involved in the conflict between the women and Immortan Joe, and only engages in it out of his own volition. When they reach the Vuvalini he is offered a vehicle and enough supplies to carry on by himself, but *he* is the one to suggest that they take back the Citadel, choosing to stay and help them even though he could leave them to their fate.

Max's role as a supporting character is not new. In *The Road Warrior,* Max is assigned a similar role: he stumbles upon an ongoing conflict between a gang of anarchists and a civilized town, the citizens of which are planning to migrate to a more hospitable part of the country. Max helps the townsfolk but acts out of his own interests and is not directly involved in their conflict. Further, in both *Fury Road* and *The Road Warrior*, Max is the only person whose psyche we access. If narratological focalization is not sufficient to make a character the protagonist, then Max is not new to the role of supporting character; that he makes way for a *female* character is incidental.

However, when men and women team up there is usually a romantic aspect, the nature of which differs depending on their strength in relation to one another; an inferior female partner can act as a prize for the male character as their joint mission culminates in romantic engagement (Brown, *Beyond Bombshells* 67). Couples portrayed as equals without any romantic engagements are more of an exception: professional success must be accompanied by an equally successful relationship, leaving romance as the ultimate goal for women (Brown, *Beyond Bombshells* 77). In one way, this can be seen as something positive: since less attention is paid to female sexuality, immediate sexual attraction receives less attention than the possibility of a fulfilling and mature relationship with reciprocal respect and support. The downside of this is that professional and romantic elements are not allowed to be separated: women are not permitted to enjoy professional success without romance (Brown, *Beyond Bombshells* 74–77). However, Furiosa runs no risk of becoming a romantic reward. As Stewart points out, the "most romantic moment involves a woman using a man to steady her rifle." Furiosa is not a damsel in distress to be saved before a romantic conclusion, and her masculine looks indicate her nonconformity right from the start. Inness argues that this paucity of romance does not automatically imply equality, at least not in older depictions of action heroines, because even when the relation is not romantic, it can still decrease the heroine's toughness: Sarah Connor in *Terminator 2: Judgment Day* has no romantic affiliation with the terminator played by Schwarzenegger, but is unable to take care of herself as well he does, and the threat she poses is thus reduced (*Tough Girls* 131).

Tasker reasons similarly to Brown but examines different aspects of cooperating couples and says that a female sidekick's reversal of femininity can be made comical (*Spectacular Bodies* 27–29). This point clearly does not apply to Furiosa as she retains her air of seriousness throughout the movie. The element of comedy is mostly absent in Furiosa's and Max's relation: they lack the frequent exchange of witty comments not uncommon in other couples, nor are they depicted in a "campy," facetious way. Yet another possibility Tasker mentions is that the female character is there to reassert the male hero's heterosexuality, but she can also be raped and/or killed to become a motivation for vengeance (*Spectacular Bodies* 15–16). Furthermore, emphasis on a woman's heterosexuality can undermine her toughness, as this implies submissiveness to a man (Inness, *Tough Girls* 43). In the case of *Rambo: First Blood Part II*, Tasker explains, the male protagonist has a momentary liaison with Co Bao, a strong heroine refusing conventional femininity. She is almost as skilled as Rambo, but eventually dies as the narrative logic of the movie cannot "reconcile its outsider-loner rhetoric with the positioning of the hero in terms of heterosexual romance" (Tasker, *Spectacular Bodies* 27). The function of the female sidekick up to this point seems to be to acknowledge the protagonist's superiority, either through demise (removing any possible competition), or through a romance making him a reliable hero, but neither is the case in *Fury Road*.

Still, some critics emphasize Furiosa's strength in relation to Max and how they differ from "conventional" couples. Tasker's examples of heroine sidekicks as love interests, comic relief or carriers of the spectator's gaze directed at the hero (*Spectacular Bodies* 26–29) indicate that it is not that common for a hero and a heroine to get an equal share of attention in the way Max and Furiosa do, meaning that the movie distances itself from couple dynamics in older action movies. One scene regarded as emblematic of Furiosa's superiority is when Max misses two shots with a rifle, Furiosa grabs it and supports it against Max's shoulder to stabilize her aim. Both Coning and Stewart emphasize Furiosa's use of Max in this scene. Coning even goes as far as saying that Max is never presented as a typically masculine hero (175). *New York Post* critic Kyle Smith interprets the scene differently, noting that while Furiosa cannot beat Max in terms of muscles, she is resourceful enough to use him as a tripod, thus acknowledging a difference between them in terms of masculinity instead of desperately trying to adopt it at all costs.

It is easy to see this particular event as some kind of "concession" on Max's part, but Coning, Stewart, and Smith all neglect that Furiosa merely *injures* the Bullet Farmer with the rifle, Max is the one dealing the final blow. Furthermore, Max kills *two* of the three patriarchs pursuing them, with relative ease one might add. By contrast, Furiosa kills but one, and is severely wounded in the process. Moreover, after Furiosa's confrontation with Immortan Joe, she is fatally wounded and in dire need of medical attention, so on the road to the Citadel, Max carries out a blood transfusion which saves her life. One could see this as a final confirmation of masculine superiority, a reminder just before the credits that Furiosa represents the weaker sex which ultimately cannot manage without a strong man by her side.

However, it is evident that one character seems stronger than the other if one neglects scenes proving the contrary, but that is too simplistic an analysis. It is misleading to place Max and Furiosa in opposition with one another as if they were competing in killing people and/or rescuing each other. By contrast, an interpretation of the movie becomes more fruitful if one considers this a *joint effort* where both are essential. Thus, it is incorrect to see Furiosa as using Max as a sniper tripod, taking advantage of him to ameliorate her aim, nor is it any better to see this as a proof of her resourcefulness, as if that would make her more versatile and ingenious than him. They have a common goal which they eventually reach together, so the battle between the sexes is ostensible. Furiosa's strength is not her marksmanship, nor her resourcefulness, but, ironically enough, her humility. Unlike Max, she is humble enough to acknowledge that the task at hand is beyond any one person's capacity, forcing them to cooperate. Neither is able to hit the target from afar on their own, so she acknowledges her shortcomings and make sure they work together, forcing him to give up, not his masculinity, but his volition to do things alone, like the lone-wolf he insists on being. A different and novel path to success is outlined through Furiosa's subversion of the "solitary myth." This is further emphasized by how Max and Furiosa rescue each other throughout the movie. The main point of the movie is *not* that women are strong and independent (even if this is indeed showed time and again); on the contrary, the movie illustrates what can be accomplished when the sexes *cooperate* instead of insisting on acting independently of one another in infantile attempts to "one up" each other. Furthermore, Max and Furiosa constantly take turns in saving each other's lives in equal cooperation, not competition, so the point is that both of them are capable warriors; it is only through *cooperation* that they ultimately succeed in defeating Immortan Joe. The fact that both men and women in their team meet an early demise shows that the movie refuses to take sides in the feminist discussion; no one sex is depicted as superior to the other. (Note that this does not automatically entail a nihilistic and/or antiscientific view on sex, where differences between the sexes are seen as conventions created by society; the movie makes no comments regarding the importance of sex. In this respect it is neither prescriptive, nor descriptive of how people of each sex do/should behave.)

It is perhaps better not to consider this a competition in which sex gets the most screen-time and/or attention. From a narratological perspective, Max and Furiosa are arguably equally important to advance the plot. They often share screen-time, and in several respects they are similar: both of them are skilled drivers and mechanics, and they take turns in commanding the gargantuan truck; both of them are fierce fighters, and defend themselves, the helpless, and each other; both are haunted by their past, since Max is trying to find a new home, escaping the memories of his old, destroyed one, and Furiosa wants to return to hers. Both have a vaguely outlined background leaving many questions about their past unanswered.

Seeing how rare it is for a couple to be as equal as Max and Furiosa while at the same time refusing romantic and/or sexual relations, it is no wonder that Furiosa seems all the more strong and independent in contrast with other *heroines*, but she does not seem to be portrayed as stronger than *Max*, nor is he for that reason stronger than *her*. Max is reproached, not for being inferior, but for being too narrow minded, neglecting the necessity of cooperation. This conclusion should not be all that surprising. George Miller himself stated in an interview in Cannes that the film did not have a feminist agenda (Stewart). As for Ensler, she too downplays the dimension of pure emancipation, explaining that when planning the film, they decided that it was not going to be like conventional movies where a man and woman fall in love, but instead that they were "going to fight side by side, and the woman will save the man one moment and he'll save her the next" (Dockterman). Relating this to earlier action heroines and to Inness's negative evaluation of *Terminator 2*, it could be objected that Sarah Connor and the terminator also cooperate rather than compete, but with the important difference that Schwarzenegger's character is a *cyborg*, which still leaves Sarah as the toughest *human* character, and which explains the lack of romance between them. What makes *Fury Road* different is that it allows two *humans* to be equal in this way, even without romantic attraction. Similarly, Ripley cooperates with male marines for a large part of *Aliens*, but they are successively killed or incapacitated until Ripley ultimately ends up as a lone heroine in the final confrontation with the xenomorph queen. In *Fury Road*, on the other hand, the cooperation is emphasized and maintained until the very end.

Conclusion

This essay has showed that the issues of gender in *Mad Max: Fury Road* are comparatively complex. The categories of women depicted are diverse, with characters embodying femininity to varying extents, but no one embodiment is seen as better than another. Together they provide a more holistic perspective of what it can mean to be a woman, where the juxtaposition of different individuals does not work as an evaluation of any one specific kind of woman, but rather as an image of how polysemic the notion "woman" can be, which stresses the futility of evaluating different kinds.

Nor is the depiction of the relation between the sexes normative or judging. The juxtaposition of the male and female protagonist does not aim to emphasize the competition between the sexes; on the contrary it stresses the importance of cooperation, while at the same time ignoring the debate on sex altogether. Instead it shows that reliance on one another is more beneficial for everyone. No obvious correlation between sex and strength is presented, as the characters themselves are regarded as more interesting and worthier of attention than their respective sex.

Ultimately, this means that it is hard to assess in what sense the movie can be labeled as feminist, as it does not defend women's emancipation, female empowerment, or gender equality as much as it does away with questions about gender altogether, rejecting them as uninteresting. However, one could argue that this is something positive, as cooperation implies reciprocity, not dependence but *inter*dependence, not between sexes but between *people*. *Mad Max: Fury Road* cannot be reduced to something as simple as a step forward or backwards, but provides a refreshing step in an entirely new direction, where the characters themselves are seen as more interesting than their sexes.

Works Cited

Alien 3. Directed by David Fincher, Brandywine Productions, 1992.
Aliens. Directed by James Cameron. Brandywine Productions, 1986.
Brown, Jeffrey A. *Beyond Bombshells: The New Action Heroine in Popular Culture.* University Press of Mississippi, 2015.

_____. *Dangerous Curves: Action Heroines, Gender, Fetishism, and Popular Culture*. University Press of Mississippi, 2011.
_____. "Gender, Sexuality, and Toughness: The Bad Girls of Action Film and Comic Books." *Action Chicks: New Images of Tough Women in Popular Culture,* edited by S.A. Inness, Palgrave Macmillan, 2004, pp. 47–74.
Buffy the Vampire Slayer, created by Joss Whedon. 20th television, 1997–2003.
Coning, Alexis de. "Recouping Masculinity: Men's Rights Activists' Responses to *Mad Max: Fury Road.*" *Feminist Media Studies*, 16:1, pp. 174–176.
Dockterman, Eliana. "Vagina Monologues Writer Eve Ensler: How *Mad Max: Fury Road* Became a 'Feminist Action Film.'" *Time,* 7 May 2015 http://time.com/3850323/mad-max-fury-road-eve-ensler-feminist, Accessed 15 May 2017.
G.I. Jane. Directed by Ridley Scott. Buena Vista Pictures, 1997.
Hill, Kathryn. "Buffy's Voice." *Feminist Media Studies*, vol. 13, no. 4, pp. 725–744.
Inness, Sherrie A., editor. *Action Chicks: New Images of Tough Women in Popular Culture.* Palgrave Macmillan, 2004.
_____. *Tough Girls: Women Warriors and Wonder Women in Popular Culture*. University of Pennsylvania Press, 1998.
The Long Kiss Goodnight. Directed by Renny Harlin. Forge, 1996.
Mad Max: Fury Road. Directed by George Miller. Village Roadshow Pictures, 2015.
Rambo: First Blood Part II. Directed by George P. Cosmatos. Carolco Pictures, 1985.
The Road Warrior. Directed by George Miller. Kennedy Miller Productions, 1981.
Schubart, Rikke. *Super Bitches and Action Babes: The Female Hero in Popular Cinema, 1970–2006.* McFarland, 2007.
Smith, Kyle. "Why *Mad Max: Fury Road* Is the Feminist Picture of the Year." *New York Post,* 14 May 2015, http://nypost.com/2015/05/14/why-mad-max-fury-road-is-the-feminist-picture-of-the-year Accessed 15 May 2017.
Stewart, Sarah. "Oops! I Made a Feminist Manifesto: George Miller and *Mad Max*." *Indie Wire*, 16 May 2015, http://www.indiewire.com/2015/05/oops-i-made-a-feminist-manifesto-george-miller-and-mad-max-203671, Accessed 15 May 2017.
Tasker, Yvonne. *Spectacular Bodies: Gender, Genre and the Action Cinema*. Routledge, 1993.
_____. *Working Girls: Gender and Sexuality in Popular Cinema*. Routledge, 1998.
Terminator 2: Judgment Day. Directed by James Cameron. TriStar Pictures, 1991.

Section II

Deconstruction

From Traditional Slasher to Fourth Wave

Fantastical Reconversion in The Final Girls *and* Happy Death Day

FERNANDO GABRIEL PAGNONI BERNS,
CANELA AILÉN RODRIGUEZ FONTAO
and MARIANA S. ZÁRATE

At the turn of the new millennium, Angelina Jolie seemed the perfect Tomb Raider. Strong-willed, butt-kicking and glamorous, she was the embodiment of the reformulation of feminist discourse in terms of female empowerment. Powerful as she was, however, the film cannot avoid the pitfalls of sexualized femininity. Indeed, Jolie's Croft "fights with impressive strength" but she is "highly sexualized while doing it" (Sutherland 155). She was a real icon of the "girl power" momentum. In turn, the new *Tomb Raider* (Roar Uthaug, 2018), a film wrote partly by a woman (Geneva Robertson-Dworet), indicates, both visually and narratively, the passage from postfeminism to fourth wave feminism: intelligent, unglamorous, and strong, the new Lara Croft is, arguably, a creature of her own era.

The new *Tomb Raider* is just the latest example illustrating a shift between mentalities as depicted in popular culture. As fourth wave feminism establishes itself as a stable, permanent movement, more and more heroines within fantastic cinema struggle to fit within the new zeitgeist, abandoning bad—but depoliticized—attitude and glamour as central attributes to embrace, instead of nuanced forms of female empowerment.

Some films put this passage between decades, ideologies and feminist collectives at center stage. Rather than appearing through the analysis of two different films—as with *Tomb Raider*—this passage *is* the main film. Genre cinema, always tapping into cultural and social anxieties, can use fantastic narratives as metaphorical depictions of this shift from postfeminism to the fourth wave. In the horror-comedy film *The Final Girls* (Todd Strauss-Schulson, 2015), Max (Taissa Farmiga) attends a tribute screening of a '80s slasher film that starred Max's late mother (Malin Akerman), who has died in a grisly car accident. Through the screening, Max and her friends are sucked into the fictional world depicted by the silver screen. Trapped inside a slasher movie, mother and daughter must team up with the fictional characters to battle the film's masked killer. *The Final Girls* offers what the classical slasher and the Reaganomics-era Final Girl of the 1980s strongly rejected: female bonding, especially between mother and daughter.

Happy Death Day (Christopher Landon, 2017) goes even further, deconstructing misguided "girl power." A college student must relive the day of her murder over and over again, in a loop that will end only when she catches her killer and masters real female power that goes beyond being "nasty" to others. Landon's film can be read as a fantastical reenactment of this passage from a feminist ethos to a wiser one.

In this essay we will analyze both *The Final Girls* and *Happy Death Day* to point the ways in which genre cinema is currently illustrating the changes taking place in both feminism and society. The fantastic devices framing the films (meta-narrative and temporal loop) must be read as metaphors of the conversions from the politics of neoliberal 1980s feminism and 1990s "girl power" to the more nuanced and still nascent ethos of the fourth wave feminism.

The Reaganomic Final Girl: Slashing Sisterhood

Second wave feminism was a movement that continued and, in some ways, also opposed, the traditional feminism of the first wave. Whilst first wave feminism looked for equality for women within the confines of society, Second wave feminists proposed the movement of "women's liberation" as completely revolutionary. It can be said that the first wave was liberal in its approach to society, while the second wave was more radical. While first wave feminism attempted to "fit" women within a world of men, second wave asked for a process of consciousness raising and rejected this process of sameness.

In the second half of the 1970s, the waning countercultural movements shifted toward disillusionment, consumerism and escapism (Hamilton viii). Within this scenario of decline, neoconservative Ronald Reagan was elected president in 1980 and again in 1984. As the 1980s were dominated by Reagan's "neoliberal" politics (emphasizing militarism, family values, and small government), feminism in general suffered a severe backlash at the hands of right-wing media and institutions that blamed many social problems on feminism's "exaggerated" claims. Together with this backlash came internal differences within the feminist movement itself (Thornham 35), which helped carry the second wave to its apparent end.

While scholars such as Sara Evans argued that second wave feminism "retained its radical edge through the conservative backlash of the Eighties" (60), it is undeniable that the governments of Ronald Reagan in the U.S. and Margaret Thatcher in the UK were successful in translating their conservative agenda to popular culture. Through the 1980s, the ideological backlash presented feminism as outmoded, since women of the world had achieved, supposedly, what they wanted. Soon enough, the word feminism was turned into a "bad word," a situation still present. By the late 1980s, feminism was dead, or so the media claimed.

The 1980s were a hard time for any kind of radicalism, but, as Jason Brock observes, "It is probably no by accident that the more conservative of the times give us the more extreme entertainment" (163) in the form of the slasher film. The basic formula of the slasher film is as follows: a group of characters, all of them teenagers (but represented by actors in their early thirties) are stalked by a (usually male) foe wearing a mask. One by one, all of them are killed until only one girl survives and even beats her foes: the Final Girl. This trope was the perfect embodiment of Reaganomics; she was beautiful but modest in appearance, strong, resourceful, virginal, and friendly, with no vices of any kind. She was the perfect antagonist of both the masked killer and the stereotypical "blond bitch" among the group. She survives not only because she is strong, but also because she is a good American girl. There was never an explicit reference that the Final Girl of the 1980s despises feminism, but her strong appliance to the rules suggests so.

It is amidst this social and cultural momentum that the term "Final Girl" was coined. Horror scholar Carol Clover wrote *Men, Women and Chainsaws: Gender in the Modern Horror Film* in 1992, elevating her idea of the "final girl" from academic halls to common knowledge within the borders of genre fandom. The final girl, Clover argues, is the only survivor of the massacres portrayed in the slasher formula of the 1980s, the boyish female "who is chased, cornered, wounded" (35) and who, at the film's climax, finds strength enough to kill the killer. "The killer's phallic purpose" (47) comes to an end when the final girl takes for herself a phallic weapon—thus, becoming masculinized—and kills the murderer, ending both the bloodshed and the film.

Time has passed since the first edition of Clover's text (1992) and the final girl has become the Final Girl, a character larger than life. In the new millennium, horror cinema has declared its love for her, to the point that this figure now occupies center stage. Already from its title, *The Final Girls* plays homage to both the 1980s slasher film and its main heroine. Still, the film does so with a millennial sensibility that reveals more nuanced portrays of femininity within the horror film. *The Final Girls* opens with a trailer for the fictional film *Camp Bloodbath*, which comes off as a wink to the "Friday the 13th" franchise. There is even a Final Girl who faces the masked killer with the phrase "You just messed with the wrong virgin," thus emphasizing her status as a "good girl." When the trailer is over, audiences realize that they were watching the film's trailer on a smart phone together with a teenage girl, Max Cartwright, daughter of scream queen actress, Amanda Cartwright.

The passage from a "1980s style" trailer to a cell phone prefigures more pressing changes as the neoconservative thinking of the 1980s shifts to the fourth wave of feminism. Max even shakes her head in disbelief after watching the trailer on her phone, a smile in her face. Clearly, she has found all the proceedings depicted in the trailer a little ridiculous. Waiting in the car and out of boredom, Max checks her mother's CV, where she finds titles such as *Co-Ed Massacre*, *Slay Bells* and *Chopping Mall* (the latter was a real film, directed by Jim Wynorski in 1986). Amanda suffers typecasting as "horror scream queen," a fact that distresses but also bonds mother and daughter.

Max and her mother do not share a traditional hierarchical relationship where the maternal figure is the ruler while the daughter tries to come out from her mother's shadow. Rather than antagonists, Max and Amanda share a relationship based on sisterhood, one of the most important political articulations of the second wave of feminism. Sisterhood was the belief that women, despite their differences, shared a unique voice *as women*. Thus, women should protect each other against all the oppressions generated by the patriarchal mindset regardless of differences of race, class, religion, or all other social categories. "But despite a unity around 'sisterhood' forged within activism, theoretical differences and political exclusions were always in evidence" (Thornham 35). Sisterhood was hard to keep alive, especially through the backlash and the Reagan years. The concept of sisterhood was, in fact, *oppositional* to the neoliberal 1980s. For Reagan, the political value resided in the individual, not in society. Classical neoliberalism asserted that the highest virtue of a society is the degree to which its individuals are allowed to compete and gain their pleasures in the form of commodities. The individual "is seen as standing separate from and prior to society. The so called 'free' individual is regarded as the basic unit of political order and the safeguarding of the individual's life, liberty and property as the state's fundamental purpose" (Peters 124). Neoliberalism was the death of the social state and the enthroning of competition and individualism. Within the neoliberal agenda, sisterhood was a relic: it had been fun, but it was long past necessary.

Sisterhood is contested in the neoliberal age with the depiction of the relationship between mother and daughter as based on competition and uneasiness. The neoliberal mother is both "overcontrolling and overindulgent" (Cain 297) and shares with her daughters a toxic relationship. This kind of bond also restrains the freedom of younger generations. Max and Amanda, however, share an egalitarian relationship based on sisterhood as it is Max who accompanies her mother to an audition. Later in the car, both women chat about where to go to eat, how much they enjoy rock and roll music and how much money they owe to the electric company. Amanda tells her daughter about her last romantic disillusionment:

> AMANDA: You remember Frank? He told me he was going to take me to Palm Springs this weekend. No message. No text.
> MAX: No surprise.
> AMANDA: You know, it's just he said we were exclusive.
> MAX: Well, he said it, but he doesn't act like it (…).
> AMANDA: You must think I'm a total zero.
> MAX: Screw him, Mom. And screw his shady hotel in Palm Springs.
> AMANDA: Oh my God. Look at you taking care of me.

From a traditionalist point of view, this conversation would fit better if shared by friends rather than between mother and daughter. Max and Amanda even have an "our favorite song" (Kim Carnes' "Bette Davis Eyes") they listen to together, thus evoking kinship rather than the traditional competition taking place between daughter and mother as is traditionally depicted in popular culture. To enhance this parallel, the scene cuts (after the accident that kills Amanda) to present day, three years later. Max goes to school sharing a car with her best friend, Gertie (Alia Shawkat). Like Max and Amanda, the two female teenagers chat about romance but also about more serious issues such as psychological therapy. There is little difference in the way Max shares her intimacy with friends and the way she did so with her late mother.

This "sisterhood" does not involve just the 1970s, but also prefigures the fourth wave. The activities of the #MeToo collective basically involves a reformulation of the concept of sisterhood, as women across the globe share experiences of abuse or harassment suffered in their lives. Through the #MeToo movement, women become sisters one more time, recuperating a bond of mutual support practically eliminated through the 1980s and 1990s.

This sisterhood continues with other characters as well. After been sucking into the movie *Bloodbath Camp*, Max becomes a Final Girl. Even her name, "Max," is androgynous, one of the characteristics that Clover notices in all the classic Final Girls. However, Max is a millennial Final Girl cast in a parody, so she is perplexed to find a group of "teenagers" (the fictional characters within the film) whose characterization is completely one-note, 1980s style: there is the "black guy" who is named "Blake" (Tory Thompson), Kurt, the hunk (Adam Devine) who calls all the girls within the camp "funbags," Tina, the blonde bitch (Angela Trimbur) who flirts with any man, Paula, the

Final Girl (Chloe Bridges) and the supporter character (Max's mother). This group mirrors Max' friends: the silly joker Duncan (Thomas Middleditch), hunky Chris (Alexander Ludwig) and Vicky, the "bitch" (Nina Dobrew) of the group. There are strong differences, however, which mark the passage of time: unlike macho Duncan, sensitive Chris presents a more nuanced portray of masculinity as he offers Max his companionship through her mother's death anniversary. Meanwhile, Duncan is the first one in the group to deduce what is happening after they are all sucked into the film, rather than being just a source of awkward jokes. There are the female characters, however, the ones who most strongly illustrate the passage from the Reaganomics times to the fourth wave of feminism.

Tina feels that flirting with any cute boy is the right thing to do as a path to empowerment. Her sense of femininity and freedom is inextricably linked to sexuality. As Cris Mayo argues, there are pro-sex feminists who too easily presumed that sexual freedom translated into general freedom (137). Tina is constantly opening her blouse to attract male attention; further, she flirts with Chris even when he has come to the camp with Max. It is clear that she does not find any meaning in sisterhood. In turn, Amanda (named "Nancy" in the film-within-the-film) opens herself to Max: she is ready to get drunk and lose her virginity without any further explanation on the why of her urgency except some vague desire of feeling "special." Nancy, like Tina, only can think on female agency as linked to (heteronormative) sex.

Since they all are trapped within a slasher film, Max must assume the position of the Reaganomics girl and keep her mother, Amanda/Nancy, virgin as a way to keep her alive. Through an ironic twist, it is the daughter who wants to keep her mother's virginity intact while the mother reaches through the text to explain to her daughter that sex "does not kill." This displacement parodies the conservative nature of the 1980s, in which any sign of "badness" was exaggeratedly punished with death.

Vicky, the millennial "bad girl" presents a more oscillating take on misbehavior. She flirts with Chris and other boys, but her sexiness is not attached to evil. She flirts with Chris, but he and Max have no romantic relationship right up to that point. After falling within the *Bloodbath Camp*, Vicky resists Duncan's idea of leaving the fictional world running exactly on schedule (to get quickly to the film's end) since that means passively watching how the killer hacks to pieces his different victims (especially other girls). Still, Vicky can be cruel to Max on occasions, as when she coldly calls Nancy/Amanda just part of the film's "body count." When the time comes to face the main killer, however, Vicky takes the opportunity to apologize to everyone whom she has hurt before, a genuine move to kinship that definitively displaces her from the "bitch" role.

When this final confrontation arrives, there are two Final Girls: Max and her mother Amanda/Nancy. Both take turns in attacking and hurting Billy, the boogeyman of *Bloodbath Camp*, with the intention of saving each other rather than just themselves. The concept of the lonely Final Girl is supplanted by sisterhood, mother and daughter working together against the evil of the masked man.

Finally, Max fails to save her mother from the carnage perpetrated in *Bloodbath Camp*, even if the former character has stopped the main killer. As a consequence, all of them return to real life. There is a change, however: since all the girls were previously able to open up in the face of death, they are now closer to each other than ever.

Rather than perpetuate the heterosexual status quo, the film ends enhancing sisterhood. There is not even a final kiss between Chris and Max, leaving their relationship open to interpretation. With this, *The Final Girls* takes the trope of the Reaganomics era Final Girl and turns it into sisterhood, thus disrupting the flow of history while, at the same time, prefiguring times to come with the arrival of the #MeToo collective.

Happy Death Day: *From Postfeminism to Fourth Wave*

The fantastic shift effected in *The Final Girls* is further elaborated on in *Happy Death Day*. There is a difference, however; rather than a shift from conservative values to sisterhood, Landon's film illustrates the uneasy passage from postfeminism—an answer to the end of traditional feminism at the 1980s—to new forms of female empowerment.

Before continuing, we must establish what postfeminism is. Second wave feminism was followed not by one collective, but two, in the 1990s: Third wave feminism and postfeminism. These were not two complementary movements but oppositional to each other. Third wave—the term "third" indicating continuity—expressed unease at the "totalizing" effect of the term "woman" (King 138), favoring rather multiculturalism and difference. Postfeminism, in turn, marked an end—the prefix "post" indicating "superseding" (Pilcher and Whelehan 107)—to traditional forms of feminism.

The most significant definition of postfeminism was given by Susan Faludi in her book *Backlash: The Undeclared War against Women* (1991). Faludi portrays postfeminism as running in parallel with the right-wing 1980s' backlash against the ground gained by second wave feminism. Through media, women were told not only that their struggle for equality had been won, but also that they were paying the price for radicalism in broken relationships and bitterness since there were no kids nor husband to keep them company. Hollywood joined the "backlash" in the late 1980s and 1990s, with the return of the *femme fatale* who came back from classical cinema to reiterate the popular image of empowered women as evil.

Postfeminism is complemented by a media-saturated world, where images of pre-fabricated "girl power" and free sexuality prevail as the crucial goal for young women. In postmodernity, "girl power's brash glamour is paired with laddishness in a period where girls must act like boys to get ahead" (Carson 95). At the center of the ideal of girl power lies an immensely profitable fashion and beauty industry, as the basis of girl power is the neoliberal pleasure that came with the creating of self-aware identities of femininity. Images of women's empowerment are, then, commodities to buy and dispose of. It is interesting to note that the final credits of *Happy Death Day* rolls over greeting cards-like images, including a female figure (presumably, that of Jessica Rothe, the main actress) in underwear with different styles of clothing at her right to cut along the dotted lines and dress her in. Furthermore, postfeminism is obsessed with girlhood (no matter the real age), sexuality, sassiness and brassiness. The word "slut" even has had a particular role in the iconography of postfeminism (E. Evans 79).

"Slut" disrupts the traditional image of passiveness and obedience to enthrone, in turn, the aggressive bad girl with attitude. All this postfeminist sassiness and attitude, however, is mostly a "depoliticised product of backlash rhetoric" (Faludi 14). This particular discourse surrounding female empowerment is articulated, circulated and legitimated through media, thus running the risk of responding, mostly, to a male sense of business and hegemony. Postfeminist girl power becomes a depoliticised shrill voice spitting claims of power to society as a whole rather than a medium to direct the energy toward those who killed feminism in the first place.

Tree Gelbman (Jessica Rothe) is the perfect embodiment of the rhetoric of postfeminism. She is a sassy girl who does not allows anyone step on her. However, she confuses independence with selfishness and attitude with bossiness to the point of being cruel to others. The film starts with her waking up on her birthday after passing out from too much alcohol in the dorm room of sensitive guy Carter Davis (Israel Broussard). He has taken her to his dorm after a party where she drank too much but she is completely indifferent to the help he has given her. Aware of her sexual appeal, she changes clothes before him—it is he who turns away to give her a privacy she has not asked for—and retires without even a thanks. For her, Carter is a loser, someone with whom she is ashamed to be seen. When he reaches her later in public to return a bracelet she forgot in his dorm, she is angry rather than grateful.

Tree is part of a university sorority where all the girls calls themselves "bitch" or "whore," wear tight-fitting clothes to (hyper)sexualize their bodies and have no time to waste with the less popular girls. She attends all-female meetings where all the popular girls contrast their privileges with their classmates such as African American Becky (Cariella Smith) or the anonymous Asian girl that Tree ignores in many of her "incarnations." In fact, all the girls are never there to support each other but to sharply point to the other's mistakes and defects, calls each other names and gossip behind their backs. This lack of female solidarity is further enhanced when audience learns that Tree is sleeping with a married man. She is also angry with her mother, who died some time before Tree started college.

Within this context, it is not surprising that the "loop effect" that Tree suffers, being hunted down and killed repeatedly by a masked killer, is the product of serious competition between her and her roommate Lori (Ruby Modine) over a guy. Lori wants to kill her roommate basically because she is sick of Tree's nastiness while also reinforcing the status quo of heterosexual romance. This exaggerated dependence on men is mocked by Tree after she learns the truth: "Wait … you've been killing me over some stupid guy?!"

Still, for Tree to come to this conclusion, she must first deconstruct her behavior. As the film progresses and she tries to discover her killer and stop the temporal loop, audiences see a clear evolution. She creates more emphatic links with those around her because she needs them to help her; in the process, she starts to know these people. This new kind of relationship eschews mere bonds sustained on power, dismantling thus any hierarchical logic.

Tree suffers a process of "feminist deconstruction," which implies the gradual destruction of old patterns associated with postfeminism. According to Hélène Cixous and Catherine Clément, we live, read and exist through a "double braid" (63), a differentiating process that entails opposition to an other, a structure where women are solely the construct of patriarchy. Feminist deconstruction implies disarming all these binary structures (male/female, god/bad, superior/inferior, etc.) to generate a third element which rises from the ruins of old patterns. This process of deconstruction necessarily implies a new reading of the world.

Happy Death Day is constructed from a spiraled logic of repeated patterns. The sequence is only altered when Tree decides to act in different ways, modifying her original behavior. Tree therefore undertakes a journey of self-consciousness where she discovers behaviors that are corrosive for her and those around her. She must learn to deconstruct the hierarchical dichotomies separating "losers" from "popular" and "good" from "bad." Only in doing so she can embrace a new bond with Carter or come to terms with the maternal figure, thanks to being reunited over and over with Carter by leaving her mother's bracelet in his dorm.

This destruction of old patterns reflects the changes that are taking place in the fourth wave of feminism, alterations that empower women and make their problems visible. It is not the destruction of man that is sought but the fall of patriarchy, the base of the binary system that Tree must downplay to reach her goal of surviving the day. This process requires her to overcome, disarm and unlearn old dichotomies. In the first instance, there's the idea of life/death as self-excluding elements, but also others associated with her false superiority. Tree must work with people she despised as "inferior" in her other "lives" to discover the killer. Further, in the film's climax, Tree kills Lori without appropriating any "phallic" weapon, thus retaining her femininity without evoking any process of masculinization.

Still, Tree falls victim to the binary logic as she tries to become a "good" person, friend, neighbor and girlfriend. The process of unlearning old patterns truly begins at the end of the film, when she kills Ruby after calling her "bitch," a call to her previous incarnation though she is a "good" character now. There lies the escape from the loop. Tree's real freedom comes when she accepts life without any of the constraining rules of being popular/unpopular or bad/good. She must learn to be bad solely against those who, like the male bogeyman, try to hurt her rather than being nasty to everyone, an energy misdirected and, as such, useless.

Conclusions

The Final Girls and *Happy Death Day* contend with the ideological conservatism of the Reaganomics girl and the depoliticized effects of "girl power." Both films celebrate femininity but take feminism closer to the nuanced aspects of the fourth wave and a return to the ideological commitment of 1970s' sisterhood.

We are not here arguing that postfeminism/third wave feminism is dying—or already dead—but, arguably, there is a shift toward a visibility of new forms of female kinship that do not involve the neoliberal trappings of modesty (the Reaganomics girl) or slutty identity (girl power) but serious apprehension of the difficulties that women have been facing in the first years of the new millennium.

Neither film can be considered as a "feminist" product per se; however, we can read both films from the perspective of our fourth wave era. The result of the analysis is interesting but contradictory since we are talking about two films constructed upon the stereotypical Final Girl. What the films attempt to do, however, is deconstruct the meanings of being "strong" as politically correct (the Reaganomics girl) or nasty (girl power). The superficial and uncommitted empowerment is disarticulated from a critical level, a process that parallels the raise of a new consciousness still forming.

Like Tree herself, feminism has the opportunity of reviving and modifying its own death, fixing previous mistakes and accepting the journey as an instance of learning. While doing so, feminism must exhibit, with pride, all the scars of the previous incarnations. Only this way can the collective become stronger and better each time.

WORKS CITED

Brock, Jason. *Disorders of Magnitude: A Survey of Dark Fantasy.* Rowman & Littlefield, 2016.
Cain, Ruth. "Just What Kind of Mother Are You? Neoliberal Guilt and Privatised Maternal Responsibility in Recent Domestic Crime Fiction." In: *We Need to Talk About Family: Essays on Neoliberalism, the Family and Popular Culture,* edited by Roberta Garrett, Tracey Jensen and Angie Voela, Cambridge University Press, 2016, pp. 289–312.
Carson, Fiona. "Feminism and the Body." *The Routledge Companion to Feminism and Postfeminism,* edited by Sarah Gamble, Routledge, 2006, pp. 94–102.
Cixous, Hélène, and Catherine Clément. *The Newly Born Woman.* Translated by Betsy Wing. I.B. Tauris, 1996.
Clover, Carol. *Men, Women and Chainsaw: Gender in the Modern Horror.* Princeton University Press, 2015.
Evans, Elizabeth. *The Politics of Third Wave Feminisms: Neoliberalism, Intersectionality, and the State in Britain and the US.* Palgrave Macmillan, 2015.
Evans, Sara. "Beyond Declension: Feminist Radicalism in the 1970s and 1980s." *The World the Sixties Made: Politics and Culture in Recent America,* edited by Van Gosse and Richard R. Moser, Temple University Press, 2008, pp. 52–66.
Hamilton, Neil. *The 1970s.* Facts on File, 2006.
King, Jeanette. *Discourses of Ageing in Fiction and Feminism: The Invisible Woman.* Palgrave Macmillan, 2013.
Mayo, Cris. *Disputing the Subject of Sex: Sexuality and Public School Controversies.* Rowman & Littlefield, 2004.
Peters, Michael. *Poststructuralism, Marxism, and Neoliberalism: Between Theory and Politics.* Rowman & Littlefield, 2001.
Pilcher, Jane, and Imelda Whelehan. *Key Concepts in Gender Studies.* London, 2017.
Sutherland, Jean-Anne. "Constructing Empowered Women: Cinematic Images of Power and Powerful Women." *Cinematic Sociology: Social Life in Film,* edited by Jean-Anne Sutherland and Kathryn Feltey, SAGE, 2013, pp. 149–161.
Thornham, Sue. "Second Wave Feminism." *The Routledge Companion to Feminism and Postfeminism,* edited by Sarah Gamble, Routledge, 2006, pp. 25–35.

Annihilation, HeLa and the New Weird

Destruction as Re-Creation

ALEXIS BROOKS DE VITA

Annihilation explores earthly application of the interstellar reality of violent disintegration and regeneration as reproduction, replicating how the known universe is theorized to have come into being. *Annihilation* vaporizes Earth's ozone layer—or substitutes for it an earthbound intergalactic replication zone where the known laws of physics and biology do not apply, similarly to the mind-bending Visitation Zones of *Roadside Picnic,* but short-lived, purposeful, and this time called The Shimmer—and experiments with what quantum physical dynamics might look like if interjected into an isolated slice of the settled, predictable, procreation-regenerated Earth. In creating this storytelling arena, *Annihilation* sets the stage for playing out what Toni Morrison describes as "these concerns—autonomy, authority, newness and difference" (44) in the claiming of "absolute power called forth and played against and within a natural and mental landscape" (45). To survive or come to re-exist after annihilation, each woman entering The Shimmer will have to find a way to lay verbal claim to her own absolute power. In breaking down hierarchies of power and control on a "raw and savage" (45) stage, Morrison argues, "Silence from and about the subject was the order of the day" and calls for "excavating these pathways" to analyze "what they contain and how they contain it" (51). In short, Morrison calls for the women confronting terror to analyze the fearful object, their fear-filled responses, and what it is that they are learning or becoming, in these confrontations. Rather than giving in to being overcome, feminist and womanist theorists exhort women to face, describe and claim their transformative roles in what Julia Kristeva conceives as, "A universe of borders, seesaws, fragile and mingled identities, wanderings of the subject and its objects, fears and struggles, abjections and lyricisms" (135), as if foretelling the journalistic sojourn of the women exploring The Shimmer as an ideal conception of the *Powers of Horror*.

In *Sister Outsider,* feminist Audre Lorde states that women have been taught to hold fear in awe, not acting until fear has dissipated. Contending that silence in the face of fear holds women in a condition of static helplessness and argues that giving voice is vital to combatting petrified stillness, Lorde explains that women "have been socialized to respect fear more than our own needs for language and definition" and taught to "wait in silence for that final luxury of fearlessness" (44). Since silence perpetuates the fearful conditions, wordless waiting is futile, if not self-destructive: "it is not difference which immobilizes us, but silence" (Lorde 44). Embracing voice is a first step toward activism. This voicing process is transformation; each feminist's part in "the transformation of silence into language and action" is the need to "establish or examine her function in that transformation" and "recognize her role as vital" (Lorde 43). Every outspoken feminist voice advances women as a collective through whatever fearful conditions they confront, toward each woman's claiming of her own individual power. Explaining "the dialectical relationship linking oppression and activism" in *Black Feminist Thought,* Patricia Hill Collins calls for "an ongoing dialogue whereby action and thought inform one another" (30). Collins describes "different patterns of experiential knowledge that in turn shape individual reactions to the core themes" (27). In *Frontline Feminisms: Women, War, and Resistance,* Jennifer Rycenga describes "a dialectic of revolutionary feminism" (297) as "actualization" of "a struggle for the mind of humanity" (317). Rycenga argues that the restructuring of a hierarchized world into a humanist one requires anti-hegemonic women's voices in dynamic dialogue about their individualized experiences "in the exercise of individuality in action" (299). In contrast to the anti-feminist social conditioning of individual silence that perpetuates group stasis, the filmic version of *Annihilation* takes on the feminist challenge to give voice to fearful confrontations, following a team of activist women through their verbalization of terrifying transformations in their exploration of destruction and monstrous regeneration.

The Shimmer suggests a sliver of astrophysical reality on an Earthly scale, transforming complex physical matter into something else, but according to cosmic laws. In The Shimmer are replicated the subatomic transformations that created the worlds scientists are just now coming to know—including the Earth—from pre-stellar hydrogen and interstellar gases and fog. Unstable particles of matter touch, fuse and replicate their new DNA, becoming something that has never been known to exist. Putting the nascent cosmos, with its black holes and quasars creating galaxies, into an Earthly bell jar, as Jeff VanderMeer and Alex Garland, the respective novelist and film director of *Annihilation,* succeed in doing, appears to lead to an unintentionally womanist spiritual reflection on the cellular transmogrification of an African American woman who died of a particularly virulent cervical cancer. The voracious disease that killed Henrietta Lacks in the known world lives on as HeLa, a self-perpetuating helix that has given innumerable human lives immunity from disease and a chance for existence, long after its carrier died.

The viewer of *Annihilation* comes awake as a comet, like hurtling sperm, blazes from the cosmos to pierce Earth's protective ozone layer. This particle of creation blasts a cervical opening into the base of a phallic lighthouse, the first of a series of the film's ambisexual images. Through the sojourn in terror and shock, advancing upon the Lighthouse, that makes up *Annihilation's* fantasy sphere, the viewer shares the wonder and blind resolution of an investigative team of women whose lives have been disrupted or threatened by cancer and habits of self-harm, as they and viewers are drawn to contemplate the cosmic possibilities of obliteration as rebirth and continued existence. "I'd say you're confusing suicide with self-destruction," the suicide mission team's leader, Dr. Ventress, explains. "Isn't self-destruction coded into us?" Among this band of conflicted, dedicated women warriors and scientists, *Annihilation* plunges the viewer into an experiential maelstrom of destructive/creative cosmic laws injected into an experimental dissection of the delicately evolved, atmospherically sheltered Earthen petri dish. "Once, it would have terrified us. But now we realize that, without the dangers, there would be no wonders. Without the nightmares, there'd be no dreams" (*Evolution of Everything*). This essay follows the women's team, its trials and discoveries, and focuses on its anti-heroic heroines, amplifying what voice is given to their transformations: The Shimmer itself, a matrix which seems ultimately to have destined itself to undergo the annihilation it offers other living matter; Ventress, who will surrender not only the life she is already losing but the mind she has carefully shepherded through Area X toward her goal of understanding The Shimmer; Lena, the secretive main character; and two African American women who seem to pass under critical radar—Josie Radek, the film's physicist, and Henrietta Lacks, the unwitting and involuntary source of HeLa.

The team awakens realizing that time has warped unaccountably, as if in entering The Shimmer it has entered the event horizon of a black hole. The women cannot account for gaps in their awareness. The journey toward the Lighthouse darkens and deepens into incomprehensible species integrations encountered as the women advance through the Zone, beginning with multiple blossoms riotous on a single vine and a crocodile/shark attacking shy Radek. Lena's flashbacks, in addition to a recorded fatality of the previous all-male team that disappeared in The Shimmer, offer tantalizing evidence of the principle of destructive regeneration at work. A film left in their abandoned shelter shows a soldier's solar plexus carved open by Lena's husband, to reveal what should be the soldier's intestines, but whatever is inside him is surging like rapidly growing vines. Fleeing the video and the questions it raises about the men's fate, the women stumble upon splattered remnants of the soldier's corpse. His dissected torso, from belt to skull, is plastered to a wall in similarity to patterns of third stage cervical cancer by the mushrooming form that must have exploded his body in its exuberant growth: another ambisexual symbol. Had the soldier consumed something grown in The Shimmer that bonded, fused with and transformed his digestive tissues into a human/plant hybrid that his body could not contain?

Contact evolution and rapid cell proliferation are the keys to re-creation as something uniquely adapted in The Shimmer. In this specialized environment, deliberate or unintentional self-destruction, such as the prolific cell-splitting of cancer, seems to offer fertile and rapid regeneration. The women's cancers are the key to their flowering explosions of assimilation, cells propelled into repurposing by their own virulent self-reproduction. The viewer is never allowed to forget that Lena suffers like Henrietta Lacks from cervical cancer because the biologist nightly sets up her microscope to examine her rapidly dividing cells, proliferating as she progresses through The Shimmer. However, the biological obliteration promised by cancer is not the only self-destruction Lena has carried into the Zone. After asking throughout the film's genesis why Lena's loving husband, Kane, volunteered for a suicide mission into Area X the previous year, the audience discovers in a panning shot of Lena rapt in lovemaking that his reason may have been her passionless sexual betrayal with a colleague at Johns Hopkins University. Between Lena's study of her proliferating cells and her memory of reading *The Immortal Life of Henrietta Lacks*, it becomes clear that Lena, like Henrietta Lacks, seems to have suffered from cervical cancer, but, unlike Lacks, Lena's cervical cancer may not have been transmitted through a philandering husband's sexual infidelity. Instead, Lena's own philandering may have simultaneously introduced into her body an HPV virus and led her husband to accept his suicide mission. Both these not unforeseeable outcomes—potential loss of her husband through his desire to escape his pain and the introduction of a human papillomavirus from which she might have protected herself with condoms if not with monogamy—indicate filmic Lena's potential willingness to risk violent self-degeneration.

Whether her infidelity preceded or succeeded her husband's disappearance, filmic Lena is not the victim of marital infidelity; she is its perpetrator. Lena's tendency toward voluntary self-destruction, as Ventress lists the symptoms—the ruination of her idyllic marriage and the troubling of her professional life, as Lena and her paramour awkwardly work together—explains why Lena may be drawn to Area X and its crucible of destructive regeneration. Lena has apparently wanted to self-destruct for some time. Therefore, Lena persistently, persuasively risks every member of her team and, eventually, her own safety to approach the stamen-shaped, phallic Lighthouse where Ventress is convinced that the origin and explanation of The Shimmer are to be found.

Psychologist Ventress, anthropologist Cass Shephard, and paranoid paramedic Anya Thorensen have all contributed since the team's first meeting to explaining to Lena the self-destructive problems of the women's team members. Lena's and Ventress's cancers, Thorensen's drug addiction, Radek's self-cutting, and Shephard's attempted suicide upon the death of her daughter from leukemia are self-destructive behaviors uniting their team and, the viewer may suspect, drawing the women, hive-like, toward the alien matrix. These women may each nurse a desire to surrender to self-disintegration, perhaps unaware of The Shimmer's repurposing. Shephard has explained to Lena that she "lost" herself with her daughter's death. However, in The Shimmer, disintegration is neither destruction nor absolution; disintegration leads to immediate repurposing, a science fiction metaphor for immortality explored in the transformation of works such as *Doctor Who*. "It's sort of a way of cheating death," Christopher Eccleston's Doctor explains to Rose his impending regeneration, "except it means I'm going to change. And I'm never going to see you again" (*Doctor Who*).

In *Annihilation*, destructive contact generates assimilation and cross-species evolution. This key to understanding the film's growing evidence of jarring imagery is thus explained by Ventress: "We are disintegrating." Ventress is determined to lead her team to the Lighthouse while still in her right mind or go there alone while still capable of learning its lessons. "If I don't reach the Lighthouse soon," Ventress explains to Lena in preparation to abandon her team's survivors, "the person that started this journey won't be the person that ends it. I want to be the person that ends it." Ventress wants to understand the recreative force that seems greater than obliteration. As the women suffer The Shimmer's misadventures, they are being biologically and psycho-emotionally altered, as in the landscape called forth by Morrison. Like an earthbound quasar spreading particles of creation on radioactive tidal waves, the film moves from the self-regenerating potential of cancer to vines that blossom from Radek's scars. Most horrific are Shephard's screams as a bear's mauling victim, repetitively echoing on the bear's breath from its skull-like muzzle, its head evolved by continual contact with carcasses into a semblance of the skeletal remains of its kills and scavenges. Following Shephard's mauling and the team's encounter with the skull-headed bear that breathes her dying shrieks, Radek philosophizes, "Imagine dying frightened and in pain and having that as the only part of you which survives. I wouldn't like that at all." Lena's and Radek's efforts to sit still while they are sniffed by the slavering white bear hints at the Norwegian folktale upon which Lena's quest through The Shimmer may be based: "East of the Sun, West of the Moon." In this Nordic retelling of Aurelius's myth of Eros and Psyche, the bride betrays her white bear husband by lighting a candle as he sleeps, to see if she has married a monster. The wife's betrayal of her husband's trust sends her, repentant, upon a harrowing quest to retrieve him from an evil queen's castle by performing a series of seemingly impossible tasks.

In some European versions of the Eros/Psyche tale such as "The Unseen Bridegroom," the tasks include the bride's descent into Hell. In Lena's case, betrayal of her husband's trust is shown in her sexual acting out rather than in yielding to doubt. Baha'i theologian Rhett Diessner compares Psyche's search to the awakened soul's yearning to be consumed in God, summarizing that her success will require "selflessness as detachment from lower forms of development" (Savi xvi). The soul must be willing "to forsake her life in 'certain destruction'" (Diessner 195). Among the achievements of Garland's *Annihilation* is his capturing in Lena both the bride's Thanatos longing and her determination to be reunited with the monstrous husband who represents ultimate love.

No matter what the team does to understand or resist the forces that surround it, the only outcome facing them all, once they enter The Shimmer, appears to be particle fragmentation and re-assemblage: annihilation. Radek's prism theory empowers her by giving her a way out of the team's suicide mission from which, early on, there has seemed to be no way out: choosing what of her will remain after death. Radek neither wants to face nor fight the mysterious prism she theorizes is animating The Shimmer: "Ventress wants to face it. You want to fight it. But I don't think I want either of those things," Radek confides. Radek's prism theory reflects her realization that her only choices are resistance with inescapable, disastrous consequences or acquiescence, whose consequences are unknown. Radek does not want her terror to be what survives of her, even if she would be unaware of her new existence. Radek exercises her full capacity for serenity so that she may die in a state of peaceful self-acceptance. Radek's peace of mind and spirit will be the particles of her that refract into the prism, blending with whatever else is captured in the prism's lens. Radek's intent to embrace her destruction at a time and in a manner of her choosing means that her death will make The Shimmer a reflection of the best of herself. Radek is empowered by her realization that there is neither malice nor meaning motivating The Shimmer's destructions and reassembling. She chooses to embrace her death as affirmation of her theory. If The Shimmer refracts biological matter like particles tumbled in a kaleidoscope, then Radek's contribution of flowering vines and peaceful spirit will beautify Area X. Radek's purposefulness demonstrates Ventress's separation of suicide from self-destruction. Radek chooses to make her death the ultimate self-affirmation. Radek bets her life on her theory, bares her scars, and disappears into the forest, there to die in a state of grace, vanishing in sunshine as part of The Shimmer's riotous botanical growth.

Lena cannot find Radek's remains. Radek's unresisting death turns out to be the most peaceful of the annihilations of the self-destructive women who do not have a biological cancer to feed to the regenerative force at the heart of The Shimmer. Without the need for a sexual act of procreation, species absorption and overlap in Area X have become inevitable, echoing the explosive assimilation of elements that created and made habitable the Earth. This destructive/regenerative rather than procreative concept appears as the surviving women near the Lighthouse see twinned deer feeding and startling like a single body with a shining, speckled, three-dimensional shadow, deep in The Shimmer forest. The bizarre deer duo are replicates in size and movement. Their elongated antlers have apparently grown saplings where the original animal rubbed its budding horns against tree trunks. The Earthly deer, unconcerned about the laws of physics and biology, has become so accepting of, or unconscious of, the presence of its less-than-identical twin that it ignores the other's mimicry. Only because the women observing the deer startle the original do the Earthly animal and its shadow-self flee in balletic synchrony. This scene offers the women and the viewer an image that does not raise reactions of horror or fear but helps develop understanding of the process of contact regeneration in The Shimmer. The original deer's horns have sprouted buds from the plant life they have contacted; its shadow self is learning by mimicking the original deer to live on Earth. This scene foreshadows and contrasts with Lena's eventual encounter with a terrifying Other-self.

Cancer may prove to be the best agent of destructive regeneration in *Annihilation*, seeing the welcome with which the matrix draws, nurtures and embraces the transformations of Lena and Dr. Ventress, However, a willfully self-harming drive will turn out to be the strongest catalyst of The Shimmer's obliterating force as it repurposes biological matter into more viable crossbred forms. This counter-intuitive potential for regeneration through destruction may be understood through the lens of cancer research in the real world. Pre-med Texas Southern University biologist Emmanuel Obi once recounted to this writer, who had never heard of HeLa cells, the seemingly incredible story of Henrietta Lacks. Obi explained her cervical cancer cells as being so virulent that scientists who carried them in a test tube in a lab pocket might come down with some type of cancer, raising questions for this writer of the cells' having a quality similar to radioactivity, like the destructive/regenerative forces now at work throughout the known universe. HeLa's ability to cause cancer upon contact is like a meteor's causing atomic destruction of Earth's crust as it crashes and introduces its cosmic gift of life-bringing water ("Monsters and the Milky Way"). Does HeLa change the nearest human cells, acting as particularly virulent subatomic particles that could penetrate barriers of test tube glass and researchers' clothing? Or did the cells' kinetic energies change contacted materials into conduits of their own peculiar reproductive patterns? Although the film does not openly discuss the restructuring possibilities of cancerous cells, its idyllic shot of Lena reading about HeLa cells while still with the original Kane suggests that the film utilizes these fatal but regenerative theories. Just as the real-world Lacks' explosively violent cervical cancer has taken on such a transformative life of its own that her HeLa cells are no longer recognizably human, in the same way, the cancerous leader of the women's team, Ventress, will, upon descending into the extraterrestrial force's uterus through the cervical hole it has opened in the Lighthouse, erupt like a quasar or a regenerative Whovian Doctor into glowing spore-like particles.

Discovering another film that documents her husband Kane's blended-identity farewell to his Shimmer doppelganger, Lena learns that the man who returned to her bleeding internally from multiple organ failure—evidently the unavoidable consequence of regeneration via self-explosion with a phosphorous grenade—is Kane's alien copy. Kane's name recalls the biblical first fratricide, Cain, and adds poetic understanding to his double's destruction of the men's team. *The King James Bible* recounts in Genesis 4:8 "And Cain talked with Abel his brother: and it came to pass, when they were in the field, that Cain rose up against Abel his brother, and slew him." Two videos documenting two deaths of the men's team members "in the field" of The Shimmer show Kane's double talking with them, like his biblical prototype, and helping them record their experiences of destructive change. Spurred on by the discovery of her husband's suicide, Lena crawls through the Lighthouse's cervix into its uterine darkness (Bishop, Carroll, Doane, Embry, Sperling), its corrugated vaginal walls sparkling with streaming particles of reproductive potential, like computer code. There, Lena will both face and fight the process of destructive regeneration The Shimmer offers before she returns, with her new understanding, to the quarantined clone of Kane the Lighthouse sent home to her at the start of the film.

At this point, the viewer may suspect that Kane's double was the matrix's bait to draw Lena to the Lighthouse. With her unique combinations of cancer, investigative scientific curiosity, self-destructive sexuality, and Army training, Lena might be uniquely capable of offering the matrix its own opportunity for annihilation and Earthly repurposing. Like Kiyomi Nagashima in *Parasite Eve*, it seems that Lena may have become destined to carry out a special reproductive mission.

The Lighthouse's uterus is a play on the concepts of matrix. A rippling data screen of strings of information glows against the black walls like shining bloody rivulets. Lena creeps through this tunnel toward the metamorphosing Ventress, seated deep in the blackness, becoming a voice for the lessons taught by the extraterrestrial force: "It's the last phase. Vanished into havoc. Unfathomable mind." Ventress and the matrix are mutually embracing the dialogic transformations exhorted by Collins and Rycenga; but Ventress is returned to herself just long enough to explain to Lena, "I don't know what it wants or if it wants, but it will grow until it encompasses everything." In this space of reductive reassignment and reconstruction, Lena witnesses Ventress's eruption and disintegration into pollen-like possibilities of existence, becoming a reflection of the matrixial force described in her last words: "Our bodies and our minds will be fragmented into their smallest parts until not one part remains. Annihilation." Ventress's Doctor Who–esque explosion is followed by Lena's gaze into the flowerlike kaleidoscope that is Ventress reassembled. This gynoecium swirls open its carpels and pistils like layers of vulvae to expose the locus of potentiality deep inside. This cataclysmic climax of Lena's and the alien matrix's converging journeys recalls Kristeva's "sublime point at which the abject collapses in a burst of beauty that overwhelms us" (210). The yearning force of her gaze draws from Lena's face a bloody tear, her own spiritual/biological essence of self-expression. This is absorbed into the alien core to fashion an inchoate Lena-Other. The extraordinary cell-splitting witnessed in Lena's microscope takes place to emit a three-dimensional chthonic silhouette.

Lena's unsteady Other comes into being in the Lighthouse's uterus, shifting through the appearance of androgyny with the exaggerated vulva and flat chest of a developing fetus or the simultaneously stamen-and-pistil-bearing Lighthouse where it has been generated. Focused on its creative source and voraciously needy, like Mary Shelley's nascent monster, Lena's double pursues its original. Lena-Other crushes Lena against the Lighthouse door as she tries to flee, the copy mirroring the prototype's actions as they fight, fall and rise in a choreography of confrontation and rejection.

Mummy-like Lena-Other evinces the annihilation that her original has enacted. Its exaggerated vulvae hint at sexuality while its flattened chest indicates a lack of nurturance, the double reflecting not only Lena's body but her employment of its destructive sexuality like a three-dimensional *Picture of Dorian Gray*. This ambisexual symbol promises fecundity without nurture: production of life that cannot survive. Faced with her double, Lena wants to escape. But her copy tries to blend with her, to become more evidently Lena by embracing her into oblivion, a cancerous version crowding out the original. The viewer may resist such determinism, remembering the coexistence of the doubled deer in the woods. Despite that animalistic live-and-let-live modeling, Lena's sense of this Other-self as a threat to her own existence leads her to place an unplugged phosphorous grenade in her double's hands like a peace offering. The bemused doppelganger's pacific responsiveness to Lena's apparent gesture of acceptance briefly sparks its evolution into fully human appearance, smiling at Lena before the grenade explodes.

Lena escapes the Lighthouse seconds before the ignited grenade spreads fire through the fascinated doppelganger and all that it touches as it stumbles back toward its matrix, carrying its destructive new gift. Perhaps Lena's Other-self instinctually expects the matrix to offer regeneration, even in this extremity. Exploding from its hands upward, it touches the remains of Kane's head and the Lighthouse's helix stairway before it crawls back into the cervical hole, as if to devolve and reconstruct. But the surrounding crystal trees flare and crumble as The Shimmer dissolves, annihilated and reassembled in its new world.

Phosphorous destruction of highly evolved biological material is apparently ash, not more building block particles of matter. The newly returned third team that grills Lena after exploring Area X reports that only ash remains of the Lighthouse and The Shimmer. Lena's fantastic account of how her team and the extraterrestrial force perished remains uncorroborated, unprovable and indisputable. Reunited with Kane's duplicate, who healed from his coma when The Shimmer obliterated, Lena embraces him and reveals to the film's viewers that she and her husband have irises that evanescently glow, indicating that they have both become extraterrestrial Earthlings. Evidently, Lena metamorphosed completely as she journeyed toward the Lighthouse and did not need to be further duplicated.

What remains of Lena and Kane is apparently a cosmically recreated Adam and Eve outcast from the Edenic Shimmer to transmute life on Earth by contact. Like Lilith Iyapo, whose alien partner seeded her womb with her deceased human lover's sperm in Octavia Butler's *Dawn*, have these destructively reproduced new versions of Lena and Kane become the alien matrix's Earthly carriers? Will all Earthly matter now begin to blend and transmogrify upon contact with other living matter, no longer procreating and destined to die but cyclically self-annihilating, destined to redefine and repurpose itself? *Annihilation*'s regenerative force does not offer benign alien healers forming sexual trinities with human survivors of the apocalypse, as in Butler's *Xenogenesis*. Butler posits an androgynous third partner joining in duo-gendered human sexual unions to eat and treat self-destructing DNA, particularly favoring cancers, enabling and enhancing procreation among Earth's sterilized survivors. In *Imago*, one of Butler's androgynous parents explains the aliens' regenerative philosophy as "A world of life from apparent death, from dissolution. That's what we believe in" (138), seemingly in agreement with *Annihilation*'s Shimmer. However, in proposing an ambigendered recreative force that infects and affects through violently destructive contact rather than seducing with pleasure, *Annihilation* gestures toward more aggressively millennial media such as the *Parasite Eve* game with flaming horses in Central Park, in exploration of a post-millennial Weird. The sublimity of *Annihilation* reminds viewers that U.S. millennials and post-millennials did not grow up believing they could rely upon a caretaking government to provide healthcare, dental care, education, and public safety. Like today's manga, *animé* and video games that start in the second half of the story and devolve to its conclusion, *Annihilation* unravels the pistils of its flower-petal storytelling as it positivizes the brutality of utter destruction by giving obliteration its own creative credit, its own regenerative reason to be. As Novella Brooks de Vita explains,

> For millennials and post-millennials, it's not *if* we're going to experience illness and suffering that we wonder about; it's what specific illnesses we're going to have and which ones will kill us. It's not *if* we're going to die but *how* we're going to die. All my friends are making suffering and death a part of their daily lives. The Uncanny Valley isn't uncanny anymore.

For two generations raised with the assurance that disability and destabilization will form integral daily components of their lives, families and global communities, *Annihilation* asks a question that few profit-driven films dare present as twenty-first century entertainment: what is death?

Particularly for generations raised without faith in man-made simplifications of complex spiritual messages, *Annihilation* allows an immersive space to contemplate what may come as one's life ends: "Incomparable beauty from total destruction" (*Evolution of Everything*). Must the embracing of inevitable destruction be brutal as it rips one from the only existence one has known, *Annihilation* asks. Might death feel unremarkable in the commonality of its occurrence, even if the unique being who is now dying will face it only once? What is it like to neither pursue death, as with Kane's ultimate suicide, nor confront it, as with Lena's dogged stoicism, but to become one with it, as in Radek's scar-baring acquiescence and Ventress's self-sacrifice to gather knowledge, shatter, reform, and briefly incarnate the alien recreative force, itself?

The Shimmer offers no reassuring tales of transcendence. Even submission comes only after spirit-crushing trauma. In the final analysis, Radek's philosophically articulate refusal to fight or face the threat of annihilation becomes not only the most peaceful way to enter death but also the most life-embracing: her acceptance of her shame blossoms as she walks into the prism she perceives. Watching these transformations, the viewer wonders if annihilation would have to hurt. Could letting go, as modeled by Radek and the glorious surrender of Ventress, be beautiful in its inevitable flowering into regeneration? Inundated by the matrix's kaleidoscopic images, viewers may consider whether consciousness ceases upon death or evolves into something diffuse, chthonic or selfless: unimaginably Other. "There is order in this chaos, pattern behind the infinite variety. An endless cycle of birth and death, of creation and destruction" (*Evolution of Everything*). Few films prompt their audiences to contemplate as does *Annihilation* if the dying person ceases to be profoundly alone and finally experiences oneness with all that exists. In advising a Baha'i facing "grievous calamity," 'Abdu'l-Bahá counsels him to "deliver to the flames the veil of moaning, sighing and lamentation" with "assurance and certitude" and "glow with the light of radiant acquiescence," recalling for this viewer Radek's and Ventress's rejections of "sadness and grief": "In truth were man to attain the stage of certitude in his spiritual development, no affliction could ever depress his spirits" ('Abdu'l-Bahá 662).

Analyzing *Annihilation* at ICFA 2018, fantastic scholars Bishop, Carroll, Doane, Embry, and Sperling considered how to define the New Weird. VanderMeer's definition in his *New Weird* anthology introduction at the *Borne Central* website explains that "New Weird has a visceral, in-the-moment quality that often uses elements of surreal or transgressive horror" that relies upon the audience's "surrender to the weird" (VanderMeer). Any effort to define the New Weird should account for storytelling media that have mushroomed into global popularity since the 1990s: video and online gaming, *animé* and manga. If the Weird told stories beyond the control of realism, limited only by the speculative structures of the storyteller, then the New Weird eschews chronology and synchronicity to immerse its audience in disorienting Otherness. The New Weird demands of viewers Radek-ean refusal to fight or face and requires submission to the sublime possibilities of an experiential plunge into transcendence.

Having neither read the books nor seen the film *Annihilation* before enjoying Bishop's, Carroll's, Doane's, Embry's, and Sperling's discussion, this writer approached the movie incapable of being disappointed by its divergence from VanderMeer's texts or readers' expectations. In this space of convergent openness and willingness, perhaps this viewer experienced a different film than was seen by the scholars who introduced it. For example, while the panel seemed not to particularly note or mention the film's referential paeans to Henrietta Lacks and her contribution to modern medicine of HeLa cells, this analyst found HeLa to be key to understanding *Annihilation's* screaming bear and blood-fed blossoming lotus petals. Nor did the panel link the film's similarity to Rabbit Ears' visually entrancing *East of the Sun, West of the Moon* while this writer was present, a pivotal association for this analysis. Finally, though several members of ICFA's "The (New) Weird in Film" panel, like many early reviewers, expect that several questions should remain after viewing *Annihilation*, this writer has only one. Having approached the film with little background noise, this viewer wonders only why Garland named the heroine Lena with an N instead of Leah with an H. "LeaH" would have been a perfect anagram of Henrietta Lacks' death-defying HeLa helix, which *Annihilation* brilliantly queries.

The known universe throbs beyond Earth's fragile ozone layer and its heliosphere's bubble wrap with violent radioactivity that creates new worlds with energy derived from the destruction of others. Earth's ecological imbalances will one day be obliterated into the larger atmosphere of the cosmos, perhaps hurtled far away by a pulsar like a beating heart, seething with radiant beauty and the potential for new life. All will be repeatedly made new. Everything, to its infinitesimal degree, starts and ends as a scintillating iota of energy: pure, finite, and reusable. This anti-intuitive potential is fourth wave feminism in the immersive art of the New Weird: the aggressive miracle in the suffering body of an abandoned mother; voluntary exile from known laws of gravity and time into the unknown and inscrutable that deconstructs as it recreates; confrontation with concepts that both animate and decimate. Artist strips viewer of provable science embedded in chronological time as both become suspended and spaghettified, staring in amazement at the back of one's own head, hurtling feet-first toward the limit of what can be understood.

WORKS CITED

'Abdu'l-Bahá. *Excerpts from Fire and Light in Writings and Utterances of 'Abdu'l-Bahá*. Baha'i Publishing Trust. 2001.

Annihilation. Alex Garland, Director. Paramount Pictures. 2018.

Asbjornsen, Peter Christen, and Moe, Jorgen. "East o' the Sun and West o' the Moon." Edited by George Webbe Dasent. Dover. 1970. Reprinted from Asbjornsen and Moe. *Popular Tales from the Norse*. Edinburgh: David Douglass. 1888. www.surlalunefairytales.com/eastsunwestmoon/stories/eastwest.html. Accessed July 8, 2018.

"Big Bang: the Dark Secrets." *Space's Deepest Secrets*. The Science Channel. 2018.

Bishop, Katherine E., Siobhan Carroll, Bethany Doane, Jason Embry, and Alison Sperling. Benjamin J. Robertson, Moderator. "The (New) Weird on Film." Thirty-Ninth International Conference on the Fantastic in the Arts. *200 Years of the Fantastic: Celebrating Frankenstein and Mary Shelley*. Orlando, Florida. March 18, 2018.

"Black Holes of Doom." *Space's Deepest Secrets*. The Science Channel. 2018.

Brooks de Vita, Novella. Private conversation. Houston, Texas. March 24, 2018.

Butler, Octavia. *Dawn: Book One of the Xenogenesis Series*. Warner Books. 1987.

_____. *Imago: Book Three of the Xenogenesis Series*. Warner Books. 1989.

Collins, Patricia Hill. *Black Feminist Thought: Knowledge, Consciousness, and the Politics of Empowerment*. Second Edition. Routledge. 2000.

Diessner, Rhett. *Psyche and Eros: Baha'i Studies in a Spiritual Psychology*. George Ronald Baha'i Studies Series. 2007.

Evolution of Everything—Space Documentary HD. the All-Seeing Eye. October 2, 2017.

Immortal Life of Henrietta Lacks, The. George C. Wolfe, Director. HBO Films. April 2, 2017.

Jacobs, Joseph, editor. "The Unseen Bridegroom." *European Folk and Fairy Tales*. G. P Putnam's Sons, 1916. www.surlalunefairytales.com/authors/jacobs/european/unseenbridegroom.html. Accessed July 8, 2018.

King James Bible Online. www.kingjamesbibleonline.org. 2018.

Kristeva, Julia. *Powers of Horror: An Essay on Abjection*. Translated by Leon S. Roudiez: Columbia University Press. 1982.

Lorde, Audre. *Sister Outsider: Essays and Speeches*. the Crossing Press, 1984.

MacHale, D.J. *East of the Sun, West of the Moon.* Max von Sydow, Narrator. Rabbit Ears Entertainment, LLC: We All Have Tales. 1991.
"Monsters of the Milky Way." *The Planets and Beyond. the* Science Channel. 2018.
Morrison, Toni. *Playing in the Dark: Whiteness and the Literary Imagination.* Harvard University Press. 1992.
Myers, Danyelle. "The Immortal Life of Henrietta Lacks." *The Griffon News,* 22 March 2018. www.thegriffonnews.com/2018/03/the-immortal-life-of-henrietta-lacks.
"Ninth Doctor Regenerates/Christopher Eccleston to David Tennant/*Doctor Who*/BBC." 2005. www.youtube.com/watch?v=qa3NM9Jhkn0. Accessed June 23, 2018.
Obi, Emmanuel. Private Conversation. Texas Southern University. Houston. 2010.
Parasite Eve. Square. March 29, 1998.
"The Quasar Enigma." *How the Universe Works.* Discovery Communications, LLC. 2018.
Rycenga, Jennifer. "Maria Stewart, Black Abolitionist, and the Idea of Freedom." *Frontline Feminisms: Women, War, and Resistance,* edited by Marguerite R. Waller and Jennifer Rycenga. Routledge. 2001.
Savi, Julio. "Introduction," *Psyche and Eros: Baha'i Studies in a Spiritual Psychology,* edited by Rhett Diessner. George Ronald Baha'i Studies Series. 2007.
Sena, Hideaki. *Parasite Eve.* Translated by Tyran Grillo. Vertical, Inc. 2008.
Shelley, Mary. *Frankenstein.* 1818. www.planetebook.com/free-books/frankenstein.pdf. June 23, 2018.
Strugatsky, Arkady, and Boris Strugatsky. *Roadside Picnic.* Translated by Olena Bormashenko. Chicago Review Press. 2012.
VanderMeer, Jeff. "Working Definition of New Weird" September 27, 2007. *Borne Central.* www.jeffvandermeer.com/2007/09/27/working-definition-of-new-weird/. Accessed March 24, 2018.
"What Happens When a Star Dies?" *How the Universe Works.* Discovery Communications, LLC. the Science Channel. Accessed March 24, 2018.
Wilde, Oscar. *The Picture of Dorian Gray.* 1890. Project Gutenberg. Accessed July 23, 2014.

"Hello, beasty"

Uncompromising Motherhood in Disney's Maleficent

Melissa Wehler

As details about Disney's *Maleficent* began to appear online, hopeful fans grew concerned that the all-powerful villain of their childhoods was about to get a Disney-princess makeover. Such concerns appeared to be further substantiated once the filmmakers revealed that a scorned-love plotline was at the heart of the production. Fans feared the Maleficent who once commanded "all the powers of hell" would be reduced to another female characters that some critics could easily decry as a "man-hating feminist." What the film delivered instead was a story unimaginable in the world of fairytales: Maleficent, a woman forged by destruction, war, and revenge, finds love again, but not in the form of a lover but rather in the form of a daughter. As the film winds its way through the origin mythology, *Maleficent* is a modern narrative about the power of mother-daughter relationships. Maleficent learns that loving the little "beasty" in her life helps her also learn to love herself again, making a powerful statement about self-love outweighing traditional Disney romance.

Critics have framed *Maleficent*, the film and character, as a challenge to traditional fairytales and the equally traditional female gender norms they depict. Benjamin Justice, for instance, sees "Maleficent reborn" by breaking from traditional gender roles and asserting her authority and autonomy. Joe Hatfield and Jake Dionne position the Maleficent at the confluence of a variety of contemporary discussions, including fourth wave feminism, queer identity, and ecofeminism. They contextualize her feminism within an international dialogue surrounding popular culture's roles in human rights and environmental ethics. Pop-culture critic Jordan Shapiro likewise views the film and character as rebuking the patriarchal norms of fairytales. Shapiro argues that the film's essential message is about "valuing others: community, sustainability, caretaking, and social equality" ("Why Disney's"). While Maleficent does indeed challenge traditional fairytale gender norms, the most revolutionary aspect of the film is redefinition of motherhood.

Maleficent behaves as a thoroughly modern mother who combines traditional maternal roles such as protector, mentor, and companion with a more nuanced understanding of women's identities. First, we see that motherhood does not consume Maleficent; it enhances her. At one end of the traditional extreme, we see mother figures who are unloving beings who "learn to love" by having children. Aurora, Maleficent's adopted daughter, does not teach the fairy to love herself. The Maleficent we see from the beginning of the film already knows and loves who she is herself. Rather, Aurora allows Maleficent to own the parts of herself that have been "lost" during her entanglements with failed lovers. On the other end of the extreme, we see mothers who sacrifice themselves, metaphorically and literally, for their children. Maleficent does not sacrifice herself, but instead, she draws power by having a gynocentric relationship. Second, Maleficent recognizes and asserts the complexities of motherhood as neither classically comedic nor classically tragic. At times, she articulates repulsion at the sight of the baby and rejects the narrative that motherhood is natural. In these moments, she also defies characterizations that define women as sideline supporters of their children. Still, at other times, she articulates a selfless, reaffirming love for Aurora that transcends obligatory familial affection. Third, Maleficent, as a fourth wave feminist character, asserts the importance of having her own identity that includes being a mother as one of the many ways she understands herself. Aurora neither creates nor detracts from Maleficent's personhood. Instead, she gives Maleficent the support to expand herself and learn new ways to love. In these ways, the film engages with conversations in fourth wave feminism that demand to see realistic interpretations of women's relationships with their children represented in media.

Protector of the Moors: The Unwomanly Warrior Mother

From the film's opening, the writers establish Maleficent as a mother figure whose identity is tied to the supernatural world and the beings that inhabit it. Before we are given Maleficent's name, she is introduced healing a broken tree branch by cupping her hands, closing her eyes, channeling her magic, and whispering "There you go" (Stromberg). This moment establishes her as a redeemer, life-giver, and healer. She is reproductive in its most essential and magical meaning. We are told that the Moors do not need a "vain and greedy king," or queen for that matter, as the strange and wonderful folk who live there "trust in one another," which allows Maleficent to flourish as an unofficial ambassador and eventually "protector" (Stromberg). The beings of the Moors benefit from her metaphorical and literal loving, healing touch, and the writers establish Maleficent as a mother-nature figure whose identity is rooted in fertility, compassion, and sympathy. This initial iteration of Maleficent's maternal identity presents as uncomplicated, and while appealing, it is ultimately unsustainable.

The world around Maleficent is changing, which requires a new paradigm of motherhood. The Moors are under constant attack by the human kingdom who seek to exploit their natural wealth. Protection is paramount to Maleficent's maternal role, and as Hatfield and Dionne have argued, is aligned with seeing her as a mother-nature figure whose responsibilities are reflected in the landscape she safeguards against invaders (91). The Moors, in other words, are Maleficent's first child. They are crafted as a direct contrast to the patriarchal space of the human kingdom, which is run exclusively by men who wage war, enact revenge, and disregard women. When King Henry, the first king we encounter, brings his army to the border between the two kingdoms, Maleficent fully embraces her role as mother of the Moors, crafting a new maternal identity as a warrior mother. Disney historically has sidelined mothers, keeping them as saintly dead angels or monster-like evil stepmothers. This film for a new era, however, does not blame the scheming stereotypical witch for her cruelty, but considers her damage at the hands of the patriarchy and her own quest for wholeness.

As a warrior mother, a new archetype for Disney, Maleficent reclaims classically masculine attributes of fierceness, assertiveness, and power. She is given license to speak, act, and defend like her male counterparts in the human kingdom. We know that King Henry fears Maleficent's power and influence and uses that fear to justify his aggressions. On the battlefield, his initial reaction is to assert his own dominance and undermine her power. He shouts, "A king does not take orders from a winged elf," which draws laughter from his soldiers (Stromberg). Misnaming her as an elf, something he views as less than a fairy, allows him to discredit her, to rename her according to his own values, and to cast her as the other. Yet, she refuses to yield her authority to this king or any other and denounces his authority, "You are no king to me" (Stromberg). She is not cowed by his attempt to belittle her, and instead, she metaphorically castrates him—in front of his own army no less. Her assertiveness, however, only reinforces his fear and this emasculation cannot be allowed to go unremarked. He answers her metaphorical castration with one of his own: he demands that his men cut off her head. Throughout this repartee, Maleficent demands to be seen as a warrior mother who will protect her child, the Moors, at any cost. She appropriates the language of masculine oppression, reclaiming it as part of maternal model for passionate protection and transforms the dialogue of war into a dialogue of love. Moreover, this scene and subsequent battle complicate the seemingly straightforward narrative of motherhood as strictly reproductive that the film's beginning suggests. Unlike the mother-nature figure we see at the beginning, this Maleficent is bellicose, aggressive, and unyielding. Her maternal instincts allow her to nurture and heal, but they also allow her to protect and destroy.

Unmaking of Maleficent's Maternal Body

Maleficent's body is constantly under threat by the male rulers of the human kingdom who use violence to intimidate, control, and destroy the locus of her power. King Henry and later King Stefan fear her growing influence manifested by her increasing physical strength. When King Henry threatens her with beheading, we see the first attempts to defile her body and the power it symbolizes. However, it is not until King Stefan's violence that it becomes clear how fearful the male rulers are of her warrior mother's body. Under the guise of trust, friendship, and love, Stefan returns to the Moors to warn Maleficent of the king's command to kill her. Maleficent embraces him as a trusted friend and accepts him as her lover. He then betrays his ideals, Maleficent, and himself when he drugs her in a moment of surrender and intimacy in a plot to kill her and take over the kingdom. While she is comatose, he attempts to murder her, but in a moment of sheer impotency, his cowardice outranks his greed. Instead, we watch him violently sever her wings with a hacksaw.

The violation and mutilation of Maleficent's body impacts her ability to be a mother and see herself as one. In speaking about this moment, Angelina Jolie, the actress who plays the adult Maleficent, explains how crucial this scene was to the creation of the character's complexity: "In essence, the question was asked what could make a woman become so dark and lose all sense of her maternity and her womanhood and her softness? And something would have to be so violent, so aggressive, and so of course for us, we were very conscious, the writer and I, that it was a metaphor for rape and that this would be the thing to make her lose sight of that" (*Woman's Hour*). Joan Acocella, culture critic, further suggests that not only was this scene a metaphor for rape, but that "someone involved must also have had clitoridectomy in mind. A piece of the girl's body, and a source of power and happiness, has been sliced off" ("Love's True Kiss"). Maleficent's body is forever altered by the experience. It carries the signifiers of a violent rape—scars, callouses, and bruises—that mirror her traumatic memory.

We see the physical ramifications of this metaphorical rape when Stefan presents the wings to King Henry as evidence of his destruction of Maleficent. Of course, the king sees the wings as evidence of her literal death whereas Stefan knows them to be the evidence of a figurative one. They become a trophy of his conquest and a lasting reminder of the violence he has perpetrated on Maleficent's body. When we next see Maleficent, we realize that the violence done to her body has also changed the way she sees her maternal protection of the Moors. The once-reproductive mother is replaced by a destructive, wicked force. She isolates herself in the Moor's abandoned ruins, a metaphor for her equally broken and discarded body. While there, she learns of Stefan's coronation, realizing that "he did this to me so he would be king" (Stromberg). Without the wings that had made her the mother of the Moors, she turns into a tyrant much like the kings in the world of men and covers them in darkness. She builds herself a crown, subjugates its creatures, commands an army of dark creatures to maintain, and uses fear to maintain control.

No longer their loving, protective mother, she builds a wall of thrones, like the walls around King Stefan's castle, so that the Moors, and her, "might never again suffer the touch of any human" (Stromberg). In doing so, she emulates the power structures of the human kingdom, gaining authority through violence, fear, and tyranny. The maternal protection of the Moors has been betrayed, defiled, and severed by patriarchal authority and the systems of oppression it engenders. Maleficent, no longer a warrior mother, becomes a warrior king.

A Different Kind of Fairy Godmother

Audiences familiar with Disney's *Sleeping Beauty* know Maleficent as an arch-villain, capable of nothing but revenge, cruelty, and despotism. In the retelling of this tale, the writers of Maleficent had to conjure not only an origin story for an otherwise one-dimensional archetype of evil but also provide an opportunity for redemption. According to Jolie who was also an executive producer on the project, the writers considered this existential riddle: "And then at a certain point, the question of the story is what could possibly bring her back? And it is an extreme Disney, fun version, but at the core it is, it is abuse and how the abused then have a choice either abusing others or overcoming and remaining loving, open people" (*Woman's Hour*). The answer comes in the form of Aurora, King Stefan's daughter. She gives Maleficent an opportunity to craft herself into a different kind of mother than either than the Mother Nature or warrior mother identities she had previously inhabited.

Aurora is the symbolic daughter of King Stefan and Maleficent and their failed union. At the beginning of the film, it is Stefan that offers Maleficent the chance at a very traditional motherhood. Having supposedly fallen in love with her and given her true love's kiss, they, according to the prototypical fairytale narrative, would be wed and start a family. When Stefan betrays her, he robs her of this "happily ever after" narrative of motherhood both meta-phorically and physically. After this trauma, Maleficent turns so completely away from motherhood that she is willing to punish the infant Aurora with a curse that replicates the sleeping potion that Stefan used to rape her. Malefi-cent further acknowledges their failed union by creating a loophole in the curse that alludes to Stefan's original lie: the curse can be broken by "true love's kiss." Aurora is reborn through the curse as a living reminder of Stefan's betrayal and remade in the image of Maleficent's pain. Witnessing Aurora's rebirth, Stefan is forced to confront the horror of his action, and he abandons her just as he has her metaphorical mother. Seeing Aurora as the illegitimate offspring of their traumatic union also helps to explain why, later in the film, we see Maleficent reluctantly become her protector, saving Aurora from a traumatic fate in a way that no one did for her. This also helps to understand the most remarkable—and consequently, perhaps the most unrealistic—part of film: why Maleficent steps in to parent the daughter of the man who raped her.

Aurora becomes the vehicle through which Maleficent is able to recon-nect with herself, confront her trauma, and begin to heal. On the first night of Aurora's retreat to the forest, Maleficent comes to her windowsill and snarls, "It's so ugly, you could almost feel sorry for it" (Stromberg). In this line, Maleficent shows a flicker of compassion and certainly the most seen since the night with Stefan. These gradual moments become the foundations for a complex relationship that is forged through deep emotional ties rather than mere blood relation and familial obligation. For her part, Aurora merely smiles at Maleficent, a small sweetness that catches Maleficent unawares as she has not been the object of kindness in many years. Maleficent responds with a declaration: "I hate you. Beasty" (Stromberg). For the first time since her rape, Maleficent is actually able to articulate her hate. As an infant, Aurora has little agency. Her presence in this scene is to be a neutral body, a vehicle for Maleficent's need to articulate her pain and seek catharsis. A similar process defines their second encounter when Maleficent tells Aurora to "go away" (Stromberg). Instead of leaving her, Aurora hugs her, prompting Malef-icent to declare, "I don't like children" (Stormberg). This declaration proves meaningless to Aurora who demands to be picked up, and Maleficent unen-thusiastically acquiesces. In a stunning moment, the young girl runs her hands over Maleficent's horns and touches her cloak. This is the first time we see Maleficent touched by another being since the night Stefan hacksawed off her wings. Maleficent appears put off by Aurora's touch yet allows her to continue. In these moments, Aurora functions as Jung's child-self archetype, helping Maleficent to reconnect with her younger, innocent self. She reminds Maleficent that her child-self still exists, and that by remembering that self, she can heal.

Aurora is no longer a simple sounding board for Maleficent's pain. She is becoming an active participant in their relationship. She challenges Maleficent to accept her, her touch, and her affection. By acquiescing, we see Maleficent acknowledge Aurora's agency as well as slowly accepting her own role as a mother figure. These moments eventually result in Maleficent coming face-to-face with a teenage Aurora. She warns that she must keep to the shadows lest she frighten the girl. Aurora retorts, "I know who you are. [...] You're my Fairy Godmother. [...] You've been watching over me my whole life. I've always known you were close by. [...] Your shadow. It's been following me ever since I was small. Wherever I went, your shadow was always with me. I remember you" (Stromberg). No longer the silent baby nor the curious toddler, Aurora acknowledges Maleficent's fundamental being by affirming it for her: "I know who you are." She defines her as watcher, shadow, and protector. She also names Maleficent and bestows the title of "Fairy Godmother" on her. She demands that Maleficent now listens to her: "I remember you." Once again, the proud Maleficent acquiesces. She literally steps into the light, allowing herself to be fully seen and acknowledged. She lets herself be vulnerable, risking rejection, for the first time since Stefan's betrayal. Aurora does not flinch at her sight, but rather marvels at her body—torn and scarred—and accepts her.

Maleficent and Aurora's budding relationship demonstrates the complexities of modern motherhood where traditional narratives about maternal instincts and mothering dynamics must be examined, questioned, and rewritten. An example of this is early on in their relationship where Maleficent makes a decision about Aurora's autonomy. As the soldiers prepare for their assault on the wall of thorns, Maleficent catches them unaware. In one of the more symbolic moments in Maleficent and Aurora's budding relationship, Maleficent uses her magic to suspend the girl in mid-air and put her to sleep. Aurora's unconscious form glides alongside her as she attacks the soldiers. It appears that she does so out of maternal instinct to protect the young girl from the realities of war and the viciousness of the fight, but this decision also allows her to shield Aurora from the realities of who and what Maleficent has become. In Aurora's eyes, Maleficent is still beautiful, fascinating, and tender. However, like most elements of this mother-daughter relationship, this scene challenges the fundamental feminist ethos of the film. Maleficent does protect Aurora, but she does so partially out of fear and self-preservation. Aurora is not given the autonomy to make a decision about something as fundamental as her own body, but rather, this is made for her under the guise of being for her best interest. Aurora not only lacks agency in this scene but simple consent as Maleficent takes her to the Moors. Certainly, the scene recalls the rape-scene earlier in the film where Stefan uses a sleeping draught to take advantage of the comatose Maleficent. Maleficent's decisions about a vulnerable, trusting person's autonomy, while made out of love, uses disturbing means that call into question the film's otherwise positive female messaging. It reinforces power dynamics between mothers and daughters and the concern for a woman's safety over and above her autonomy, a common theme in traditional fairytales.

The film further explores autonomy and agency in mother-daughter relationships by questioning the equally important relationship of truth and power. As previous discussed, Maleficent protects Aurora from physical danger, while also shielding her from a possibly ugly truth. Later, when Aurora learns about Maleficent and her curse, she confronts her: "Don't touch me. You're the evil that's in the world" (Stromberg). Aurora rejects Maleficent's comforting, loving, and protective touch that she had sought her whole life, recasting that intimacy as false and evil. She also rejects Maleficent's maternal wise and advice about the "evil in this world, and I cannot keep you from it," turning it back on her as a rebuke (Stromberg). Maleficent has wielded her authority over Aurora by denying her access to the truth and circumscribing her agency within their relationship. She has shaped Aurora's narrative about her by only providing her with the information that Maleficent feels she needs to know. However, by protecting Aurora from the truth, she actually loses the control over her narrative, exposes them to danger, and makes them more vulnerable. Maleficent's lie of omission costs her place in Aurora's life and the only "true love" that she has ever known. Worse yet, Maleficent imperils Aurora's physical safety as the grief-stricken girl flees her maternal protection and absconds to the world of men. As Maleficent knows all too well, the world of men is a dangerous place for women, especially because of those like Stefan. Aurora finds herself unprotected when she reaches the castle. Stefan, who imprisons her in an attempt to wait out the curse, unintentionally creates the very conditions for the curse to come to pass. Having lost control of her narrative and Aurora, Maleficent runs headlong into Stefan's trap, and the resulting fight almost kills her. We are reminded that truth and power have significant, physical consequences for both women, and these consequences reinforce the importance of honesty, transparency, and trust in a mother-daughter relationship.

That is not to say that motherhood in the film is about being perfect or living up to idealized version of true womanhood. Instead, we see motherhood defined through acknowledging mistakes and owning lapses in judgment. A repentant Maleficent tells the seemingly lifeless Aurora: "I will not ask your forgiveness because what I have done to you is unforgivable. I was so lost in hatred and revenge" (Stromberg). In this scene, Maleficent enters a moment of deep reflection. She articulates the truth of her trauma and takes responsibility for her actions. She also recognizes how being responsible to Aurora has changed her: "Sweet Aurora, you stole what was left of my heart. And now I have lost you forever" (Stormberg). For the first time in the film, she has to face herself, her trauma, and her actions. She sees through the fog of her "lost" years where she forfeited her fundamental identity to hatred and revenge. She works through the series of traumatic events that have led her to become someone that she no longer understands and through this path, lost Aurora. She can now fully assert that motherhood is not about sacrificing identity, but about becoming more fully oneself. At the end of this deep reflection, Maleficent realizes how Aurora was and is the only person who can guide Maleficent to deep love and deep fealty instead of hatred and revenge. In this moment, the film argues that motherhood cannot assert itself as control, dependence, and deceits. Rather, it has to be defined through mutual respect, responsibility, and autonomy, grounded in an honest sense of personal identity.

Having reclaimed herself, Maleficent leverages her maternal relationship to empower herself and Aurora. After Maleficent admits to her failures as a traditional mother figure, she is free to pursue motherhood on her own terms. She no longer has to hide behind the false narratives she created to protect both her and Aurora from the terrible truth. She can be authentically herself: a healer, destroyer, protector, and defender. Motherhood does not subtract these identities in her, but adds to them. This self-acceptance also allows her to offer unconditional love and break Aurora's curse. In doing so, however, she also discovers that she has broken her own. After all, Maleficent's curse on Aurora mirrors Stefan's curse of Maleficent, and it allows her to manifest her trauma and hatred for him. When Aurora is awakened from her curse, Maleficent is also freed from the burden of her trauma. This is concretized in the film when Aurora unlocks Maleficent's wings and literally and figuratively releases her from Stefan's imprisonment. With Aurora's help, she defeats Stefan and receives the closure that has longed eluded her. As the film ends, we see Maleficent taking off her crown and giving both kingdoms to Aurora in a gesture that is a political and symbolic acknowledgment that Maleficent is not empowered through controlling Aurora, but through sharing her experiences with her.

Maleficent's Other Mother

Motherhood is the most significant theme in *Maleficent* not only because of its centrality to the film's plot, but also because of its role in the critical discussion about the film. Angelina Jolie, the film's starring actress and executive producer, played a significant role in shaping the film and the discussion around it. Jolie has spoken about Maleficent's identity as a female and mother as key factors in reclaiming the classic villain character in this retelling (*Woman's Hour*). In these discussions, the actress and producer framed the film's questions about womanhood and motherhood by contemplating their deeply personal intersections. This framing is understandable given that Jolie has certainly been cast in the media as a "celebrity mom" whose identity has been fodder for public discourse and discussion. Thus, in a film about motherhood anchored by a "celebrity mom" and marketed to families, it was perhaps unsurprising when the filmmakers announced that Jolie's five-year-old daughter Vivienne would be joining the cast as one of the young Aurora actors. Jolie explained this casting as a decision of necessity: "The other 3- and 4-year-old [actors] wouldn't come near me. [...] It had to be a child that liked me and wasn't afraid of my horns and my eyes and my claws" (Lee, "Angelina Jolie's Daughter"). The real relationship between mother and daughter seeps into the scene as an unafraid Aurora, Vivienne Jolie, caresses Maleficent's face. In her media appearances, Jolie also openly talked about having her entire family on set to help coach Vivienne and perfecting her Maleficent voice while bathing her children (Finn, Gonzalez). We even see two more of Jolie's children, Pax and Zahara, making cameos in the christening scene. Of course, the inclusion of Jolie's actual children was not without its critics who felt that it took them out of the internal narrative of the film and who saw the decision as "play[ing] to the public's voyeuristic fascination with this famous family" (Doty). Still, Jolie's decision to blur the lines between her identity as a mother and Maleficent's identity as a mother does help to reinforce the ways that a woman's identity is not circumscribed her role as a mother. In the scenes with her daughter, the audience literally sees Jolie embodying the duality of maternal identity. She is both a famous actor and a mother. She is a real body and a fictional one. She inhibits the space of both person and character. She is Angelina Jolie and Maleficent just as she is mother to Aurora and to Vivienne. By casting her own daughter as her character's daughter, Jolie engages in a unique metacriticism of the ways that modern women and mothers inhabit multiple identities that can both overlap and contradict.

Lately, films have rejected the archetypes of perfect princess and wholly evil villainess seen in the original Disney's *Sleeping Beauty*. Instead, they deconstruct these narratives with developed female characters, emphasizing the damage of the patriarchy and women's search for wholeness. With this, the film's final message further reinforces this reality of the modern mother by casting Maleficent as a contradiction. We learn that the prophecy at the beginning of the film was wrong: That the two kingdoms were brought together not be a "great hero or a terrible villain," but by Maleficent who was both hero and villain. The film's ending demands that we see Maleficent through a nuanced understanding of what it means to be a mother: not saintly dead mother or cardboard villainess but complex person. We watch as Maleficent loses herself in hatred and revenge. We see Aurora's thoroughly disrupt her plans for revenge, forcing her to investigate herself and reclaim her purpose. We see her reflecting on what it means to love someone and how that love expands her sense of self rather than detracting from it. We see the power she draws from loving Aurora and from Aurora's love, which allows her to reclaim herself. We see that "true love" does exist—not through the union of two romantic lovers as fairytales tell us, but through honesty and trust between mothers and children. For fourth wave feminists, Maleficent gives us a modern definition of motherhood that accounts for all of the complicated, conflicting, and powerful emotions that result from loving a little "beasty."

WORKS CITED

Acocella, Joan. "Love's True Kiss: *Maleficent*'s Complex Sexual Politics." *The New Yorker*, 2 July 2014, https://www.newyorker.com/culture/culture-desk/loves-true-kiss-maleficent-s-complex-sexual-politics. Accessed 22 August 2018.

Doty, Meriah. "Why Angelina Jolie's *Maleficent* Scene with Her Daughter Took Me Out of the Movie." *Yahoo! Entertainment*, 2 June 2014. https://www.yahoo.com/entertainment/why-angelina-jolies-maleficent-scene-with-her-87342939702.html.

Finn, Natalie. "Angelina Jolie Describes Daughter Vivienne's First Day on *Maleficent* Set—Brad Pitt and the Whole Family Were Put to Work!" *E! News,* 20 May 2014. https://www.eonline.com/news/543813/angelina-jolie-describes-daughter-vivienne-s-first-day-on-maleficent-set-brad-pitt-and-the-whole-family-were-put-to-work.

Gonzales, Erica. "Angelina Jolie Perfected Her Maleficent Voice While Giving Her Kids Baths." *Harper's Bazaar,* 11 September 2017. https://www.harpersbazaar.com/celebrity/latest/a12221850/angelina-jolie-maleficent-practicing-with-kids.

Hatfield, Joe, and Jake Dionne. "Imagining Ecofeminist Communities Via Queer Alliances in Disney's Maleficent." *Florida Communication Journal* vol. 42 no. 2, 2014, pp. 81–98.

Jolie, Angelina. "Angelina Jolie, William Hague, and Sexual Violence in Conflict." *Woman's Hour.* BBC Radio 4, 10 June 2015. Radio.

Justice, Benjamin. "Maleficent Reborn: Disney's Fairytale View of Gender Reaches Puberty." *Social Education,* vol. 78, no. 4, September 2014, pp. 194–198. EBSCOhost, centralpenn. idm.oclc.org/ EJ1045156.

Lee, Esther. "Angelina Jolie's Daughter Vivienne Jolie-Pitt Joins Mom in Maleficent as Princess Aurora." *US Magazine,* 14 March 2014. https://www.usmagazine.com/entertainment/news/angelina-jolies-daughter-vivienne-jolie-pitt-joins-mom-in-maleficent-as-princess-aurora-new-pictures-2014143.

Shapiro, Jordan. "Why Disney's *Maleficent* Matters." *Forbes Online.* 5 June 2014, https://www.forbes.com/sites/jordanshapiro/2014/06/05/why-disneys-maleficent-matters/#2659388 73901.

Stromberg, Robert, director. *Maleficent.* Walt Disney Pictures, 2014.

SECTION III

CHILDREN'S STORIES

Katniss, the Naive Virgin

Fourth Wave Heroines Recentering Neoconservative Values

Paula Talero Álvarez

Introduction

> No one will forget me. Not my look, not my name. Katniss.
> The girl who was on fire.
> —Katniss Everdeen (Collins, *The Hunger Games* 70)

Katniss Everdeen, the protagonist of the dystopian fiction series *The Hunger Games*, was certainly right when she asserted that she would not be forgotten. Her words now sound premonitory: since 2008, "the girl who was on fire" has shaken up the realm of young adult dystopian fiction. Besides launching entire shelves of imitation novels, she is the protagonist of three novels, stars in four film adaptations, and is responsible for a fan fiction world created around her persona and experiences. Katniss Everdeen has not been forgotten—she is here to stay.

The successful film series *The Hunger Games,* based on the young adult fiction trilogy by writer Suzanne Collins, has made a striking impact on the film industry over the last decade. The four films have been distributed widely throughout the United States and around the world, becoming an important part of our science fiction repertoire. The story takes place in Panem, an imagined dystopian future country where racial mixing and hybrid gender roles *seem* to be the norm. Film critics A.O. Scott and Mahnola Dargis argue that the dystopian world of Panem in the first film of *The Hunger Games* has its utopian moment "in that race and gender stereotypes have become seemingly irrelevant," which may largely account for the film's popularity. However, a closer analysis of the saga reveals that gender, sexual, and racial normativities are still entrenched in the narrative inequality. While it is true that the saga has challenged archetypes by placing a strong, not-sexualized fourth wave heroine at the center of the narrative, these sexual, racial, and gender tropes still pervade—and are crucial to—the figure of Katniss Everdeen and the larger story of *The Hunger Games*.

Katniss stands as a strong female representation within mainstream cinema. She is presented through the films and novels as a complex, well-developed character; an epic heroine who defies the systems of oppression that threaten her community, seeks and achieves justice and becomes a revolutionary symbol. Although empowered girls could be found in young adult literature throughout the twentieth century (Brown), the figure of Katniss has enjoyed a striking popularity in both the literary product and the film adaptations. Her representation fits the current state of Hollywood's film industry and the neoliberal cultural landscape at large, in which young audiences demand empowering young female heroines. Consider, for example, the remarkable anticipation and success of films such as *Mad Max: Fury Road* (dir. George Miller, 2015), *Wonder Woman* (dir. Patty Jenkins, 2017), *Atomic Blonde* (dir. David Leitch, 2017), *Black Panther* (Ryan Coogler, 2018), and *A Wrinkle in Time* (Ava DuVernay, 2018). *The Hunger Games* saga features a female strong protagonist whom we can associate with the fourth wave, yet who sometimes is not decisively feminist. Overall, the saga tries to dismantle stereotypical ideas related to femininity. Katniss is forced to perpetuate ideas about her femininity in order to survive, but those are "stereotypically feminine associations" that she does not choose (Hansen 168). However, her lack of sexualization, although a positive aspect at a first glance, can also work to recenter hegemonic ideals about female virginity and virtue.

The Hunger Games—*A Multifaceted Story*

As Mary Pharr and Leisa Clark have stated, the epic story of *The Hunger Games* saga contains multiple and sometimes contradictory narrative genres, i.e., "a war story that is as well an antiwar treatise, a romance that is never unreservedly romantic, a science fiction adventure that also serves as grim social satire, an identity novel that is compellingly ambivalent about gender roles, and—like other great epics—a tragedy depicting the desperate human need for heroes and the terrible cost of heroism" (Pharr and Clark 9). This multiplicity of layers allows the novels and their film adaptations to offer complex commentary on critical issues and moves the research on *The Hunger Games* in exciting and manifold ways. The saga has fostered reflection on a variety of critical issues taken up by scholars and film critics, namely neoliberal globalization, governmental and media power, social asymmetry, horror as spectacle, audience manipulation, the impact of reality television and the hegemony of totalitarian governments (Moore and Coleman 949). For Suzanne Collins, *The Hunger Games* trilogy is a war story. She expressed during an interview that the trilogy is part of a larger goal, which is to write a war-appropriate story for every age of children (a feat she has accomplished when her other series, beginning with *Gregor the Overlander,* is added to the mix). However, she welcomes different interpretations: "You know, for me it was always first and foremost a war story, but whatever brings you into the story is fine with me" (Grossman).

Still, the novels also incorporate other angles, as the research of many scholars has evidenced. The classic love triangle as Katniss chooses between her childhood companion Gale Hawthorne and her fellow tribute Peeta Mellark is secondary to the main war story. Notwithstanding, it is strung along from beginning to end. In spite of its many attempts to discredit, problematize, or discard normativities about romantic love, desire and sexuality; *The Hunger Games* saga—novels and later on, films—sometimes cannot avoid those very normative conceptions. These hegemonic ideas about romantic young love, desire—or lack thereof—and sexuality are portrayed especially through the films, namely through Katniss Everdeen's romantic and sexual innocence and potential purity and her relationships with Peeta and Gale.

The Innocence of the Heroine: Two Readings

The non-sexualization of Katniss Everdeen might be read by many as a sign of optimism. Katniss's representation opposes common ways of representing women as sexual objects to be desired, admired, and ultimately possessed by men. In contrast, she is particularly not sexualized or exploited by the publishing or film industries. As many mythic women do, "Katniss clings to her eternal virgin status well into teenagerhood" (Frankel 25), and she is also aligned with the image of heroines in science fiction, who are oftentimes portrayed with a lack of eroticism. Katniss's representation is also reaction against a sex-saturated culture and an overtly sexualized media setting. This last has been explored by scholars such as Rosalind Gill and Angela McRobbie. According to Gill, our postfeminist neoliberal setting encourages young women to display a certain sexual knowledge and practice. In this context, sexual agency has become normative, and a "technology of sexiness" has replaced "innocence" and "virtue" as the commodity that young women are required to provide "in the heterosexual marketplace" (Gonick et.al 2–3). McRobbie shares a similar view and asserts that women must now perform a "post-feminist masquerade" "where they are subject to more intensified technologies of bodily perfection and visual display as 'feminine subjects' in a current 'fashion and beauty' system that privileges oppressive forms of idealized white femininity" (Ringrose and Renold 461).

The non-sexualization of Katniss Everdeen also fosters a different reading, one that understands her virginity and naiveté as a lack of sexual agency in the heroine's own terms. This essay explores the myth of the naive virgin in film through the figure of Katniss Everdeen and shows that discourses that engage with teenage sexuality in film often fall into conservative patterns. These discourses, linked to the neoliberal rhetoric of choice, sometimes promote disempowered models of female sexuality. Katniss's purity and innocence in the saga exemplify how tales of virginity operate through film and other media, a recent trend that coincides with the rise of conservative sexual ideologies in popular culture. The heroine makes herself an "asexual warrior" (Frankel 27). She is presented as being uncomfortable with romance, and uninterested in physical intimacy with any of the male characters—first her friend Gale and later her opponent Peeta—who manifest a clear interest in her, especially in the film adaptations. Her "distaste for the role of desirable woman" is also shown throughout the novels and films (Hansen 168).

The Cult of Virginity and The Hunger Games

Despite superficial assumptions about permissiveness and open-mindedness in our current socio-cultural context, virginity is still an important social trope. While a trend of hypersexualization pervades our media with highly sexualized images of women and men, another movement leans toward the celebration of innocence and lack of sexual experience as virtue, as the analysis of Katniss' innocence demonstrates. Virginity and sexual chastity may seem old-fashioned topics, yet they still enjoy currency within popular culture and the various cinemas that serve it (McDonald 1). The treatment of young sexuality in *The Hunger Games* follows these conservative patterns. Neither the novels nor the films explicitly reference Katniss's sexual agency, and they include very little talk about sex. This approach echoes what professor of Rhetoric and Public Culture Casey R. Kelly calls "abstinence cinema," a conglomerate of films that transform virginity into a progressive and feminist ideal and represent the historical convergence of conservative sexual ideologies and contemporary postfeminist culture through the discourse of choice. Promoted through neoliberal cultural products that locate sexual innocence as a virtue, the trend that equates sexual naiveté with virtue facilitates young women's adhesion to neoconservative values and tries to prevent them from engaging with their sexual agency. However, Kelly asserts that films that celebrate conservative sexual ideologies provide a disempowering model of young femininity, since they reduce the individual morality of adolescents to whether they have sex before marriage. These films, he continues, sell audience members the new traditionalism, "inviting them to believe that chastity and sexual repression are the newest form of personal empowerment" (Kelly 7–23).

The *Twilight* franchise, based on the novels written by Stephenie Meyer and a best-selling literary phenomenon before *The Hunger Games*, exemplifies this new attitude toward sex displayed in film and other media. The romantic hero and vampire Edward Cullen is the ultimate embodiment of "abstinence cinema" as he prides himself on his strict sexual abstinence until marriage, distancing himself from the "bad" promiscuous vampires. His choice exemplifies the long-held association between virginity and self-discipline. In this context, virginity turns into the ultimate expression of self-control and assertion of the will, a commonsense choice in societies that promote aspirational striving (Bernau, "Eternally Virginal"). *The Hunger Games*, often studied in opposition to the *Twilight* franchise, shares with the vampires' fantasy saga several elements, such as a love triangle and a central teenage heroine. Katniss has enjoyed greater appreciation from feminist readers and writers, who oftentimes consider her a modern feminist heroine. Bella, on the other hand, has been derided as the traditionally feminine antithesis to Katniss Everdeen (Firestone 209). Both sagas present their heroines as virginal, inexperienced girls and situate chastity—as abstinence before forming a long-term relationship and monogamy thereafter—as a virtue (Siegel 10). Although in *The Hunger Games* this abstinence is not celebrated like in *Twilight*, there is still no sexual activity that involves the main heroine, no references to the protagonist's sexual agency, and very little talk regarding premarital or extramarital sex (Heartfield).

While *The Hunger Games* films do not glorify abstinence, they use a handful of resources to idealize sexual innocence and purity, and to represent Katniss as an inexperienced virginal hero. Virginity—or the lack thereof—is often held as a private, sometimes secret aspect of a person's history, hence *The Hunger Games* films need to render visible what has not been disclosed; they need to offer visible signs for the invisible state of Katniss's virginity. In order to show what cannot be seen, a common technique in the film industry has been to displace virginity from overt dialogue onto the bodies of the actors or the mise-en-scène, or both (McDonald 2–3). In *The Hunger Games*, Katniss's virginity and innocence is rendered visible to audiences through a multiplicity of strategies. First, she is characterized by her romantic and sexual innocence and potential purity. She is an innocent and virtuous *white* virgin, like most virgins in contemporary cinema. While her character in the books is described as having olive skin and black hair, onscreen she was assigned a lighter skinned, naturally blonde actress. This ongoing cultural association reaffirms the reading of Katniss as the innocent virgin (Kelly 130, Blank 9–11). Second, she is presented as being uncomfortable with romance and uninterested in physical intimacy with any of the boys—first her friend Gale and later her opponent Peeta—who manifest a clear interest in her. And third, she is clearly uncomfortable with expressions of sexuality overall. During the Quarter Quell Games, for instance, she admits her discomfort with Finnick's closeness, "especially since he's got so much bare skin exposed" (Hansen 163).

Her "distaste for the role of desirable woman" (Hansen 168) is also consistently shown through the films and novels, crystallizing once again her lack of sexual experience. For example, before she meets Cinna, her stylist, she thinks: "My stylist will dictate my look for the opening ceremonies tonight anyway. I just hope I get one who doesn't think nudity is the last word in fashion" (Collins, *The Hunger Games)*. The heroine is unaware of how to please and amuse, and how to present herself as desirable. In the first film adaptation, she confesses this concern to Cinna, as she says: "I don't know how to make people like me." Sexual desirability can increase her chances of survival, but her naiveté makes her unaware of this fact. We find multiple examples of Katniss's naiveté through the saga. In the first movie, for instance, she gets infuriated when Peeta professes his love for her in a televised interview before the Games. Her mentor, Haymitch, explains how love can be exploited to her benefit, how it can be marketable, and eventually save her life.

> HAYMITCH: He did you a favor.
> KATNISS: He made me look weak.
> HAYMITCH: He made you look desirable, which in your case, can't hurt, sweetheart.

Peeta notices, and praises, Katniss's innocence as well: "It's like when you wouldn't look at me naked in the arena even though I was half dead. You're so … pure" [Collins, *Catching Fire* 216].

Peeta's expression of surprise and awe elevates her innocence to a noble status that resembles a goddess' trait (Hansen 163). It further entrenches the myth of the naive virgin in film, perpetuating the religious notion that women's virginity is linked to their virtue. Peeta's statement perpetuates the ongoing association of virginity with qualities such as purity, innocence, and naturalness; a centuries-old pairing that still pervades our media and popular culture today (Bernau, *Virgins* xiii and McDonald 2). In *The Hunger Games*, ideals of virginity as linked to purity and innocence are not explicit, but located in the subtext: Peeta's suggestive statement helps to invoke them. Through the aforementioned techniques, Katniss's body is constructed as pure and virginal, and naiveté and innocence are idealized, constructed as the right choice or deemed heroic. The saga features a strong fourth wave female protagonist who is nonetheless incompetent, naive or uninterested in sex. This representation perpetuates the idea that sexual naiveté (and, by extension, lack of sexual agency) is a virtue in young women, and that the moral choice is not to have (or even think) about sex. A dismissal of female sexuality surreptitiously centers virginity as virtue. As a result, young women are encouraged to be virginal, and are contrived to remain oblivious to, or uninterested in, the agency of their own bodies.

In spite of Katniss's representation as a naive young woman, *The Hunger Games* trilogy appears as one of the most frequently challenged young adult books in the American Library Association's list for being "sexually explicit." Other reasons to challenge the novels include their supposed unsuitability to age group and the violence contained in the plot (Pharr and Clark 11). Although it is true that the series is violent (the plot is centered on children killing other children), the claim that *The Hunger Games* is sexually explicit is a gendered reading that understands female violence as sexual. Here, the female protagonist metaphorically penetrates (with arrows), which constitutes a subversion of traditional tropes involving male violence. This figurative and gendered reading does not match, however, the factual absence of the discourse of sex in *The Hunger Games*. In spite of their inclusion in the ALA's "Frequently Challenged Books" list, the *Twilight* and—to a lesser extent—*The Hunger Games* franchises ultimately reaffirm the conservative message that nice girls do not feel sexual arousal, "unless they are in love with their one true mate, whom they will soon marry" (Siegel 56). This message is entrenched in a culture with a long history of punishing girls who lose virginity under the "wrong" circumstances and praising those who retain it until the "right" person arrives (Blank 22).

The figure of Katniss Everdeen shows how discourses that engage with teenage sexuality in film still fall into conservative patterns. Many scholars share a similar view. For Siegel, the industry offers a "near hysterical view of youthful sexuality" in most films made about white people for predominantly white (or unmarked) audiences (Siegel 38). Film scholar Timothy Shary agrees, highlighting that teenage sex in American cinema tends to be either unenlightened or somber. For Shary, films have not been irresponsible in showing young people that sometimes negative consequences arise from the loss of virginity, but he believes films could be more progressive if they suggested to young people the joys and obligations of sexual experience as well. As he poses, despite what seemed to be cautious maturation in the sexual initiation of teens in films from the late 1990s, the majority of youth sex in American cinema remains "woefully afflicted" well into the twenty-first century (65–67).

This approach to female sexuality contributes to promoting a neoconservative ideology that seeks to reestablish abstinence until marriage as a social and political imperative. *The Hunger Games* presents Katniss as inexperienced and uninterested in sex throughout the entire saga, a representation that fits the current neoconservative pushback against the liberalization of sexual attitudes. Kelly notes in *Abstinence Cinema* that filmmakers have recently been preoccupied with both the dangers of sex out of wedlock and the virtues of virginity in a sex-saturated culture. Films that elevate virginity as a postfeminist choice or show the disastrous consequences of teenage sexual experiences establish an ideological outpost for sexual conservatism within the terrain of popular culture. While sex remains prominent in Hollywood film and television, a strong challenge to the liberalization of sexual attitudes— especially for women—has also been observable in the last few decades (Kelly 5–6). This trend is also noticeable outside the Hollywood industry. Against the hypersexualization of women in different media, some cultural products promote neoconservative values linked to innocence and purity.

Katniss's naiveté does not only match the pushback against the liberalization of sexual attitudes, but also fits the conventions of the genre, as science fiction is oftentimes synonymous with lack of eroticism. In her article "The Virginity of Astronauts: Sex and the Science Fiction Film," Vivian Sobchack explores the subject of virginity in science fiction, pointing out that its heroes are fairly often represented as virginal. In a way, virginity seems to be an unspoken ideal for science-fiction heroes, who are often represented as chaste or simply not that interested in sex, as it is the case of Katniss Everdeen (Sjö 295–297). Libido and sexual activity are a major absence in the genre, which denies human sexuality a traditional narrative representation and expression. While there are numerous relationships and encounters that take place across the genre, they tend to be chaste and safe in their dramatization, leaving them "more obligatory than steamy" (Sobchack 41–42). These encounters are also peripheral to narrative concerns. The nature and function of sexuality are either muted or transformed. In words of Sobchack, "science fiction films are full of sexually empty relations and empty of sexually full ones" (43). The de-emphasis on human female sexuality in the science fiction film, she adds, is not limited to a specific period. It is particular to the genre, and still present in more recent films which feature central and narratively active female characters. For Sobchack, women are sexually defuse and made safe and unthreatening by various strategies involving "costume, occupation, social position, and attitude—or they are sexually confused with their male counterparts and narratively substituted for them" (45).

Whether Katniss's purity responds to genre conventions or a rise of conservative sexual ideologies in popular culture, it serves to disallow the heroine's sexual agency. *The Hunger Games*, like *Twilight*, domesticates illicit sexuality by making what was old new again (Kelly 25). Katniss's inexperience is presented as a progressive and feminist ideal: the Mockingjay, busy in her fight against the Capitol, does not have time to engage in sexual discourse or activities. Part of her strength is located within her innocence: her personal empowerment comes, precisely, from her chastity. She violently reacts when Peeta introduces a romance narrative as part of their strategy in the Games, she refuses to discuss her romantic feelings with her friend Gale, and she rejects the reduction of her life to a romantic scenario.

Katniss Versus Johanna: Johanna's Sexual Agency as Other

Katniss is visibly uncomfortable with expressions of sexuality, as her initial interactions with tributes Finnick O'Dair and Johanna Mason in *Catching Fire*, the second film of the series, show. It is important to note, however, that Katniss's characterization does not discredit or ridicule other options. Johanna Mason, a female tribute from District 7 who fully embraces her sexuality, strongly contrasts with Katniss's representation. Cynical and outspoken, Johanna shows a rebellious attitude and a clear ownership of her body and does not hesitate to strip off her costume in the elevator in the company of Katniss, Peeta and Haymitch. While Peeta and Haymitch are entertained by Johanna's subversive gesture, Katniss is clearly displeased. Nevertheless, Katniss and Johanna eventually become allies, learning to respect and support each other in spite of their differences. Johanna also helps the forces of the revolution to save Katniss from the Quarter Quell.

Although Katniss and Johanna's alliance and mutual respect suggests a potential coexistence of multiple attitudes regarding young sexuality—a myriad of options that Katniss and Johanna represent—the saga chooses for the female protagonist the innocence and naiveté of Katniss, and not the sexual agency of Johanna. This is a pervasive trend in Hollywood and television, where female friends are allowed to have sexual agency, but only because they are relegated to secondary characters. These characters add the "spice" the female protagonist does not have, and they introduce an element of comedy. Women who possess sexual agency are often respected by other characters and the female protagonist herself, but they are not at the center of the narrative. Actress Judy Green, for instance, has played the archetype of the sexually driven female friend in romantic comedies such as *27 Dresses* (Anne Fletcher, 2008), and *13 Going on 30* (Gary Winick, 2004). This trend supports conservative ways of dealing with youth sexuality and entrenches the postfeminist notion of the "right choice," equating (sexual) innocence with virtue.

The character of Johanna Mason also fits a second common trope in the film industry, one that catalogues sexual agency as erratic behavior. Hollywood often depicts women who are in charge of their bodies as mentally unstable or justifies their choices as a result of a traumatic experience. Amy, from the comedy *Trainwreck* (Judd Apatow, 2015), is a recent representative example of the surreptitious operation of these normativities. Amy, the protagonist of the film, is sexually involved with multiple partners because her father taught her not to believe in monogamy and true love. Besides, Amy accompanies this sexual activity with heavy drinking and erratic behavior, which she abandons after finding true (heterosexual) love. The film is a refreshing update on outdated rom-com clichés, yet it serves to situate multiple partnership as problematic and erratic. Johanna's defiant attitude and ownership of her body are also justified as the result of trauma: she is not ruthless and subversive because she decides to be, but only because the Capitol has murdered all of her loved ones; Johanna is rebellious only because she has nothing to lose.

Our films and other media products tend to adopt one of these two positions: either they sexualize (or hypersexualize) women, or they locate them as innocent, virginal creatures. Neither of these poles offers a satisfactory view of female sensuality and sexuality, since they continue to locate women in polar opposites that have oppressed women for centuries. These two poles echo biblical notions of the good versus the bad woman: the Virgin Mary versus temptress Eve. Katniss's representation as a virginal heroine and Johanna's depiction as a reckless fighter are exemplary of these two opposites. This polarization entrenches tropes about innocence as virtue and sexual agency as erratic and does not provide satisfactory accounts of female sensuality and sexuality. Young women do not need neoconservative depictions of sexuality that encourage them to suppress their sexual agency. The opposite is true—in order to foster healthy attitudes regarding sex, representations that feature female protagonists who engage with their own sensuality and sexuality in a multiplicity of ways are necessary. Moving forward and presenting new fourth wave heroines, the film industry does not need to sexualize these female heroines, but neither must it remove all traces of sensuality from them. It needs to give its female heroines sexual agency, and to put them in charge of their own bodies. The first edition of *Our Bodies, Ourselves* was printed in 1971. We still struggle to take ownership of our bodies, in cultural products and elsewhere.

Works Cited

Bernau, Anke. "Eternally Virginal: Rehymenisation Surgery Is the Latest Example of an Ancient Obsession with Totemic Purity." *The Guardian*, 18 July 2007. https://www.theguardian.com/commentisfree/2007/jul/18/comment.comment Accessed 29 October 2018.
_____. *Virgins: A Cultural History*. Granta, 2007.
Boston Women's Health Book Collective. *Our Bodies, Ourselves*. Simon & Schuster, 1973.

Brown, Joanne, and Nancy St. Clair. *Declarations of Independence: Empowered Girls in Young Adult Literature, 1990–2001.* the Scarecrow Press, 2002.

Blank, Hanne. *Virgin: The Untouched History.* 1st U.S. Ed. Bloomsbury USA, Distributed to the Trade by Holtzbrinck Publishers, 2007.

Collins, Suzanne. *Catching Fire* First ed. Scholastic, 2009.

_____. *The Hunger Games.* First ed. Scholastic, 2008.

_____. *Mockingjay.* First ed. Scholastic, 2010.

Firestone, Amanda. "Apples to Oranges: The Heroines in *Twilight* and *The Hunger Games.*" *Of Bread, Blood, and the Hunger Games: Critical Essays on the Suzanne Collins Trilogy.* Critical Explorations in Science Fiction and Fantasy 35, edited by Mary Pharr and Leisa Clark, McFarland, 2012.

Fletcher, Anne, director. *27 Dresses.* Katherine Heigl and James Marsden, performers. *Fox 2000 Pictures,* 2008.

Frankel, Valerie Estelle. *The Many Faces of Katniss Everdeen: Exploring the Heroine of the Hunger Games.* Zossima Press, 2013.

Gonick, Marnina, Emma Renold, Jessica Ringrose and Lisa Weemsc. "Rethinking Agency and Resistance: What Comes After Girl Power." *Journal of Girlhood Studies* vol. 2 no. 2, Winter 2009.

Grossman, Lev. "'Come for the love story, stay for the war': A Conversation with Suzanne Collins and Francis Lawrence." *Time,* 22 November 2013. http://entertainment.time.com/2013/11/22/come-for-the-love-story-stay-for-the-war-a-conversation-with-suzanne-collins-and-francis-lawrence/ Accessed 29 October 2018.

Hansen, Kathryn Strong. "The Metamorphosis of Katniss Everdeen: *The Hunger Games,* Myth, and Femininity." *Children's Literature Association Quarterly* vol. 40, no. 2, 2015, pp. 161–178.

Heartfield, Kate. "Hardly Revolutionary: *The Hunger Games* Is No Feminist Manifesto." *Ottawa Citizen,* 29 March 2012. http://www.pressreader.com/canada/ottawa-citizen/20120329/284885182445662 Accessed 29 October 2018.

The Hunger Games. Directed by Gary Ross. Performed by Jennifer Lawrence, Josh Hutcherson, and Liam Hemsworth. Lionsgate, 2012.

The Hunger Games: Catching Fire. Directed by Francis Lawrence. Performed by Jennifer Lawrence, Josh Hutcherson, and Liam Hemsworth. Lionsgate, 2013.

The Hunger Games: Mockingjay—Part 1. Directed by Francis Lawrence. Performed by Jennifer Lawrence, Josh Hutcherson, and Liam Hemsworth. Lionsgate, 2014.

The Hunger Games: Mockingjay—Part 2. Directed by Francis Lawrence. Performed by Jennifer Lawrence, Josh Hutcherson, and Liam Hemsworth. Lionsgate, 2015.

Kelly, Casey Ryan. *Abstinence Cinema: Virginity and the Rhetoric of Sexual Purity in Contemporary Film.* Rutgers University Press, 2016.

McDonald, Tamar Jeffers. *Virgin Territory: Representing Sexual Inexperience in Film.* Contemporary Approaches to Film and Television Series. Wayne State University Press, 2010.

Moore, Ellen E., and Catherine Coleman. "Starving for Diversity: Ideological Implications of Race Representations in *The Hunger Games.*" *Journal of Popular Culture* vol. 48, no. 5, 2015, pp. 948–69.

Ringrose, Jessica, and Renold, Emma. "Teen Girls, Working-Class Femininity and Resistance: Retheorising Fantasy and Desire in Educational Contexts of Heterosexualised Violence." *International Journal of Inclusive Education,* vol. 16, no. 4, 2012, pp. 461–477.

Scott, A. O., and Manohla Dargis. "A Radical Female Hero from Dystopia." *The New York Times,* 4 Apr 2012.

Shary, Timothy. "Virgin Springs: A Survey of Teen Films' Quest for Sexcess." *Virgin Territory: Representing Sexual Inexperience in Film.* Contemporary Approaches to Film and Television Series, edited by Tamar Jeffers McDonald. Wayne State University Press, 2010.

Siegel, Carol. *Sex Radical Cinema.* Indiana University Press, 2015.

Sjö, Soffa. "Saviours and Sexuality in Contemporary Science-fiction Film: Reflections on Virginity, Chastity and Gender." *Theology & Sexuality* vol. 15, no. 3, 2009, pp. 293–309.

Sobchack, Vivian. "The Virginity of Astronauts: Sex and the Science Fiction Film" *Shadows* of the Magic Lamp: Fantasy and Science Fiction in Film, edited by George Slusser and Eric S. Rabkin, Southern Illinois University Press, 1985.

Trainwreck. Directed by Judd Apatow. Performed by Amy Schumer, Bill Hade. Universal Pictures, 2015.

Winick, Gary, director. 13 Going on 30. Jennifer Garner, performer. Revolution Studios, 2004.

Contrivances of
Female Empowerment
and the Millennial Wave
in Disney Movies

ANANYA CHATTERJEE
and NISARGA BHATTACHARJEE

Introduction

Disney animated movies form a very significant part of the popular culture and thus have a considerable hold upon societies worldwide. The depictions of Disney princesses in the movies has attracted criticism from the feminists for their portrayal as "damsels in distress." For instance, *Feminism in India* opines that the "Princess paraphernalia constructs an unrealistic and stereotyped representation of an '*ideal woman*' in young minds" (Gupta). However, holding this judgment upon every animated Disney movie indiscriminately would mean being oblivious toward the recent developments that have taken place within the franchise. In movies like *Tangled* (2010), *Mulan I* and *II* (1998 and 2004), or *Beauty and the Beast* (1991 and 2017) there have always been finer nuances that deviate from the normative. In the three movies that our essay is primarily concerned about—*Brave* (2012), *Frozen* (2013), and *Finding Dory* (2016)—the defiance of gender roles and patriarchal hegemony have been achieved with a notable degree of success. Bonnie Dow explains: "Generally, hegemony or hegemonic processes refer to the various means through which those who support the dominant ideology in a culture are able continually to reproduce that ideology in cultural institutions and products while gaining the tacit approval of those whom the ideology oppresses" (262).

In these films the audience is incited into thinking of a locus outside the established order and, therefore, locates the agency for empowerment outside the hegemonic realm. The resultant agency shall not be granted by patriarchy and for patriarchy. One might, as such, hold 2012 as a watershed year in which Disney decided to be braver in using unorthodox female characters and driving a point home.

As for being "unrealistic"—which, after all, animated movies intentionally become—part of our essay's purpose is showing how the foreign and fantastic, in fact, lend force to the spirit of empowerment that these movies tend to propagate. The plots reveal that what they have in common with many of the other Disney movies is a pattern: the formation of some trouble, brought about partly due to some error caused by the protagonist; a subsequent feeling of guilt and alienation; the resolution of troubles that coincide with and partly result from the protagonist's overcoming of inner dilemmas. However, the movies selected here depart from most other Disney movies in the climax's not being a romantic conclusion. Instead, the focus is upon self-realization, and upon the ways in which these self-realizations enable the protagonists in contriving solutions for their problems. Setting the drama within imaginary lands and infusing it with fantastic elements result in making the plot-arch more elaborate, getting the audience more imaginatively involved, and therefore, increasing the chances of the audience's being influenced.

As such, a millennial with her tablet or art brush comes to relate with Merida with her bow or Elsa with her snow constructions. The millennial does not see some external agent, like a prince, coming up to save the situation for her. Instead, external agents mostly serve to make the protagonist more aware of her inner potential and equip her to interact with society. Her potential is not a given from the beginning of the movies (just as her role is not) but is developed in the course of the plot. Indeed, gender, as a consideration, is gradually suspended as new avenues of empowerment are opened.

Gender Politics Within the Hallowed Locus of Empowerment

The first three waves of feminism, all emphasized women's empowerment—specifically, they allowed women to redefine gender-roles and choose between alternate ways of being without restrictions.

In *Brave*, Princess Merida lives in the mythical kingdom of DunBroch in Scotland with her mother, the venerable queen Elinor; her father, King Fergus; and her mischievous triplet brothers, Hamish, Hubert, and Harris. Queen Elinor attempts to convince Merida to do her duty as a princess by marrying one of the three most eligible bachelors they have selected for her from three neighboring kingdoms. Merida flips the classic fairy-tale suitor test by beating them all at archery after boldly insisting, "I'll be shooting for my own hand" (*Brave*). Thus rejected, the unattractive young men quickly fade into the background. The marked absence of the typical prince charming is what makes *Brave* so different from the Disney movies preceding it. Merida is far from being a typical fairytale princess. Having flatly rejected the three suitors proposed by her family, she is apparently prepared to go through life quite happily without a husband, and we can imagine her in later years, a weathered and indomitable Amazon queen, a sort of Boudica for the Scots.

The moment of mounting conflict follows the mother-daughter conflict instead, as Merida's problem is actually her mother's insistence that she conform and marry. Merida bargains with a witch for a cake to "change [her] fate" (*Brave*), which turns the queen quite dramatically into a huge bear right in front of Merida's eyes. The psychological significance of the incident is momentous, visibly setting up the character arc and the resultant impact of the drive for empowerment in the movie.

As opposed to the apparent nonchalance of Franz Kafka's Gregor Samsa upon his metamorphosis, Queen Elinor is shocked and traumatized by her unexpected transformation into a hulking bear. While Samsa's life bears no significant changes even after turning into an insect, the queen in the celebrated Disney movie could not have been more different as she takes quite some time to come to terms with her new body. Due to her sudden metamorphosis, her power, poise, prestige and even her life hang on the line. If one is to consider the human consciousness in the animal body of the bear, into which the dainty queen gets magically transformed, we cannot but notice her shock, so very identical to the reaction of her daughter. At that point of discovery in the movie, the two women were far apart in terms of external appearance. However, the two could not be any more similar in their expressions and bodily postures. The moment she is transformed, ironically, their differences start to fade, especially in terms of opinions and psychic nuances. This irony, as we shall go on to establish, is uncanny in the truest sense of the term.

The fourth wave of feminism recognizes that the struggle is not just against men; it is also against women who have internalized the patriarchal ideals deeply ingrained within the fabric of the society and now act as the reinforcers of these ideals at the cost of other women's independence. The fourth wave galvanizes the women to take matters into their own hands and deal with the consequences of their actions with a sense of vigorous psychological strength.

Brave is indeed a feminist movie as the central characters are not the king and the triplet princes, but the princess and the queen. The two go through trials and tribulations of their own making and come out from the tangle through their own agency. Merida follows her mother into the forest where they live off the land and bond, while Merida comes to repent her mistake. Merida teaches the queen to fish, but also returns to the castle and masters her mother's technique of silencing a room with poise and feminine presence. With this, Merida gives a speech to the male lords declaring an end to the old ways of young women as prizes for confining patriarchy: "The queen and I put the decision to you my lords. Might our young people decide for themselves who they will love?" (*Brave*). The men eagerly agree. Here, Merida wraps her radical ideas in her mother's courtly civility, and they repair the insult Merida offered her suitors at the tournament. In fact, the women's independence and strength of character turn the other cast members peripheral—a shift that highlights alternate modes of resourcefulness and empowerment with which patriarchy traditionally does not agree.

Only King Fergus stands out as a fleshed-out character among the male cast, and the reason behind this is a shift in the role of the patriarch that he portrays. Part of his charm lies in the ludicrous excesses of masculinity that he seems to embody as a representative of the Scottish population. Thus, King Fergus, the unifier of the Scottish people against the Norman threat, is brave enough to take on the demon bear with his bare hands (*Brave*). He leads a people with hyperbolic acts to their credit; the suitor from clan Macintosh slayed thousand Norman invaders with his sword, the MacGuffin suitor "with his bare hands, vanquished two thousand foes," while the Dingwall representative "was besieged by ten thousand Romans, and … took out a whole armada single-handedly with one arm" (*Brave*). The macho attitude is portrayed as a ludicrous excess, as what is needed for solving the problem is a presence of mind displayed by Merida, while the males only worsen the problem. Fergus, finally, manages to stand out since, as Billy Connolly (who voiced him) notes, "He is more soft than he appears," as made evident when Fergus at one point impersonates Merida before Elinor ("Disney UK"). His portrayal, therefore, subtly subverts gender-roles while giving him a soft corner, which literally is the redeeming quality the movie requests.

After all, the happily-ever-after is obtained at the end after Merida's admission to her mother that she loves her. This changes her back, and the queen replies that they both have changed. An integral part of this redeeming element is the wholesome approach to life in harmony with not just one's family but also nature—a virtue learned under the tutelage that the fourth wave gained from ecofeminism. "Some say our destiny is tied to the land, as much a part of us as we are of it," Merida narrates as the animation pans over the Scottish landscape (*Brave*). The opening of the film pre-shadows the plot when we see a younger Merida playing with the queen who impersonates a carnivore. Merida is simply amused by this presumed encounter. This indicates how the bar of acceptability for the animal self in society has been raised higher—a nod to human coexistence with animals is provided. From the point where Fergus and his troops discover Elinor in her bear form and try to hunt her down, not knowing it is she, Merida and her siblings in fact become a nature conservationist working hand in hand with the wild.

Merida does not have any superpower like Rapunzel's magical hair, or Elsa's power of snow, but she becomes empowered in the course of the movie because of the sensibilities that connect her with her family and the wild. The creators, in this case, are going further to give Merida impressive ordinary human skills to help the audience relate and feel that they too can be empowered while being apparently ordinary human beings. Scholars like Kira Cochrane have pointed out that fourth wave feminism is "defined by technology" (Cochrane) and that is exactly what the Disney studios are employing to bring about a revolutionary approach through *Brave*. With her bow in hand, striding on her horse Angus, Merida is equivalent of the millennial geek who is obsessively tied to her books or PC and has a dog or cat as a favorite. Merida gets criticized for her obsessions by her mother just in the manner in which the millennial's parents may express their displeasure with their son's or daughter's mannerisms. However, we come to discover that this apparent handicap actually enables Merida, by giving her a deal of technical expertise with which she can contrive a solution. Reaching her happy ending involves repairing a tapestry on horseback, solving a riddle, and letting down her emotional barriers and apologizing, as well as fighting, shooting, and surviving off the land.

The year 2012 is marked for the resurgence of people's interest in feminist issues along with the renewal of movements through internet, digital and social media, and this is amply reflected in movies like *Brave*. This does not mean that *Brave*, in effect, justifies the eccentricities of the millennial. Rather, we see the signs of emotions that this lifestyle may inculcate in the millennial, including anxiety, stress, mood swings, attention deficiency, alienation and, possibly, depression, along with a path for working through them (Bahr 88). (One can argue that *Inside Out* [2015] most directly addresses the psychology of the millennial. However, it does so in such a way that the audience is left feeling that the protagonist's psyche at any given point is barely holding it together.) As Scott Degraffenreid notes in *Understanding the Millennial Mind: A Menace or Amazing?* "The fact is, they are not broken and trying to fix them is not the answer" (5). The symptoms noted above actually do have their positive counterpoints, namely that the millennials have successfully attuned themselves to the realization that change is the only constant and have very often found ways of being creative under changing circumstances. *Brave* draws upon this circumstance and, with deliberate anachronism, projects this reality into a historical era. The consequences are very significant. Not only do the foreign setting and the involvement of magic accentuate the resourcefulness of the protagonist, but also the relationship between the mother and the daughter summons the daughter back from her disarrayed state through the call of responsibility. Responsibility, in this case, is not a baggage for the daughter that curbs her potential. It, instead, motivates her to the fullest utilization of her skills, developing in her a sense of purpose. Furthermore, the sense of responsibility works two ways here, binding Merida and Queen Elinor in a bond that respects their individualities, rather than making traditional rules the guide and caprice for their behaviors. The consequence is hence a constructive sense of empowerment.

Although ruled by an alpha-male leader (who is no longer in his prime), the kingdom of DunBroch is in danger of entering a diplomatic relationship in which it would become the lesser partner, whoever may become the successful suitor, since King Fergus's sole heir is a woman. In rejecting every suitor, Merida actually prevents her kingdom from entering into an unequal relation with another nation, although that aspect may not be motivating her. As such, while her unequivocal and irresponsible rejection does initially turn the diplomatic order into chaos, in the long term, by asserting her autonomy, she actually asserts the autonomy of her nation. Apart from a statement on female empowerment, the incident is also a considerably notable statement on political empowerment. *Brave* also reflects the significance of diplomatic instructiveness in our contemporary globalized world. However, the movie indicates that while forces such as neo-liberalism make nations feel obliged to open its boundaries (Comaroff 9), this openness should actually not come from a sense of duty but out of one's own inclination. A nation needs its autonomy in order to display authentic hospitality. (This, especially, is a worthwhile issue in the movie for an Indian viewer.) Thus, the act of empowering is essentially a political act, although, again, very carefully, Disney prioritizes the personal over the political in order to show the significance of individual agency. The crux of this sentiment is presented in Merida's following lines: "There are those who say fate is something beyond our command. That destiny is not our own, but I know better. Our fate lives within us, you only have to be brave enough to see it."

The empowerment factor that starts at the very outset of *Brave* no doubt makes it a heady cocktail for the feminist viewers. However, what makes it a true feminist piece? Of course, the fact that Merida accomplishes the feat of bringing her mother back from her altered shape contributes. More, the way in which the friction between the two women, that is the queen and the princess, henceforth dissolves, gives way to a healthy level of active cooperation laced with the anxiety of losing each other. The stake is higher for the queen who would forever remain a bear if not converted back within the stipulated hours, but this would bring Merida a very personal journey into an abyss of never-ending guilt, the possibility of which makes her rise into action.

Anna-rchy: For the First Time in Forever

The action in the blockbuster movie *Frozen* owes much to Anna and Elsa, the two dynamic siblings who present a refreshing perspective on gender roles. The movie is adapted from Hans Christian Anderson's fairy tale "The Snow Queen," and from the start, Disney struggled with the evil Snow Queen character. Originally, Elsa was supposed to be the antagonist and then the script was altered so as to morph her into the adorable Snow Queen that the world loves (Gross). Does this not imply the present generation's greater level of tolerance for the so-called strong woman? *Maleficent* (2014) does draw our attention to the fact that the women who diverge too much from the feminine model typically become the Disney villain. However, *Frozen* indicates that the empowered woman need not be a threat to the well-wishing world-order. What appeared to be threatening finally becomes adorable as the character's arc runs from a premature empowerment to an empowered maturity. (Even the witch in *Brave*, for that matter, is a borderline character.) This makes *Frozen*, by far, the boldest when it comes to all-around empowerment of women.

Our argument for claiming this is that *Frozen* actively alters general perception of the millennial and does so to a degree unmatched. In Michel Serres's *Thumbelina: The Culture and Technology of the Millennials*, the title coinage is suggested as the name for the millennial female, given her proficiency in using her fingers to send text messages (Tom Thumb being her male counterpart) (7). It is telling that Serres takes recourse to a Disney character in order to indicate the technical aptitude and the reliance on technological mediums of the millennial. As an individual, the millennial female is dynamic and potentially violent: "Like an atom without valency, Thumbelina is completely naked. We adults have not invented any new social links; our generalized tendency towards suspicion, critique, and indignation had led instead to their destruction" (10). The Snow Queen's case is hence not an exception. It is representative of an entire generation of individual exiles not understood by the society of the elders around them. The orphanhood of the two primary characters comes to accentuate this predicament, although emphasized by the girls' enforced childhood isolation from each other. "An atom without valency" (10), the bottled-up anxiety finally leads to the point of outburst and destruction. At her coronation, Elsa lashes out with a wall of ice and, despairing at having revealed her hidden magic, runs up the mountain to be alone. Following the destructive outburst, however, the movie gradually works up to a better conclusion as it banks upon the millennial's capacity for self-expression, emotional bonding, and care. *Frozen* achieves a fine line in the name of care—a line that tips neither toward negative critique nor toward patronization. The result, therefore, is a constructive anarchy.

Serres further demonstrates that the millennial generation is the outcome of an unprecedented development in human civilization—"The new technologies, finally, externalize the messages and operations that circulated in our neuronal system—information and codes, which are soft" (25). While books have always thus acted as the external manifestation of human intelligence and knowledge, the fluidity and accessibility to the process of externalization and, consequently, cognitive processes, brought about by *soft* technologies, virtually, have made possible an evolutionary step forward. The transformation is miraculous in nature. Equally inevitable is a consequential drive toward defiance and anarchy, since the world of technologies is also the world of overabundance. This world integrates the individual into a web of pre-existent knowledge systems, drowning her individuality and her chances for self-expression. The pressure of the world is clearly visible in Elsa's case whose young shoulders feel the responsibility of governing an entire nation. In response to this situation, she cannot combat reason with reason. The millennial's "work defies classification" (41). She "sow[s] seeds into every wind, perpetually fertilize inventiveness" since the "only authentic intellectual act is invention" (41). The most significant message that *Frozen* offers is that there is nothing wrong in this inventiveness that requires temporarily relinquishing responsibilities. This forms the subject of the most prominent song of the movie—"Let It Go." It first recounts the bottled-up situation but soon goes on to be an obvious, blunt defiance of the Victorian ideals of silence, submission, and sacrifice (*Frozen*). It concludes with the ultimate sass as Elsa slams her new ice castle's door in the audience's face (*Frozen*).

Equally important, however, is the counterbalance of Anna that calls Elsa back to the world of responsibilities—not by appealing to Elsa's so-called better judgment but through an authentic sense of sisterhood. Thus, we find here the same principle as in *Brave*—the woman cannot enter healthy social relations without, anarchically, indulging and empowering herself through the means of individual agency. Still, the films establish the rebellious heroines as protagonists. *Frozen* has simply been braver than *Brave* in letting the female protagonists curve a disruptive space of their own.

Elsa's quest for liberation, however, does not mean that Anna is purely a foil and an agent of restoration with no creativity of her own. Possession of magic, after all, is not the only criterion. While Anna initially appears dependent on a man to take her to Elsa, she quickly disabuses the viewers of that particular misconception as she uses her both her wit and her physical strength to save herself, Kristoff, and his reindeer Sven from hungry coyotes, and later, from a fall into an abyss. The trio's team makes a sound picture of inclusion rather than dependence. Moreover, at the climax, Anna and Elsa summarily break the myth associated with the "kiss of true love" solving all problems, and Anna unhesitatingly chooses her sister over her beau. Of course, the kiss of true love finally takes place, because it is, after all a Disney animated movie, but the audience also enjoys the pleasure of seeing how Anna restrains Kristoff, who intends to deal with the scheming Prince Hans and deals with him herself, hitting him square on the face and propelling him into the water. The women bridge their emotional disconnection, just like in *Brave,* and the ending of the movie reminds us of the closing lines of Christina Rossetti's celebrated poem, "Goblin Market":

> For there is no friend like a sister
> In calm or stormy weather;
> To cheer one on the tedious way,
> To fetch one if one goes astray,
> To lift one if one totters down,
> To strengthen whilst one stands [Rossetti 119].

The Uncanny Homeliness of Finding Dory

Although not a princess or even a human, Dory's character marks a significant development in Disney's millennial wave. As we have noted, Disney's visions of empowerment banks upon the resources that the female protagonists bring in, in order to correct the situation. In case of Merida, however, her instruments belong, for the most part, to the masculine toolbox, while Elsa's skills hail from the supernatural repertoire. In a way, Anna is more similar to Dory than to the other women—they are ordinary and flawed characters who nonetheless turn out to be special individuals in a world teeming with multiplicity. (Considering that a blue tang is also called a regal tang, one may argue that Dory indeed is a princess in a certain sense.) *Finding Dory* is, as such, the most determined of the three movies since the movie's weight is shouldered by a character who has apparently nothing to distinguish herself from the crowd (and, if anything, is actually unusually capable of getting lost in the crowd).

In this movie, Dory gets separated from her parents and, due to her short-term memory loss, fails to find them for a long while. She grows up into a young adult and one day, while she acts as a teacher's assistant, she comes to know about migration, which, we are told, is about going home, to where one belongs. Migration and memory are linked in a simple and yet unique way. The season migration becomes a pilgrimage for Dory, one packed up with action like an epic voyage, where she receives help from several unlikely sources, and discovers old friends like Destiny, the nearsighted whale, and makes new ones like the seven-tentacle octopus, whom she calls "septopus" (*Finding Dory*). Flashbacks come and go, revealing precious memories of Dory with her parents who shower her with love and didactics, quite

representing the Disney morality. Thanks to these conveniently paced rec-
ollections, Dory overcomes the difficulties caused by her condition—her
meaning demented and her being a little fish in a big ocean—so as to not
only fulfill her quest but also provide release from captivity other fishes. *Finding Dory*, therefore, draws further attention to the question—how can the
unfamiliar and uncanny be the material for generating discourses of empowerment and rather than simply being the gateway for escapism for the millennial audience?

Finding Dory enables us to address an associated issue that we previously
addressed regarding *Brave*—interspecies fluidity. While the other movies have
offered a few anthropomorphic or metamorphosized animals, *Finding Nemo*
and *Finding Dory's* casts almost entirely consist of anthropomorphized animals, extending the audience's sympathy toward the animal world. As a
poignant allegory for the condition of the exile, *Finding Dory* makes its teenage audience, consequently, sensitive to issues they are otherwise not expected
to confront. Wildlife conservation, environmentalism and the individual's
relation to "homeland" are among the themes to which the film provides an
inroad.

Regarding the last-mentioned theme, we can sense the maturity in the
movie's perspective when we do note that, upon finding her parents, Dory
does not settle with them in her previous homelands but returns with them
to her reef home (to Nemo's delight). The movie strikes a balance between
the attachment to homeland and the need to move on. It takes into consideration the world of its audience in which migration, caused by political reasons, is a serious issue, and it lays focus on the (female) individual within
this scenario. The comic mold, as such, particularly enables fluid imagination
in its audience, and it, in turn, makes us particularly open to fluidity in gender
and species roles.

This development is significant for the discourses of empowerment.
Having been put under a spell and made to look at things through the other's
eyes, one learns to detect or project agency in places originally unthought of.
This holds true for not just the characters but also the viewers. These become
encounters with the "uncanny"—used here as a translation of the German
"*unheimlich*"—literally meaning unhomely. With Nemo, Marlin and Dory,
we are indeed not at home. *Unheimlich*, however, according to Freud, actually,
more specifically, denotes the presence of what is strangely familiar within
the foreign. A movie like *Finding Dory* makes us encounter that which speaks
to us from within a world that is not our own. Typically, an uncanny
encounter is frightening and unsettling. However, animation helps replace
the potential for trauma with wonder. This, we argue, makes animations a
special medium for communication. Viewing this poignant representation
of the emigrant's condition and of the disabled's attempts to cope up with

life, the audience does not feel repulsed, distressed or disturbed in coming across these problems. The colorful atmosphere of the movies provides a creative energy that makes us optimistic. *Finding Dory* drives home the point that Dory is, more appropriately, differently abled, rather than disabled. Consequently, all of us, with our own little perfections, are inspired to make a resource out of our own peculiarities. The idea here can very well be expressed through the words of Jenifer Lee, the co-director of *Frozen*—"the idea is of always looking for that girl that is more like us, you know. [She] talks too fast, messes up a bit, and yet, still can be inspirational" (HeyUGuys).

In this case, Dory's dementia actually makes her more attuned to the flow of life (the ocean being the medium of fluidity in their lives) and remarkably free of anxieties, as opposed to Marlin, who has always carried the traumatic memory of the loss of his wife. It, therefore, is quite ironic that Marlin is the clown fish. Also—a less obvious but nevertheless notable feature—Marlin, in fact, appears with feminine characteristics—a single father who worries about his household (as opposed to the carelessness of a teenager that Dory displays), his color-coat is far lighter compared to the royal blue that Dory, a blue tang, sports. Nemo has both examples at hand as he grows up, observing them both in order to emerge with a balanced personality. *Finding Dory,* however, emphasizes the ways in which Dory has a unique personality: when Dory uncharacteristically drops into a pessimistic and reflective state while considering her parents' possible attitude toward their long-lost daughter, it is Marlin who brings into notice her unique abilities.

> Dory, you know how we found you? [...] We were having a very hard time until Nemo thought "What would Dory do?" [...] Ever since I met you, you have shown me stuff I never dreamed of doing. Crazy things. [...] Dory, because of who you are you are about to find your parents. And when you do that you will be home [*Finding Dory*].

The message that one's own ability will lead one home is essentially empowering. The fact that the elements in this drama are so foreign to our reality is hardly a hurdle in our connection with the sentiments expressed here. Through Dory, we find a reassertion of the ground under our own feet, and that ground we make our own not by imitating Dory but by the virtue of our own strength—as the film explains, "you can do whatever you put your mind to" (*Finding Dory*).

Admittedly, in spite of the little haven that all the fish have found at the end of the movie, the sea creatures' lives are essentially in a precarious condition. Dory, at the end of it, is in no way relieved of her condition. What Disney nonetheless suggests is that the empowerment achieved is dominantly psychological in nature. Within the immediate range of their social lives, personal self-realization makes them well equipped to deal with every situation in life.

Conclusion

Feminism as a movement is too vast and varied to be fitted into ideologically unique watertight compartments. The fourth wave, by far, may be considered the most complex and yet, the most interesting. The advancement of technology and the resultant change in the millennials' cognitive patterns require the implementation of innovative modes of communication. As Serres notes, we need to invent "new social links" (10) to establish that communication with the millennial generation, and we can find these in the Disney movies. The intention is not that of interpolating the generation into a nexus of obedience, but that of providing a platform where their potential can be expressed in its entirety.

WORKS CITED

Bahr, Nan, and Donna Pendergast. *The Millennial Adolescent.* ACER Press, 2007.
Brave. Directed by Brenda Chapman and Mark Andrews, performances by Kelly Macdonald and Kevin McKidd, Pixar, Walt Disney Pictures. 2012.
Cochrane, Kira. "The Fourth Wave of Feminism: Meet the Rebel Women." *The Guardian,* 10 December 2013. https://www.theguardian.com/world/2013/dec/10/fourth-wave-feminism-rebel-women.
Comaroff, Jean, and John L. Comaroff. *Millennial Capitalism and the Culture of Neoliberalism.* Duke University Press, 2001.
Degraffenreid, Scott. *Understanding the Millennial Mind: A Menace or Amazing?* BigBusinessZoo.com, 2008.
Disney UK. "Brave: Billy Connolly Introduces Merida and King Fergus. Official Disney Pixar UK." *YouTube,* 17 August 2012, www.youtube.com/watch?v=VR0VS4O.
Dow, Bonnie J. "Hegemony, Feminist Criticism and the Mary Tyler Moore Show." *Critical Studies in Mass Communication* vol. 7, no. 3, 1990, pp. 261–74.
Finding Dory. Directed by Andrew Stanton and Angus McLane, performances by Ellen DeGeneres and TyBurrell, Pixar, Walt Disney Pictures. 2016.
Frozen. Directed by Jennifer Lee and Chris Buck, performances by Jennifer Lee and Idina Menzel, Walt Disney Pictures. 2013.
Gross, Terry. "Songwriters Behind *Frozen* Let Go of the Princess Mythology." *NPR,* 10 April 2014. https://www.npr.org/templates/transcript/transcript.php?storyId=301420227.
Gupta, Shagun. "How to Be a Damsel-In-Distress: A Lesson by Disney Princesses." *Feminism India,* 19 May 2017. https://feminisminindia.com/2017/05/19/disney-princesses-damsel-in-distress.
HeyUGuys. "Frozen: Directors Chris Buck and Jennifer Lee Exclusive Interview." *YouTube,* 6 December 2013, www.youtube.com/watch?v=5fHZ2Mb8Q2I&t=28s.
Pender, Danielle. "Why Millennial Pink Can Do One." *It's Nice That.* 7 November 2017. https://www.itsnicethat.com/features/why-millennial-pink-can-do-one-danielle-pender-opinion-071117.
Rossetti, Christiana. *Christiana Rossetti: Poems and Prose.* Oxford University Press, 2008.
Serres, Michel. *Thumbelina: The Culture and Technology of Millennials.* Translated by Daniel W. Smith. Rowan & Littlefield, 2015.

Making Her Own Destiny

Disney's Diverse Females

LISANN ANDERS

Waves of feminism come and go but that does not mean that feminism goes away. The metaphor of waves, introduced by Julia Kristeva (cf. Gillian and Tauchert 37), has often been criticized since it implies that feminism is just a trend that comes back from time to time, as Ednie Keah Garrison argues "[…] my own problem with the metaphor [of waves]: generations posed as suspended in conflict or separated by a gap presuppose only two conflicting factions; it feeds so well into the media's tendency to categorize feminism and feminist conflicts simplistically and oppositionally […]" (Garrison 31). Although this is a valid point, the wave metaphor also suggests that feminism stays like the water in the ocean—to extend the metaphor. It is just sometimes more prominent, more visible, more forceful because of changing circumstances, just like waves. This forceful crashing waves can be seen when the need for social change cannot be held back anymore, the need to get a step closer to a cultural and social equality between different sexes and genders. In the wake of *#metoo* or the ongoing discussion on equal payment between men and women, it is important to have a look at the fictional representation of the treatment and representation of women and men. The film industry is especially interesting to look at due to its reach and influence on viewers. In particular the Disney brand deserves special attention here since it is Disney's films and programs for kids that have an impact on the next generation of girls and boys, men and women.

Disney princess films in particular are often condemned to be anti-feminist in so far as they seemingly always end in marriage and with a need for the damsel in distress motive. While this might be true to a certain degree in Disney classics such as *Snow White* (1937) or *Cinderella* (1950) and even the Renaissance movies such as *The Little Mermaid* (1989) and maybe even

Aladdin (1992)—even though in these two there is already a great develop-
ment apparent compared to the former ones—the most recent depictions of
Disney princesses do not follow the cliché anymore. Disney movies after 2012—
Brave (2012), *Frozen* (2013) and *Moana* (2016) show a further major movement toward an independent representation of females. However, even in
The Princess and the Frog (2009) and *Tangled* (2010), these tendencies can already
be observed, as Maegan M. Davis outlines, "These films, especially *Tangled* and
Frozen, highlight the idea that women have the ability to achieve their dreams
without the help of a man" (50). Jena Stephens notes that *The Princess and the
Frog* marked a watershed for Disney princesses since Tiana "decides her own
journey and dream in life" (97). All of the modern Disney princess films from
2009 to 2016 feature strong independent girls who are trying to grow up in
a world which still seems to be dominated by traditional role models. Each
of these princesses, Tiana, Rapunzel, Merida, Elsa, Anna, and Moana, need to
go on a literal and metaphorical journey to find their true selves and rid themselves from the social but also individual constraints they are living in. In that
way, these films can be read as feminist coming of age stories or *rite-de-passages*.

However, only classifying these films as feminist because they do not
revolve primarily around the classic love story would be too short sighted.
The feminist trend in Disney started quite a bit earlier with several princesses
rebelling against their parents and trying to find their own way—be it Jasmine
in *Aladdin* or Ariel in *Little Mermaid* or Mulan in *Mulan* (1998). These are
all examples of strong modern women. Mulan deserves a special emphasis
here since she holds her ground in a clearly male-dominated anti-feminist
world but even *she* gets the guy in the end (cf. Rothschild 142–152). It can be
observed that in comparison to the classic Disney movies from the mid–20th
century, in the Renaissance Disney movies or "middle movies" of the 1980s
to early 2000s, the princesses "start a trend of working together with their
male counterparts in order to achieve happiness, stability, and health as
opposed to waiting for the male lead to prevail individuality" (Davis 50).
Disney took the feminist criticism that these movies still hold up patriarchal
values seriously though and stirred away from the classic boy meets girl plot
in the second decade of the new millennium to show how diverse individual
feminism can be and that marriage can be an option but does not have to be
the only option for a fulfilled and satisfying life. As a consequence, Disney
is broadening its definition of love to parents, sisters, nations, and oneself. It
is once again emphasized that the most important quality in characters is
that they should be true to themselves. The modern films do exactly this.
Thus, with regard to the most recent Disney princess films, an important feature of fourth wave feminism is diversity in dreams of female protagonists.
These dreams can only be fulfilled by means of a journey to the true self in
order to make one's own destiny.

Yet, this definition needs to be extended since fourth wave feminism is not only concerned with the female protagonist, but it also allows more space to an equal relationship between men and women—after all as Julie A. Nelson remarks, "'male' is also a gender" (1362). Consequently, in comparison to the classic Disney princess movies, the male characters today are less flat and are given more room for development, too. Interestingly enough, they often (with the exception of *Brave*) accompany the princess on her journey and they learn from her while simultaneously helping her, too. Hilary Radner and Rebecca Stinger comment on the gradual progression toward gender equality by illustrating that "contemporary deliberations about femininity throw into relief the ways in which masculinity as its analytic other is itself an unstable and contested category" (5). Therefore, fourth wave feminism can be regarded as a step toward breaking up gender binaries and thus true equality between the genders with acknowledging strengths and weaknesses of the protagonists and with a plot in which romantic relationships are not the main route to happiness. The route itself is interesting here also in terms of spaces, which is why the various spaces the princesses occupy are to be discussed with regard to the princesses' *rite-de-passage* since their journeys often take place in the wilderness.

When talking of spaces, Foucault's notion of heterotopia cannot be ignored. Michel Foucault coined the term "heterotopia" in his essay "Of Other Spaces" in 1967. Foucault describes heterotopias as non-spaces or anti-spaces, meaning that they offer a space that is set in reality and yet, subverts the very same by presenting their own set of hegemonic rules. Examples for such heterotopic spaces would be prisons, which are part of society and yet are removed from it, graveyards, which are inhabited by, well, dead people or the theater stage, which presents a make-believe world to a real audience. Heterotopic spaces thus challenge the boundaries between what is real and what is unreal or at least other. Foucault outlines that "[…] real places […] which are […] a kind of effectively enacted utopia in which the real sites, all the other real sites that can be found within culture, are simultaneously represented, contested, and inverted. Places of this kind are outside all places, even though it may be possible to indicate their location in reality." However, heterotopias do not necessarily have to be geographical spaces or rather places as such, which would be congruent to Foucault's claim that heterotopic spaces are not publicly accessible but are exclusive. Heterotopias can also be seen on a more abstract level. Thus, mirrors would be another example of a heterotopic space. In a mirror we see ourselves, yet what we see is just a reflection and not our real self. It is a picture of us captured in the frame of the mirror. The mirror image cannot be grasped because it only represents the real without ever being the real space.

In Disney movies, these heterotopic spaces are often closely linked to spaces of nature—especially in the most recent Disney princess films. In *The Princess and the Frog*, Tiana and Prince Neveen undergo a journey through the bayou, Rapunzel from *Tangled* is locked up in a secluded tower in the forest, *Brave*'s Merida hunts magic in the forest to reverse the curse she put on her mother, in *Frozen*, Elsa is building an ice castle on a mountain while her sister Anna tracks her through snow-covered forests and Moana (or Vaiana in Europe) restores nature's balance by means of water and a journey across the sea on nothing but a small boat. All these spaces suggest a transformation of the norm. Here, society is absent and thus different rules apply, rules that need exploring. The protagonists need to be able to stand up for themselves and defend themselves against nature's challenges. This exploration is incorporated in the princess's journey to herself. The question of "who am I" is nothing new to the concept of the Disney princess. In *The Little Mermaid*, Ariel dreams of being a human and she longs to see more of the world—similar to *Aladdin*'s Jasmine or *Beauty and the Beast*'s Belle, who wants adventure and escape, as she explains in song (00:20:27). Yet, the most famous exploration of the self in the Disney films of the late 1980s and 1990s is probably given by Mulan in her song "Reflection" in 1998. Here, in her songs, Mulan realizes she cannot be a traditional woman by her community's standards (00:11:57) and asks herself when reflection will reveal the person hiding within (00:12:30). Her rebellion against patriarchal norms of behavior through cross-dressing can indeed be regarded as the template of fourth wave feminist films and is very much in line with third wave feminism since gender roles are questioned. Third wave feminism is concerned with "young women's refusal to view themselves as victims of gender regimes, associated with notions of empowerment through sexual assertiveness and agency" ("third-wave feminism"). The difference to fourth wave feminist movies is, however, that the recent films are less concerned with a challenging of patriarchal rules and the assertiveness of female sexuality but that they build on the achievements of the third wave feminist princesses.

In fact, the movies have moved past patriarchy and toward a more liberal understanding of gender roles, meaning that female protagonists are seen as powerful and worthy leaders in these movies. Even though *The Princess and the Frog* can be regarded as the new wave of feminist Disney films, *Brave* is often considered the true beginning of a new era since it marks a turn in terms of romantic relationships in Disney films (cf. Stephens 103). While *The Princess and the Frog* and *Tangled* show strong-minded and stubborn protagonists who follow their dreams sedulously, they still end up married. *Brave*, however, addresses exactly this problem, namely that marriage is not the only option to achieve happiness. Instead, Merida tries to avoid marriage at all cost and the plot resolves around her relationship to her mother. *Frozen* follows in this regard by highlighting the relationship between two sisters whereas *Moana* presents more the protagonist's relationship with nature, tradition, and culture. Here it can be seen that the princesses of the third wave, who were all concerned with "female empowerment" (Rothschild 171), have successfully fought their rebellions against oppressing or at least overprotective fathers and social expectations—even though Merida still has to struggle with exactly this but she succeeds to set a new direction for Disney princesses, a direction in which a happily-ever-after does not have to be tied to marriage.[1] In the following, fourth wave feminist characteristics in *Frozen* and *Moana* are to be more closely examined. *Brave* would, of course, also fit into this category of new Disney princesses; however, the patriarchal element of rebellion against social norms is still too much foregrounded, which is why it is left out of the analysis. *The Princess and the Frog* and *Tangled* are likewise excluded here since they still end with a heterosexual union of the two main protagonists. Still, it needs to be stressed again that these two films already hint at a new trend in Disney princess movies, following Mulan's example, since their primary goal is not a wedding; they have in fact different dreams, which deviate from their rather passive and clichéd predecessors. Tiana would like to open a restaurant, even though strictly speaking she is only building on her father's dream—Alisa Clapp-Itnyre has criticized this goal since the restaurant then only continues patriarchal norms (14); However, Tiana is not *expected* to open a restaurant but it is her own free will to step in her father's footsteps and cook for people. Rapunzel, on the other hand, just wants to see the lights; still, it becomes clear that the lights are just an excuse to leave the tower because she does not want to be locked up anymore. Nevertheless, both "princesses"—Tiana only becomes a princess through marriage (cf. Stephens 96)—end up in a love relationship, fulfilling the audience's expectation of a classic Disney princess tale (cf. Clapp-Itnyre 14). These are the reasons why *Frozen* and *Moana* serve as a better template for an in-depth fourth wave feminist reading.

When looking at *Moana*, the first striking feature is that we do not find a princess in classical terms. Moana has a more realistic, healthy appearance (in which she is similar to Merida) and she is not a real princess but the daughter of the chief, which is close enough to a princess, according to Maui, but Moana refuses to be called a princess (00:52:08). However, Maui explains in an ironic comment that evokes the Disney princess franchise, "If you wear a dress and you have an animal sidekick, you are a princess" (00:52:10). He adds, "You are not a way-finder and you will never be a way-finder" (00:52:15) making clear that in the past, Disney princesses were confined to be just that, princesses; they had to adhere to the roles they were born into and could not be princesses and adventurers at the same time. Over the last decade, this picture has gradually shifted with the modern Disney princesses. Moana as the designated chief-to-be must go on a voyage to save her people; hence, she has to be an adventurer in order to be a good "princess" and ruler. Consequently, adventure becomes a precondition for the role of a modern princess. Furthermore, this adventure is very much intertwined with nature. The princess has to go on a journey through nature to find her way in society.

In *Moana*, the element or rather elements of nature take on a very prominent role as Moana goes on a quest to restore the heart of Te Fiti and thus bring back the natural balance of elements; she thus has to heal nature and through this she restores her own relationship with herself. Moana's relationship with nature, in general, and water, in particular, becomes clear at the very beginning when she finds the seashell or rather when she is given the shell by the sea. Not only does the ocean itself signal to her that she is the chosen one to restore nature's balance, but her grandmother supports and even encourages her in finding her own way in and on the sea. In that respect, the grandmother acts almost like the classic fairy godmother in so far as she unfolds the possibilities of what might be by means of showing Moana what was, i.e., who her ancestors were. The time element thus plays a crucial rule in the understanding of nature. One has to learn from the past in order to act in the present to shape and ensure the future. This balance of time is mirrored in nature—the future can only be ensured through the balance of nature's elements. On an individual level, Moana has to learn this lesson, too. She can only be in balance with her family and herself when she learns from the past and follows her intuition or the call of the ocean in the present, to give not only her people a future but also to become a good independent leader who takes responsibility and knows who she is. Furthermore, by restoring the heart of Te Fiti, Moana restores her own heart in a figurative way. By fulfilling her quest, she gradually learns who she is. It is a learning process that is similar to Mulan's "manning up," but Moana does not have to become a man to prove her worth and abilities; she does not have to cross-dress or to hide her femininity. Moana can be both strong and female and most importantly a leader whose gender does not matter.

The ocean plays an important role in Moana's journey as it is reminiscent of Foucault's heterotopia here. While it first seems that gender stereotypes are enforced when Moana meets Maui and the latter tricks her and steals her boat over the course of the song "You're Welcome," it is worth noting that this scene takes place on an island. While islands are also often regarded as heterotopic spaces, in *Moana* they serve as places that restrain an individual's freedom and urge for development through patriarchal rules—Moana's father wants to protect her and thus keep her away from the ocean while Maui literally imprisons her in a cave. The ocean subverts these rules, however. Even though Maui teaches Moana how to sail, it is Moana who saves her island and by extension, the natural balance. The natural balance can be understood here as a metaphor for the balance between men and women. When Te Fiti does not have a heart, she is Te Kā, an evil fire-spitting male demon made of a pile of rocks; gaining the heart back, Te Kā transforms back into Te Fiti and becomes soft, gentle, mild, and female. Moana thus has to overcome several male barriers throughout her journey: her father, Maui, Tamatoa (the shiny crab) and Te Kā—even though it needs to be pointed out again that her femininity is never a true hindrance nor does any male protagonist truly doubt her because she is female (except for Maui when he mentions that she is a typical princess but this rather refers to her social status than her gender). Nevertheless, even though she is accepted as a female leader, she needs to overcome these male obstacles. She can only restore the heart because she can bond with Te Kā as she sees through the rocky appearance and recognizes another female creature within the fiery shell. It is this recognition of female vulnerability paired with female strength that makes Moana a true fourth wave feminist heroine. Still, it is also the recognition of Maui's vulnerability and his ability to change that aligns the film with fourth wave feminism. Even though the emphasis is still on the female lead and her success, Maui is an equally important character as he assists Moana on her way, but he is simultaneously her student in human affairs and affects. He, too, has to understand his weaknesses and shortcomings and undergo a transformation through the journey across the sea. Again, the ocean performs its heterotopic power by making the male demigod dependent on a female human and by making the human more powerful in her actions than a demigod.

Similarly, *Frozen* depicts the snowy landscape of the forest and the mountain as a heterotopic wilderness, i.e., a space in which both male and female characters have to make choices and become their true selves. Elsa, the snow queen, runs away after she can no longer hide her magical powers. It is fear that drives her away from her castle, her people, and her sister. Like Moana, she wants to protect her kingdom and goes on a journey to do so. However, Elsa runs away because she thinks she is a threat to the kingdom and thus has to be removed from it. While Moana learns the right lessons from the past and is determined to make the future better, Elsa misunderstands the lesson she was taught by the trolls after she had hurt Anna accidentally. They told her and her parents that fear would hinder Elsa from controlling her powers. Thus, in a way, Elsa not only runs away out of fear but also in order to be truly free for the first time without being afraid of hurting anyone. Even though she means well, she is motivated by the wrong trigger, i.e., fear, which consequently causes more harm than it does good. She is too afraid of the past to let the present be determined by actions of the heart. Still, through her escape to the mountains, she discovers the power in herself and realizes for the first time what strength she has, which is visualized in her iconic song "Let It Go." In the heterotopic space of the mountain, Elsa is isolated from society and can thus be powerful, but she needs to learn in that very place that power can only be controlled and needs to be controlled by embracing it rather than fearing it. Only by rejecting the fear of her natural power, she can restore the balance in nature again and bring back summer to her kingdom. With regard to that, her magic powers stand in for her power as a female leader. Once she embraces her roles as the queen of Arendelle and more importantly, her role as a sister, she can be a true leader. As a consequence, Elsa resembles Moana again as both undergo a process within an imbalanced natural surrounding that needs to be restored and in which they learn to be strong (female) leaders who can rule without a man by their side.

However, the portrayal of female leadership and the lack of a romantic relationship for Elsa is not the only aspect which makes *Frozen* a fourth wave feminist movie. Anna and Kristoff seem to be the stereotypical romantic Disney couple at first glance, but in fact, they show a deviation from the classic love plot. Indeed, Anna makes her longing for a husband clear not only in the song "For the First Time in Forever," but also in her hasty engagement with Hans. The film does not criticize the longing for a romantic relationship since, in the end, Anna and Kristoff become a couple, but what is criticized is Anna's passivity, irrationality and rashness in her relationship with Hans. Therefore, what distinguishes Anna's story from princess stories of former generations is that she has to learn to first get to know the guy before getting married to him. By extension, this direction also has a positive effect on the role of the male protagonists. While many classic Disney princes are themselves rather flat, indecisive or even passive—just think of Snow White's or Cinderella's Prince Charming or Ariel's Eric, Hans is more fleshed out. This is fair enough; he turns out to be the villain of the movie, but his caring as well as his power-hungry side are equally present. Kristoff is, similar to Maui, Anna's involuntary guide. He accompanies her through the wilderness of the forest and the mountains and undergoes a transformation from the lonesome wolf to a more caring individual. In this regard he is very much in line with his fellow male protagonists of the modern Disney era, namely Prince Naveen, Flynn Rider, and Maui. All of them are allowed to show a rather feminine side; they all learn how to care for others and be less egotistic. Here, an applied fourth wave feminism is dominant since it is not only the female characters who have to learn by means of a literal travel through the wilderness, but it is also their male counterparts who need to grow.

What makes *Frozen* thus a movie of the fourth wave of feminism is that it shows alternatives for female characters. On the one hand, it shows that political power but also love is not bound to a romantic love plot but has multiple layers to it. It demonstrates that Elsa does not need a spouse to have a happy ending. Anna, on the other hand, seems to be more prone to the romantic fairytale plot as she longs to find a happy ending in marriage. Garrison argues that "the appeal to the family romance is a convention of patri-archal social organization which sustains itself and perpetuates oppressive hierarchies and aggressive competition" (Garrison 31). However, in fourth wave feminism, family romance can also be the portrayal of an equal part-nership in which neither partner is oppressed. Fourth wave feminism is thus rather close to or a continuation of the notion of post-feminism as defined by Yvonne Tasker

> Postfeminism emphasizes women's achievements—physical, educational, profes-sional—and places particular emphasis on individual choice. Contemporary women are imagined by postfeminist discourse to be free to choose; free of both old-fashioned, sexist ideas about women's limits and feminism's supposed imposition of an asexual, unfeminine appearance. The extraordinary *lack* of diversity in media images of girls and women belies that emphasis on choice [68–69].

While fourth wave feminism does all this, too and likewise highlights the element of choice, it also includes a development of male characters. In *Frozen*, neither the perspective of the strong independent woman who remains single nor the perspective of a strong independent woman who enters a romantic relationship is criticized as such; instead, it is shown that women can choose what ending they envision for themselves. The same holds true for *Moana*. Moana does not need to find a husband to fulfill her dreams or societal expectations. She can listen to her inner calling and follow her heart—not to a man but to herself. Female characters in these modern Disney films have thus the chance of making their own destiny by choice. It is this manifold choice of vocation, the need for being in balance with one's inner self, and the *rite-de-passage* both male *and* female characters have to undertake which marks a new era of Disney movies, a fourth wave feminist era.

NOTE

1. This is not to say, of course, that all Disney movies with female protagonists before 2012 focus on marriage. *Lilo and Stitch* (2002), for instance, is about family, tolerance and acceptance; however, it does not count as a Disney princess movie since neither Lilo nor her sister Nani, nor Stitch, of course, are princesses. This essay on fourth wave feminism in Disney solely focuses on the Disney princess franchise in order to see what Disney has changed in their portrayal of Disney princesses over time.

WORKS CITED

Aladdin. Directed by Ron Clements and John Musker, Disney, 1992.
Beauty and the Beast. Directed by Gary Trousdale and Kirk Wise, Disney, 1991.
Brave. Directed by Mark Andrews and Brenda Chapman, Disney, 2012.
Cinderella. Directed by Clyde Geronimi, Hamilton Luske, Wilfred Jackson, Disney, 1950.
Clapp-Itnyre, Alisa. "'Help! I'm a feminist but my daughter is a 'princess fanatic'! Disney's Transformation of Twenty-First-Century Girls." *Children's Folklore Review*, vol. 32, 2010, pp. 7–22.
Davis, Maegan M. "*From Snow to Ice*: A Study of the Progression of Disney Princesses from 1937 to 2014." *Film Matters*, vol. 5, no. 2, 2014, pp. 48–52.
Frozen. Directed by Jennifer Lee and Chris Buck, Disney, 2013.

Garrison, Ednie Kaeh. "Contests for the Meaning of Third Wave Feminism: Feminism and Popular Consciousness." *Third Wave Feminism: A Critical Exploration*, edited by Stacy Gillis et al., Palgrave Macmillan, 2004, pp. 24–36.

Howie, Gillian, and Ashley Tauchert. "Feminist Dissonance: The Logic of Late Feminism." *Third Wave Feminism: A Critical Exploration*, edited by Stacy Gillis et al., Palgrave Macmillan, 2004, pp. 37–48.

Lilo and Stitch. Directed by Chris Sanders and Dean DeBlois, Disney, 2002.

The Little Mermaid. Directed by John Musker, Ron Clements et al., Disney, 1989.

Moana. Directed by Ron Clements and John Musker, Disney, 2016.

Mulan. Directed by Barry Cook and Tony Bancroft, Disney, 1998.

Nelson, Julie A. "Make Is a Gender, Too: A Review of *Why Gender Matters in Economics* by Mukesh Eswaran." *Journal of Economic Literature*, vol. 54, no. 4, 2016, pp. 1362–1376.

The Princess and the Frog. Directed by John Musker and Ron Clements, Disney, 2009.

Radner, Hilary, and Rebecca Stinger. "Introduction. 'Re-Vision'? Feminist Film Criticism in the Twenty-First Century." *Feminism at the Movies: Understanding Gender in Contemporary Popular Cinema*, edited by Hilary Radner and Rebecca Stinger, Routledge, 2011, pp. 1–9.

Rothschild, Sarah. *The Princess Story. Modeling the Feminine in Twentieth-Century American Fiction and Film*. Peter Lang, 2013.

Snow White and the Seven Dwarfs. Directed by David Hand, Larry Morey et al., Disney, 1937.

Stephens, Jena. "Disney's Darlings: An Analysis of *The Princess and the Frog, Tangled, Brave* and the Changing Characterization of the Princess Archetype." *Adaptation Across the Humanities*, vol. 31, no. 3, pp. 95–107.

Tangled. Directed by Byron Howard and Nathan Greno, Disney, 2010.

Tasker, Yvonne. "*Enchanted* (2007) by Postfeminism. Gender, Irony, and the New Romantic Comedy." *Feminism at the Movies: Understanding Gender in Contemporary Popular Cinema*, edited by Hilary Radner and Rebecca Stinger, Routledge, 2011, 67–79.

"Third-Wave Feminism." *A Dictionary of Gender Studies*, edited by Gabriele Griffin. Oxford University Press, 2017. *Oxford Reference*, www.oxfordreference.com. Accessed September 2018.

Jack Frost and
the Heroine's Journey

Gender-Bending Back to the Goddess
in Rise of the Guardians

Patti McCarthy

In 2018, women finally stood together to say "enough." Here, the new fourth wave of feminism women with the #MeToo and HeForShe movements started to challenge a patriarchal belief system that disempowered women and other minorities. This movement shed light on the need for greater equality, inclusivity, intersectionality and empowerment of traditionally marginalized groups (Cochrane). Time for change. Time to find a way back to the feminine in balance with the masculine. Riana Manuel-Paris considers, "The discovery of the importance of intimacy, relationships and care, those things which value connection above autonomy and competition, have been familiar to women from the beginning, a legacy or gift of the Goddess.... Women's voices often illuminate the power of the feminine principle in the world today, and the essential role it must play in bringing back a sense of balance, and harmony to the excesses of an Apollonian driven ethos" (Manuel-Paris). Time to strike a balance.

When asked if there was a Journey of the Heroine, celebrated mythologist Joseph Campbell stated, "It is not necessary. That is the place all the heroes are trying to find ... the place where they all want to go" (*Power of Myth*). Indeed, men are told that if they slay the dragon, marry the princess, and get the treasure, they have made it as men. Although Joseph Campbell offered the Journey of the Hero as a prototype for self-realization, the Hero's Quest is decidedly masculine. Women need to take a journey for women, not take a journey intended for men.[1] How can a woman reclaim the Goddess if the only God the journey leads to is the one that has brutalized and buried her—an ugly spiritual wound which often manifests as misogyny, sexual abuse, casual cruelties, and degradation. Patriarchy has taught girls how to act, what to want, and what to achieve. Although the first and second waves of feminism were instrumental in getting equal rights, they still didn't achieve a sense of equal value. Unfortunately, many women did not recognize the difference, so bought into this idea. Girls said they "were as good as boys," suggesting that being a "boy" is the only way to achieve success or be valued. Seeking the approval of men, women look in the mirror only to find they have no reflection of their own, instead only the internalized projection of what the patriarchy wants them to be. Women and girls need to stop seeing themselves through the eyes of men, but through their own "I," and find value in who they are, not what they aren't. In fact, Gilgamesh and King Arthur are not the only myths out there on which to base a model of self-enlightenment, transformation and individuation; others such as the Descent of Inanna and older fairytales featuring female protagonists give insight into ways women and men can find the Goddess in themselves.[2]

Different paths to this are emerging in an era in which some fictional heroines are so strong and brilliantly created that they inspire boys. More little children *of both genders* are singing Elsa's "Let it Go" on the playground, swinging Wonder Woman's lasso, or even costuming as both on Halloween. Rey and Jyn action figures are appearing more and more in their playsets.

This in itself hearkens a return to female role-models. Indeed, men have been shortchanged by the patriarchy. Men and boys are experiencing the emptiness that is considered "winning" in today's cultural environment. The promise and definition of success today is often unfulfilling. Men have been told they will inherit a "kingdom," but it is a hollow, shadow kingdom, bereft of an equal-ruling Queen and filled with toys and baubles that have no meaning. Through the rise in powerful women's fiction, however, they can find a path to cultivating and valuing the nurturing aspects of the self. This thread even appears in male-led fiction as gentler, less violent heroes rise to replace the muscled warriors of the past, and sometimes even follow the heroine's mythic arc.

One of the more liberating tenets of fourth wave feminism is a shift away from binary systems of thought. "We divide ideas and people into hierarchies of good/bad us/them, black/white, right/wrong. We separate spirit from matter, mind from body, head from heart, science from art, good from evil, life from death, women from men, … we see the 'other' as an enemy (or those dualistic qualities within our self) and demonize them" (Murdock 171). Martin Buber recognized that human beings view the world in conflicting ways—either in terms of I–It or I–Thou (28). Joseph Campbell postulates that the I–It is an innate part of a rigid patriarchal belief system. In the past, the Goddess was alive in the Earth, and dwelled as the life force and divine within each individual (*Goddesses* 17–18). However, for the past three thousand years the Goddess has been driven from cultural memory. Hence, in our culture we are unnaturally split from both within ourselves and without from others. Including narratives, then, that foster inclusiveness and equality—both hallmarks of fourth wave feminism—will help create much needed balance and heal oppositional thinking and inequalities.

Strategies of Resistance and Change: Rise of the Guardians, *a Gender-Bending Heroine*

Rise of the Guardians, directed by Peter Ramsey and written by David Lindsay-Abaire, based on the books, *Guardians of Childhood* by William Joyce, is probably one of the most underrated films of recent years. The film acts as a feminine "call to arms" for males and females equally. The film received mixed reviews in 2012 from critics worldwide—a 72 percent on the Rotten Tomatoes Meter. The film featured an "Avengers" style story and an all-star voice cast populated with well-known characters from childhood fairytales and myths, including Santa Claus, the Easter Bunny, the Sandman, the Tooth Fairy, and Jack Frost, that battled the forces of darkness in the guise of the Boogie-Man, or as he is known in the film, Pitch Black. Still, it never really found an audience or created a sustaining fanbase. This may have happened because this is a film about questioning belief systems, always tricky in America. It's no small coincidence that the release of this film coincided with the beginnings of the fourth wave of feminism movement (2012) which challenged patriarchal belief systems.

The male hero Jack Frost, interestingly enough, takes the classic Heroine's Journey. From the very beginning of *Guardians*, Jack Frost wants to know his identity and purpose, because he can't remember. Like other heroines who take the journey, the memory of who he is has been taken.[3] This restlessness triggers his journey. Like many women, Jack is tired of sitting by the phone—eternally waiting for his life to begin. In voiceover, Jack tells the audience, "Why I was there and what I was meant to do, that I've never known, and a part of me wonders if I ever will" (Lindsay-Abaire).

The Heroine's Journey Begins: Awakening and Supernatural Aid

Typically, the protagonist on the Heroine's Journey begins living in a World of Illusions designed to protect her or him. Victoria Lynn Schmidt, author of *45 Master Characters: Mythic Models for Creating Original Characters*, observes, "This is a familiar world of things known to her and repetition brings her the illusion of security, but is a form of imprisonment" (186). Our "heroine" typically stays put because she feels she has an obligation to do so, is afraid of change, has no other viable options, or has bought into the role of martyr. Jack Frost is no exception. He kids himself into believing everything is okay when it isn't.

In a dramatic opening monologue and miraculous "birth" scene, Jack Frost emerges from the depths of a frozen pond: "Darkness. That's the first thing I remember. It was dark. It was cold, and I was scared. But then ... I saw the moon. It was so big, and it was so bright. It seemed to chase the darkness away and I wasn't scared any more. Why I was there and what I was meant to do, that I've never known and a part of me wonders if it ever will" (Lindsay-Abaire). It's clear that this signifies something breaking through to conscious thought, an "awakening." The association with the moon and water, both symbols of the feminine, suggests that a part of the feminine, or the Goddess aspect, in Jack has been sleeping, denied or repressed and is now breaking through to the light.

Campbell explains, "The Goddess is the ultimate boundary of consciousness in the world of time and space. But when reduced in emphasis, the Goddess is reduced to the elemental level. She is the cosmic water" (*Goddesses* 19). It is not unusual for protagonists who take the Heroine's Journey to take on attributes of the repressed Goddess and become associated with various symbols or metaphors that highlight her existence. Despite this shining symbolism, Jack is invisible to the nearby townsfolk. This sets up an important theme in the film—the need to not only believe in oneself, but others as well. As Jack, so the power of the Goddess in our daily lives. It's there, but only functions as a ghost of many women's true power and ability because they lack self-confidence. As "fathers' daughters," to fit into a patriarchal society and narrative, women and girls measure themselves against the masculine ideal—and like men, devalue their own femininity. This stage of the journey asks us to "awaken" to our true potential.

Tricksters in particular hold great significance for today's feminist movements. Tricksters always appear when there is a desire for change and according to Vogler, "serve several important functions.... They cut big egos down to size ... they point out folly and hypocrisy, and bring about healthy change and transformation, often by drawing attention to the imbalance or absurdity of a stagnant psychological situation. They are the natural enemies of the status quo" (77). As such, many folkloric tricksters are outliers, often portrayed as minorities, who cannot challenge the patriarchy directly but instead rely on cleverness and humor. "I laugh at what has endangered or has fought to suppress, enslave, or destroy what I cherish and has failed" (Holland 45).

If we can laugh at our fears, and our nightmares, we can overcome them. Tricksters like Jack teach others how to use humor and play as a powerful tool to quell our fears and defeat those who unjustly stand against us. This is the second major theme in the film and what Jack must learn to value in himself. Fourth wave feminists might consider developing a good sense of humor to counteract current pushback strategies. It is telling that Jack only defeats the villain later on—not, as one would expect, with violence—but with laughter, instead. Laughter is what drives the darkness away.

Early on, Jack jokes around and uses his "super powers" of humor and play for healing, transformation and change—but he doesn't know it yet. Immediately after his miraculous birth from the frozen pond under the protective light of the moon, Jack finds what looks like a stick or staff. Unlike a typical "male" hero's "weapon," such as a sword or wand, its top is shaped like a crescent moon (Goddess), a scythe (death and transformation), a shepherd's crook (protection), and an Egyptian Was scepter (power, dominion and order over chaos). Holding the powers of life, death, protective forces and the proper use of power, the staff represents not only the transformative power of the Goddess, but the ability to create proper balance in the world. This is a creative and protective object, but it also, if wielded incorrectly, has the *potential* to become destructive. Further, while winter can be harsh, rigid, ruthless, it must give way to the flexibility and gentleness of spring, creating a balance. Even within winter there is beauty. Jack soon learns the staff gives him the power to create frost.[4]

At first, he is wonderstruck by the beauty of creation and makes beautiful mosaics of ice to the delight of the people around him, but after years of being ignored, neglected, and "cursed," he begins to inflict the pain of his abandonment onto others in the form of practical jokes. This is humor turned dark (like the Joker in the *Batman* oeuvre). He makes someone slip, blows cold air through a window to ruin a stack of important papers, sticks a kid's tongue to a drinking fountain with frost, all things that spread chaos and discontent. Jack laughs at their misfortune, "Ah, now, that was fun," a phrase tellingly echoed later on by Pitch, Jack's darker side, when he kills the happy dreams of humanity. Jokes can be used as a weapon to avert feelings of pain, inferiority or anger. How many times have we heard someone say, "Ha-ha! I was just joking!" after almost reducing the intended target into tears? This is a classic case of anger and pain turned outward. In order to cope in his current situation, Jack would rather hurt others than feel his own pain. He pretends he doesn't care. "I've been around for a long time…. I love being on my own. No rules. No responsibility. It's as good as it sounds." Still, we, as well as he, know it's a terrible lie that covers an almost unbearable sense of loss and feelings of abandonment. On this journey, Jack will need to uncover the lies he's been told and in turn stop lying to himself.

Like most Trickster figures, Jack associates and identifies most with children—and this is where we mostly find him throughout the film, either playing with, or protecting children. On the heroine's journey, the protagonist typically is taking the journey to protect the weak, the young, or the disenfranchised. In an opening scene, Jack plays with some neighborhood kids, specifically Jamie, Caleb, Claude, Sophie, Monty, Pippa, and the formidable, Cupcake, before Easter. Soon the kids get into a discussion about "believing" in the Easter Bunny. All the kids, except Jamie and his sister Sophie, have doubts. When Jaime's mother tells Jamie he "doesn't want Jack Frost nipping" at his nose, Jaime innocently asks "Who's Jack Frost?" Miffed, Jack, still unseen, hurls a snowball at Jamie. "*Then we watch as his face changes ... a mischievous sparkle comes into his eyes, A big smile. Make no mistake, something magical has happened*" (Lindsay-Abaire).

Barbra Ehrenreich in her book, *Dancing in the Streets: A History of Collective Joy*, explains how we have "forgotten real fun." Ehrenreich believes that rites and festivities that have provided cohesion, joy, and power to communities, were suppressed by powers of church and state and appropriated by commerce, such as Christmas, Easter, and Halloween. Representations of these rites and festivities occur in prehistoric drawings and paintings, in medieval and Renaissance carnivals and festivals which include feasting, drinking, song, music, dancing, costuming and masking as well as role-reversals that threatened the status quo. Since they imagined the removal of those in "charge" (church and state), practices of "collective joy" were strongly suppressed. This lack, Ehrenreich speculates, most likely contributed to the prevalence of melancholy from sixteenth-through the eighteenth-century Europe (133), during which time, the modern isolated individual was separated from the healing powers of community celebration. As then, so today. When dreams, wonder and memories are oppressed, we despair. She does acknowledge that festivity "keeps bubbling up," at planned and at spontaneous festivities or protests—and important thing to remember as feminists move forward—with joy—in the campaign for equality, inclusivity, balance and interconnectivity.

The magic of play is deliciously infectious as seen in the film. As soon as Jamie is hit with a Jack's "magic" snowball, he laughs, and an epic snowball fight ensues. It's a wonderful scene full of happy mayhem, chaos, snowball fights and wild sled rides. Even the neighborhood heavy, Cupcake, can't help but join in the "fight" after getting "hit" by the *magic* of *play*. When Jamie's sled ride gets too dangerous, we see a side of Jack we haven't experienced before—He uses his frost power to guide the sled and protect Jamie thorough the dangerous metroscape. Still invisible, Jack aches for this simple connection to community—but he's still on the outside looking in (It's not surprising that many scenes in the film show Jack outside in the cold, looking in through frosted windows—much like women and minorities, the perpetual outsider).

It is at this point of the film when he tearfully pleads with the Moon, "If there is something I'm doing wrong, can you, can you just tell me what it is? Because I've tried everything, and no one ever sees me. You put me here, the least you can do, is tell me why." Jack still doesn't believe it's ultimately up to him to define himself. However, in the Heroine's Journey the mentor is usually harsh, or as in this case with the moon, absent; and may even be the villain. With only silence from above, Jack must learn on his own.

Fortunate Fall/Call to Adventure

While the previous stage was about living some form of a lie, either cloaked as complacency, coping or denial, this stage of the journey is about making the decision to change one's situation. Usually this decision is prompted after the heroine's "ordinary world" is upset and coping strategies crumble. In Jack's case he is not so much called as he is "bagged" in a "fortunate fall" by Bunnymund, aka the Easter Bunny, and two Yetis, and brought to the North Pole. It's clear there isn't much love lost between Jack and Bunnymund over a deep freeze during Winter '68. Jack soon learns amid much fanfare he's been chosen by the Moon to be a Guardian alongside North (Santa Claus), Bunnymund (Easter Bunny), the Tooth Fairy and Sandy the Sandman. "But why wouldn't he tell me that himself?" Jack is confused. The Tooth Fairy explains that it's the "job of the Guardians to watch over children of the world and keep them safe. To bring wonder, hope and dreams" into their lives. The Goddess always finds expression in those who are willing to listen and act in her name.

Jack, like most heroines before beginning the journey, has doubts. They don't believe they are strong enough, smart enough, good enough. He refuses the Call. "After 300 years this is his answer? To spend eternity like you guys cooped up in some, some hideout thinking of, of new ways to bribe kids? No, no, that's not for me. No offense." Bunnymund is relieved and tells the rest, "What's this *clown* know about bringing joy to children anyway?" Jack bristles, "Ever hear of snow day? Kids like what I do." Bunnymund pulls his ace out of the hole, "But none of them *believe* in you, do they? You see, you're invisible, mate. It's like you don't even exist ... people *believe* in *me*." And that's the bottom line. No one believes in him—most importantly, Jack doesn't believe in himself. Discounting his magic to "clowning around" and "kids like what I do," it's clear he, and the world, still don't value what he has to offer. Later, Jack says, "How can I know who I am, if I don't know who I was?" He has no sense of origin, no connection to history, no memory and thus no sense of identity. He exists, but where? Like Jack, without a connection to the Goddess, women find themselves asking the same question.

It's at this point in the narrative that North (Santa Claus)—a very buff Russian version of the man in red—takes Jack aside and asks him the most important question of the film: "Who are you, Jack Frost? What is your center?" Jack is perplexed. North grabs a Russian nesting doll and hands it to Jack to open. Each layer reveals different aspects of North (jolly, mysterious, fearless, caring), but at the center, Jack finds a small baby with very large blue eyes, representing North's sense of Wonder. "This is what I put into the world, and what I protect in children. This is what makes me a Guardian. It is my center. What is yours?" North knows his core and center. Jack, however, does not. One's core is the "true North" that points a person in the right direction. It's interesting that it is actually "North" who poses this question to Jack. Jack at this point tells North, "I don't know," but once the Guardians learn that there is trouble at the Tooth Palace where all the teeth and childhood memories are stored, Jack accepts a ride with the other Guardians in North's sled. The journey begins.

Road of Trials/Allies and Villains

The protagonist on the Heroine's Journey is tested on the Road of Trials. Jack will meet a variety of allies who will support, but not rescue, antagonists who will provoke thought, and villains that will tempt, force decisions and/or double as mentors. Schmidt writes that our heroine must face Issues of Attachment, Fear, Guilt, Lies, Shame, Grief, and Illusion (220–221). During these trials the heroine needs to: (1) learn to depend on herself and confront her fears; (2) find her voice, say "no" and overcome feelings of guilt; (3) forgive herself and others and accept her strengths and weaknesses; (4) accept love from others and love herself for who she is; (5) refuse to conform; (6) overcome denial; and (7) trust herself and learn not to blindly obey. She must also learn, through it all, to remember to ask "why?" but also "why not?"

Jack still hasn't completely committed to taking on the mantle of a Guardian, but after witnessing Pitch's destruction of the Tooth Palace, he's willing to join with the Guardians temporarily to fight against the threat and consider the Moon's offer, thus taking the first step on the journey. He makes the decision to change and that's the important thing.

His new allies offer qualities he hopes to cultivate in himself. Of course, today's childish Easter Bunny and Santa Claus were once great holy figures or their representatives. North/Santa Claus also represents a celebration of the winter solstice, the Green Man/Green Woman, or Elen of the Ways. Bunnymund the Easter Bunny represents the Vernal Equinox, and a combination of Eoster, Ostara, Frigga, Persephone, and Eos, who were celebrated for all the riches they brought to the Earth: light, growth, greenery, fertility, abundance, renewal, and second chances. Her fertility symbol is the rabbit. Eggs are the obvious symbol of new life, the Cosmic Egg, the great alpha and omega, the beginning without end—on one end of the cycle, winter represents life in death (wonder), while on the other, spring represents new life (hope) and regeneration—and so the circle of the seasons, time, life, and all things, turns. Both represent the Goddess—the circle of life, the original womb and tomb that encircles us all. Thus, the Guardians in this film also represent the tension between the patrilineal/phallocentric and matrilineal/gynocentric points of view and in doing so, open the door for creating "play" and balance between both.

Meeting the Shadow

The shadow tests our heroine and represents the energy of the dark side, the unexpressed, unrealized or rejected aspects of herself, all the dark secrets she can't or won't admit—all one's dark wishes and even darker thoughts. We think them, but as soon as they reach consciousness, we push them back down into the darkness. We tell ourselves, "I can't believe I even considered that option, thought that thought, desired that outcome": The negative face we of what we've stuffed away and refused to face, better known as the Shadow, is projected in stories onto characters called "villains, antagonists, or enemies" (Vogler 65).

Pitch Black is Jack's shadow. He is everything Jack doesn't want to be or is afraid he will become. In fact, he literally appears in the film for the first time as a shadow on the wall when Jack is first introduced to the Guardians. This proverbial boogie-man steals memories and replaces them with fear and delights in turning dreams into nightmares. "Darkness. That's all I can remember." Because this simple line opens the film in total darkness, Pitch Black is the first thing Jack, and the audience experience. Pitch represents Jack's amnesia, the disconnect from, and loss of, his core, and his lack of belief in himself—his fear that he is not "good enough" ("Jack: Am I on the naughty list? North: You hold record. But no matter. We overlook.") or worthy enough to be a Guardian. Freud once told a story about at a child who was afraid of the dark and asked her Mother to talk to her from the other room to make it lighter. "But it's still dark," the mother replied. The child said, "I know, but it gets much lighter when I hear your voice and know you are there." It's not the dark we fear, but it's the fear of being alone and unloved, unwanted. Jack believes he is an abandoned child. He has been alone and in the dark for 300 years with only the silent promise of the moon. Women have been alone and in the dark for over 3000 years, and that, any woman or girl can testify, is a very long time.

The first thing Pitch does in the film is steal the teeth from the Tooth Fairy. He wants to supplant the Guardians within children's beliefs. This is a sin of omission, erasure, and replacement. Pitch also functions, on a deeper level, as a shadow of our culture. He has stolen the teeth from the Tooth Palace and in doing so, has stolen childhood memories—thrown them into darkness and replaced the happy memories with fear and nightmares. Sound familiar? History is written by the winners. As the winner, patriarchy has tried to erase the memories of the Goddess and replaced them with their own. Cultural memory can, over time, be replaced with new narratives that oppress people instead of uplift them, destroy instead of create, and dominate with fear and self-interest instead of creating narratives that support equality, freedom and inclusivity. Here, we see a negative patriarchy at work (Pitch: "Everyone frightened. Miserable. Such happy times for me. Oh, the power I wielded.")

Pitch explains how an erosion of belief occurs. "Such a little thing ... but to a child?" First children discover the Tooth Fairy isn't real, which can gradually lead to mistrust, self-doubt, hopelessness, disillusionment, and on and on, until there is no trust in the world at all. Although distrust can force change, more often in the world it breeds incivility, crime, cheating, lying, and aggressiveness. This represents the shadow of society—its darkness that rises with mob mentality, hatred, or fear. Only open community forums, which allow the freedom to air concerns, without shutting others down with anger or name-calling, dogma, or extreme prejudice, will allow distrust to dissipate and allow trust to grow in fertile ground. Current fourth wave feminism has opened the door to inclusivity but must be vigilant to remember not to exclude those with differing opinions. Difference strengthens truth—and truth, as the erasure of the Goddess from memory reminds us, has many faces.

The Tooth Fairy's significance in this film is also multi-faceted. Teeth, the mouth, and orality are often tied to the Mother who first nursed us at her breast. Teeth in real life, or in symbols and dreams, can represent two periods in human life. The first is growing up and coincides with the loss of milk teeth. This stage emphasizes independence, vitality, energy, nourishment, and the power to feed ourselves. Eventually, the teeth will grow back even stronger than before, just as one will grow stronger after facing a challenge. In old age, when the teeth fall out, this represents the opposite, since the teeth are permanently lost. This suggests helpless and impotence, and inability to take a bite out of life's challenges. Pitch steals the teeth in the hope they will never grow back, weakening the Guardians, primarily the Tooth Fairy.

Teeth, especially their relationship to the mouth and Mother, have other, deeper, more profound mythic significance and represent the fear men have of powerful women, first embodied in the Goddess. This is the personified fear of the vagina dentata, or a vagina with teeth. Barbara Walker explains that this myth proliferates in overly masculinized patriarchal cultures. "The more patriarchal the society, the more fear seems to be around by the fantasy.... Stories of the devouring Mother are ubiquitous in myths, representing the death-fear which the male psyche often transformed into a sex-fear.... The archetypal image of 'devouring' female genitals seems undeniably alive even in the modern world." In other words, the patriarchy fears female power and, thus, demonizes and degrades it. Jack, and the others, when they arrive at the Tooth Palace, are too late to do anything. The crime, the stealing of the teeth and feminine power, in the film, as in our own cultural past, has already been committed.

North comes up with a plan to counteract the predations of Pitch and collect the children's teeth to restore belief in Toothiana, the Tooth Fairy. Again, it becomes a wonderful game between the Guardians to see who can collect the most teeth, building common admiration and comradery while finding pleasure in the simple, collective joys of working together to get a job done well. While this is going on, the Sandman accidentally puts all the Guardians to sleep except Jack. An opportunist, Pitch intervenes with his army of nightmares (culture of the Blade) in the physical form of horses when the Guardians literally have their guard down. Using these dark horrors, he overpowers the Sandman and tries to kill him, successfully ensuring these children only have bad dreams, diminishing their belief in Sandy, while strengthening their belief in Pitch. It's important to note that the Sandman is decidedly androgynous. Dreams, although mostly reserved for men and boys in a patriarchal culture, aren't exclusively theirs. The ambivalence of the Sandman/Sandy's gender reflects this duality—but also the integration and blending of the two.

Seeing Sandy succumb to the bad dreams, Jack faces Pitch. However, Pitch has been around for millennia, and he is at least the match for a boy who doesn't believe in himself. Pitch has the advantage. To destroy the Goddess, one must omit her from memory (teeth/Tooth Fairy), then take away the dreams of those who might try to imagine her (dream sand/Sandy). Fourth wave feminists realize it's important that girls—and all people—to have the same opportunity to dream the same dreams that boys and men have had in our culture. It's one thing for a girl to see a picture of Rosie the Riveter and another whole thing to actually *believe* she exists. How can a woman and others without equal access, *believe* they can do the things men can do until they actually *see* it in real life—in the world around them. Representation is a powerful. Without it, the under-represented, women and minorities, don't "exist" and are invisible in society like Jack. Even though he might not yet believe in himself, Jack *does believe* in Sandy and all that s/he represents—the dream of being recognized, the dream of being "seen." Completely engulfed in nightmares, Jack's too late to save Sandy, but against horrific odds, without the help of the other Guardians, his staff becomes a light in the darkness. Although he knows he might fail, Jack fends off and completely destroys Pitch's nightmares with his staff. The others arrive in time to see a "massive wave of ice and frost rocket back up the stream of dark nightmare sand, culminating in an explosion of ice and snow" (Lindsay-Abaire). Jack is as shocked as they are with his "power." When the tooth fairy asked how he did it, he responds, "I, I didn't know I could."

Belief is a controlling theme in this film, and, in many ways, also acts as a controlling theme in the Heroine's Journey. In fact, North is caretaker of a giant Globe of Belief that dominates his workshop and shows how many human children still believe and thus keep the Guardians alive. This isn't so much about believing in Santa Claus or the Easter Bunny per se, but what they represent. They as Joseph Campbell would say "wear the mask of God," or act as a springboard to divinity. Divinity in this sense, is a recognition of the sacred, in ourselves and others. North represents Wonder, Bunnymund represents Hope, the Sandman, Dreams, and the Tooth Fairy protects Memories. It's the belief that these things exist in the world, and the internalization of, and continuation of, these things, that are important. It is the job of the Guardians to protect these qualities, but also show how people can attain this sense of wonder, hope, and hold on to their dreams and happy childhood memories in the world as adults.

It's been said that the way to experience divinity is through the sublime acts of others. It is interesting that each of these characters are involved in gift giving in some form. When we see someone do a good deed, we feel good ourselves—a warm, glowing, open type of feeling, physically tied to the release of oxytocin associated with bonding with other people. This elevated feeling, experienced as love and trust, makes people more receptive to new relationships and active altruism toward strangers (Haidt 198). This desire to "pass it along," do good for others, opens our hearts in positive ways—a collective elevation. This is what the Guardians represent. Pitch's "gift" on the other hand, sows discord. This is the erosion of that trust that occurs in a society when there is no reciprocity. This is where we find ourselves today in a consumer society that feeds on our fears and preys on our weaknesses and self-doubts. It is also another form of enslavement for women who have been most impacted and distracted by an unobtainable patriarchal ideal promoted in our Western "cult of beauty."

Allies

Some of the most emotional and heart-touching scenes are when both North, portraying very masculine traits, allows himself to say and feel what might be considered feminine. The same goes for Bunnymund. There are especially moving scenes when Bunnymund is preparing his eggs for Easter in his Warren. Sophie, Jamie's sister, accidentally finds her way into the company of the Guardians. At first Bunnymund is fearful Sophie will ruin Easter, but it's Jack, who is still only visible to the child through the snowflakes he creates, who teaches the Guardians the true meaning of the season. "When was the last time you guys actually hung out with kids?" North blusters, "We are very busy bringing joy to children! We don't have time…." North hears his own words, and stops, embarrassed. Jack walks toward little Sophie and forms a snowflake which floats over to her. She tries to grab it. "If one little kid can ruin Easter, then … we're in worse shape than I thought." Sophie follows the snowflake as Jack magically leads it over to Bunnymund. When it falls on his nose, Bunny "turns to Sophie and remembers the JOY and HOPE of the season, instead of his worries" (Lindsay-Adaire).

A wonderful, fanciful and tender montage follows—eggs are colored, flowers bloom, Sophie is delighted and happy, and during this celebration of Spring the Guardians grow closer than ever. Jack has *all* taught them something important. It's an intense moment of healing for Jack and Bunnymund. Bunnymund is just as masculine as North, and part of the fun of the film is watching the two try to outdo each other in their machismo (jokes and jibes about Christmas as being more important than Easter), but Bunnymund, a gruff, Australian six-foot Pooka (rabbit), is one of the most tender and caring of all the Guardians when it comes to nurturing and preparing his eggs to deliver into the world, as it should be when guarding the hopes, dreams and wonder of children and new generations.

On the Heroine's Journey, our protagonist will meet allies that they must integrate. Jack who has forgotten where he came from (birth/spring) and where he is going (death/winter) must reconcile these opposite experiences. They also must reconcile splintered aspects within the self, both anima/feminine and animus/masculine. Each Guardian contains a duality like Jack. They all act as gestalts that flip back and forth to create play between masculine and feminine energies—erasing the boundaries and shaping liminal spaces where change occurs.

The Shadow always shows up in the heroine's quest when she needs to confront something she has stuffed in her big black bag of insecurities. If North's bag is filled with gifts in this film, Pitch Black steals them away and stuffs them deep into his bag of shadows and nightmares, hiding them away from memory. Typically, on this journey the heroine will meet both a Green Man or Green Woman, who supports, but doesn't rescue and helps her find her way back to her core, and a Blackbeard, who does everything he can to hobble, unseat, and dominate or brutalize the protagonist into complete submission. In *Guardians*, the Green Man is North (and sometimes Bunnymund) and Blackbeard type is Pitch. It is between these two "clashing rocks of opposites" that Jack must find his way back home and remember who he is and why he is here.

Tempted to Abort the Quest

After his defeat of Pitch and his visit to Bunnymund's warren, Jack's feeling more secure, but still isn't sure "who he is." This is what Pitch is counting on and waiting for, to prey on Jack's insecurities. The Guardians caution him about leaving, worried they will fail to keep Pitch at bay without him. It's clear, however, they believe and trust him. This is something new for Jack. It throws him off guard. Basking in the admiration of his new support system, he gets a little cocky, maybe neglectful. He tells the Guardians to "trust him," and takes off with Sophie and Baby Tooth (one of Toothiana's helpers) and soon puts the child safely to bed.

Suddenly, out of nowhere, Jack hears a woman calling his voice—a voice from a memory: "Jack..." He recognizes that voice and begins to follow it, while Baby Tooth trails behind. Over the rooftops, through the city, into a dark forest, Jack follows the voice to the "decrepit remains of a rotting frame from a child's bed" that has been abandoned in a clearing. Baby Tooth tries to get Jack to leave this place—this horror from a child's nightmare, but he doesn't listen to her. Under the bed frame, he finds a "hole leading deep underground." This dark pit leads directly to the shadow realm—the fears that hide beneath our conscious thought ... that fear that always threatens to bubble up into reality at the most unexpected times. Jack hears the voice from memory call his name again and, throwing caution to the wind, he plunges into the darkness. He must know! Within the cavern, he finds cages filled with all the mini tooth fairies Pitch had stolen from the Tooth Palace. It's not unusual to find cages, chains and other things that literally or symbolically restrict or bind in close proximity to the Shadow. These are things that keep us from moving forward, keep us locked in the past—prisons of our own making. Hearing the voice, again, Jack looks down and sees mounds of tooth drawers from Tooth's Palace. "In an instant he forgets his duties, and the fairies, and the Guardians and everything except those teeth, and the chance to finally get his memory back."

At this moment, Pitch appears in shadow form. It's time for Jack to confront him again. Pitch taunts him with the tooth drawer. "Do you want them, Jack? Your memories? Everything you wanted to know.... Why did you end up like this? Unable to reach out to anyone ... you want the answers so badly ... but you are afraid of what the Guardians will think ... of disappointing them." The Shadow tries to shame us. Jack listens with sickening fascination—almost expecting what comes next. "They'll never accept you. Not really. You are not one of them." Jack shouts back, "I don't know what I am!" Pitch is relentless. "Of course you do. You're Jack Frost. You make a mess of everything. Why, you're doing it right now." Pitch has tapped into his deepest secret fear, a fear built on shame. Too late again, Jack realizes what he's done, his mistake—that he isn't responsible enough to possibly be a Guardian. Horrified, he tries to fly out of the dark hole, and find Baby Tooth and escape, but he appears, with the "help" of Pitch, back at the Warren where he sees destruction everywhere. Jack watches a nightmare unfold in front of him. Children are waking up and finding no eggs. Bunnymund rushes from one child to the other with empty baskets, but it's clear that they no longer "believe" in Easter, or him. Within minutes, the spark of childhood winks out in these children, and so does their belief in Bunnymund. The children, disappointed, walk through Bunnymund, the Guardian of Hope, as if he weren't there. "They don't see me, they don't see me." Jack is watching all this unfolding and it's heartbreaking because he knows it's all his fault. Externalizing his guilt, the Guardians confront Jack. It's clear they now distrust him. Jack no longer trusts himself and hates himself even more.

Confronting the False and Impotent Father

Jack leaves the Guardians in disgrace. He flies to the farthest reaches of Antarctica. He's never been so alone in his life. Of course, Pitch shows up again. The False Father always does when the hero is the most vulnerable and alone. For Jack, his Shadow appeared when he slacked off from his duties and responsibilities, the negative repercussion of too much play—irresponsibility and an overblown sense of self-entitlement and self-interest. This may be the result of not taking things seriously enough, or, most often, it could be the nagging sense of guilt women feel when they finally take a few minutes for themselves instead of taking care, as they've been told they must do, of others' needs. During the Journey of the Heroine, the protagonist must confront the powerless and impotent Father, a representation of the patriarchy. On the road of trials, she will discover that he is fallible. In fact, in many instances he is the perpetrator of that lie that tells our heroine she needs to obey him in order to survive. Before she can truly participate in the Hieros Gamos, the sacred marriage of the masculine and feminine in herself, she must abandon the father and learn to look within for approval.

Recently, abuse in the workplace, especially in Hollywood, has been the focus of feminists, in particular, the #MeToo movement. Over and over again, we hear the historically challenged ask, "Why do women allow men to abuse them, i.e., succumb to casting couches or other workplace abuses?" "Allow" is not the proper term. It wasn't that long ago that women were forced to be—by law and by culture—completely and totally dependent on men for their survival. Restricted from making a living, or owning property, or voting, women have been taught over time that they are literally and figuratively "nothing without a man." Women may still unconsciously believe they need a man to survive, or they are not good enough [fill in the blank] to make it on our own. This is a lie of the patriarchy. Women need to reclaim faith in themselves and realize they have the power to allow what they decide to allow.

It is at this point in the narrative when Pitch tries to convince Jack he needs to "join his team" to survive. Jack fights Pitch with everything he has. Wind and ice, snow and sand all the elements of cold and dark push and slam against each other. However, Pitch preys on Jack's tender vulnerabilities. "All those years in the shadows, I thought no one else knows what this feels like. But now I see I was wrong. We don't have to be alone, Jack. I believe in you and the children will too." Like the hole under Pitch's bed, the Father promises one thing—love and acceptance—but the bottom always falls out from underneath. The False Father wants desperately to be loved, but this is love on his terms only. He always takes, and there are always strings attached to any offer of help or support that strangle the unwary and gullible. Our heroine/hero must learn that no one has the power to make her happy, feel loved, but herself. Jack accordingly rejects him. "No, they'll fear us both. And that's not I want."

On the Heroine's Journey, the protagonist must choose for herself goals and limits, while saying "no" to others' commands. Transgressive redemption is one of the tests on the Road. However, saying "no" is a dangerous narrative because it is subversive. It threatens the status quo and those in authority. Still, the heroine figure must say no at four stages: when she decides to follow her own quest not an assigned one, when she refuses to let a man rescue her, when confronting her own or a False Father and rejecting his authority, and finally, denying her deepest fears when she faces her Supreme Ordeal and finds that what she thought were weaknesses are, in truth, her greatest strengths. Each refusal pushes the heroine from external expectations toward inner strength and wisdom.

In retaliation, for saying "no," Pitch threatens to kill Baby Tooth unless Jack gives him his staff. He agrees, but Pitch breaks Jack's staff and throws him and Baby Tooth down into a chasm, leaving Jack powerless, trapped, dejected and abandoned—again.

Atonement with the Mother

Campbell describes the hero descending to the innermost cave to face his supreme ordeal. However, our heroine must learn on the road and during her descent into the cave that she is the cave. All she has ever had to do was look inside herself—and recognize her own power. She is giver of life and vessel of death. As womb/tomb, the center of the labyrinth, she needs to realize and accept she is the Mother of her own life, is one with the Goddess and the divine, makes her own path, and creates or destroys her own reality.

Atonement with the Mother always forces the heroine to undergo a symbolic death experience. For Jack this occurs when Pitch tosses him into the ice chasm. Buried there, deep within the unconscious, is the Dark Mother. When we are thrown into the darkness—or finally confront those things that are too painful for words and have been repressed—we are forced to cast away all that is not true about our lives and ourselves. The Atonement with the Mother forces us to look at ourselves with utter, naked honesty. This is part of her Terrible aspect—she strips us bare of all illusions and false pretenses. She is our ultimate shadow sister—that bag of insecurities, fears, worries, and self-loathing that we drag behind and try to forget and repress.

At this stage of the journey, Jack hates himself. He hates that he let down his friends, he hates that he endangered Baby Tooth, he hates that he let himself be taken in by Pitch and he hates himself most of all. He despairs. He fully believes what Pitch has told him is true—believes he messes everything up and no one will ever love him because of it. Baby Tooth tugs at Jack's sleeve—she hears a voice coming from the tooth box in his pocket. A voice calling his name from a distant memory again can be heard. He opens the glowing box and unlocks his forgotten memories.

In rapid montage we see Jack as he was as a boy, part of a loving family, surrounded by warmth, good times and an abundance of joy. In fact, in every scene we see Jack clowning around, making the people around him happy, spreading love and cheer with his wonderful sense of humor. Then a final scene changes everything. As Jack's four-year-old sister Sophie stands several feet away from him on cracking ice, Jack reassures her, promising, "You're gonna be all right. You're not gonna fall in. We're gonna have a little fun instead." As he tells her, "You have to *believe in me,*" the script explains, "Jack's sister pauses a moment, *then smiles through her fear. A light is switched on inside him* and the last thing that could be happening is what is actually happening." This is Jack's greatest super power in action—helping others forget their fear and be strong in the face of adversity and help them endure their pain. He brings the light that holds all despair and darkness at bay. Jack smiles reassuringly back at his sister, "You wanna play a game? We're going to play hopscotch! Like we play every day!" Jack makes her laugh, but never breaks his gaze with her. He reaches for a familiar stick on the ice we've seen him use throughout the film and holds it out to his sister. "In one massive effort he slings her with all his might to safety. but the movement propels him into the cracked ice. He looks up to see his sister safe—smiles—and then plunges into the dark cold water" (Lindsay-Abaire).

His last memory while alive is the light of the full moon glowing brightly on the surface of the water. The memory fades with the glow of the tooth box. Jack is awestruck. He finally knows who he is and what is at his core. He died saving the life of his younger sister by using fun to calm her and distract her from her fear, giving her the courage to live. She believed in him—now it's time for Jack to believe in himself. "That's why you chose me," Jack whispers to the Moon, now in present day, "I'm, I'm a Guardian." Inspired, Jack reaches down and looks at his broken staff. It's an illusion. Pitch never had the power to break his staff, his will, or take his power at all—it was never Pitch's to take.

Reaching down into the very fabric of his being, he receives the greatest gift of all from the Mother. He finally knows who he is—a Guardian, a true hero who is willing to sacrifice himself for an innocent without any expectation of reward. He grabs both ends of the staff and wills them into wholeness. Everything the False Father told him was wrong, he finally realizes with glaring clarity; his "flaw"—his love of play and sense of humor used to give courage to others when they are afraid, is his *greatest strength*. This is what the Goddess and Mother teaches us. These "flaws" are what women have been taught by the False Father that make them, "unclean, sinful, and terrifying," when in truth they are the very attributes that make them strong. (Frankel, *Buffy* 132). As the patriarchy came to fear these qualities, women were persuaded to abandon them, and the Goddess was buried. Thus, heroines descend into the darkness, seeking to reintegrate what they had lost.

While the Guardians are having trouble of their own fighting a newly empowered Pitch, Jack travels to the home of Jaime Bennet, who is on the verge of losing hope in Bunnymund. We learn that his is the last and only light still glowing on the Globe of Belief in North's workshop. Darkness and despair engulfs the Earth. In his bedroom, Jaime asks for a sign, any sign, that the Easter Bunny is real—but nothing happens. Just in time, Jack shows up and creates a delicate frost bunny that leaps magically around Jamie's room. This is the sign Jamie was asking for, the answer to his prayer. Jack's magic is at work again! Jamie sees Jack at last. "You see me!" Jack almost can't believe it. "So cool!" says Jamie. "Right?" Jack replies, and in doing so finally acknowledges his gift as valuable. Finally, Jack is no longer part of the shadows, as a nuisance or a mess, but as a light that breaks through, bringing laughter and joy to the darkest moments, helping restore faith and belief. It's not surprising that when Jack is finally "seen" it's not when he is promoting himself but supporting the work of others. The Heroine knows that by supporting others, she's really helping herself as well. All people are uplifted when we "pass it on." Jack soon assembles the weakened Guardians and a handful of Jaimie's friends to battle Pitch and his nightmares. Armed with this new-found self-knowledge and the strength of purpose, against Jack, Pitch doesn't stand a chance.

Supreme Ordeal

Now is when the heroine on the journey must test her mettle against her biggest foe, the Biggest Bad—in truth, a personification of herself. Jack is no exception. Just acknowledging his fears isn't enough; now he must actually publicly face them and own them as his greatest strength. Pitch has gained strength, much like a dark Chronos, glutting himself on the despair, lost hope, and dreams not only of the young, frail, and disenfranchised, but the entire world. His patriarchal dominion is almost complete. When they arrive to fight Pitch, the Guardians have all been reduced to weak, pitiful versions of what they once were. Much like the traditions have been gutted by commercialism today, the things that give meaning to life are almost gone, the traditions and light of the Goddess fading into memory. Pitch has made the shift from Shadow (that creates shame within the self), to False Father (who tries to seduce with lies from without), to now a Dark Lord, embodying all the negativity of toxic Patriarchy.

With all his force, Jack attacks Pitch who is taunting the weakened Guardians and wreaking havoc in the city with his nightmares. Pitch hits Jack with "a roaring fury of Nightmares" and slams him down to earth with nary a struggle. Jack is hurt. The Guardians are shocked, horrified, scared. Jack tells them, "He is stronger. I can't beat him." Touched by what Jack did for him with Jamie, Bunnymund, now reduced to a cute bunny rabbit, stands up to Pitch and tells Pitch, "You want him, you're gonna have to go through me!" Although they have had their differences, Bunnymund has had a change of heart. It was Jack who helped Jamie believe in him when no else did. That is the *definition* of hope: To stand up for another, to believe enough in our own self to trust our inner judgment, and then not be afraid to share it with the world. Still, Pitch is still too strong. He can't be defeated with threats, posturing or violence. This is something the hero taking the Hero's Journey might do to overcome the Dark Lord, but not the heroine. This is a journey inward. Violence alone will not work here and must be discarded with all the rest.

Jamie tells Jack he is "scared." This is Pitch's greatest power. Jack pauses. Jaime's words are hauntingly familiar. In sudden flashback, Jack remembers his sister frightened on the ice. Jack hears himself tell her, "We're gonna have a little fun." As he sees her smile, Jack has finally discovered, "That's it. That's my center." Jack hits Jaime with a snowball. BOOOF! Blue magic lights up

Jaime's face—he smiles. North chuckles. The tide has turned. Jack's magic begins to spread. Laughing at our fears shows how absurd they really are, how silly we've been to be so afraid. Pitch's darkness suddenly weakens. Quickly, Jack and Jaime gather all the other kids in the neighborhood. They are amazed when they see the Guardians assembled. They do exist! When asked who will protect the Guardians, in a scene reminiscent of that in *Spartacus*, the children, although frightened, stand together before Pitch, each saying, with strength of conviction, "I will." This moment of inspiring the next generation, raising them up to be strong, emphasizes the epic heroine's grounding in community—fighting to strengthen her people, not only as a lone warrior.

The Guardians are amazed. Pitch taunts the children, "Still think there's no such thing as the boogeyman?" Jaime steps forward, "I do believe in you. I'm just not afraid of you." Magic fills the air. Pitch sends all the nightmares screaming toward the children, but when Jaime reaches out his hand and touches it, the dark sand turns to gold dream sand. Sandy is back! Thanks to Jack's use of joy and his personal connection to the children, Pitch and his influence have weakened, resulting in the Sandman's resurrection. Fear has no power here anymore. The Guardians are restored to full strength. Together, the children, the Guardians, the Yetis, the elves and mini-tooth fairies all work to overcome Pitch and his minions. Outnumbered and no longer believed in, Pitch tries to retreat, but his nightmares drag him down into the dark hole of his, and sometimes our own, making.

Women need to remember who they are and believe in their abilities. As long as one woman speaks out, the darkness—fear itself—can be held at bay. Soon, others will listen, trust in their own worth, and follow suit. If a woman can laugh, in spite of the fear, that's the definition of courage and a sign of the Goddess at work. Humor, like the moon, will always light the darkness.

Apotheosis

Jack Frost has survived the cold and winter and it has given him strength; he knows the winter—its bleakness and loneliness, but it has made him stronger. He's no longer a victim, he is a survivor. His ordeal and encounter with the Mother gave him strength and courage to defeat the darkness within. Now, he owns it, instead of it owning him. A child of the moon, he finds the dark side holds no fear for him anymore. He's cried alone but has learned how to laugh with others instead. This is his core, his center. Pitch defeated, Jack pledges to "watch over the children of the world, to guard them with his life, their hopes, their wishes and dreams" and agrees that "they are all we have, all that we are, and all that we will ever be."

Most heroines make the decision, after saving themselves and those around them, to go home. Where once this land was filled with fears, villains, and impossible tasks, now it is populated with friends and allies. The demons have been tamed and the tasks completed—for now. After they battle Pitch, Jamie and the kids worry that after Jack leaves to go "home" they might stop believing again. "You tell me you stop believing in the moon when the sun comes up? Do you stop believing in the sun when the clouds block it out?" Jamie smiles; he knows better. "We'll always be there, Jaime." Jack points to Jamie's heart. "And now we'll always be here." The journey for Jack was always about loving himself enough to believe in himself. He passes his hard-won knowledge on to the children he has come to protect.

In the end, Jack learns that belief is not "out there," but must come from within. Jack's final voice over sums it up well, "When the moon tells you something, believe it." Mary Daly, the mother of current feminist religions, in her book, *Beyond God the Father*, called for a return to the Goddess, to a culture that embraced the feminine and offered equal representation of sacrality for women and men alike (Cartier and LaBoeuf). In *Celebrating the Seasons of the Goddess*, feminists call for a way back to the Goddess tradition in three ways: (1) feminism, which allows for an awakening of spirit to connection and purpose, (2) the need to resist the patriarchy through activism, and (3) the push to reclaim the Creatrix, or Goddess spirituality (3). Fourth wave feminists already recognize these steps as a way back to the core (Kore). Women just all need to remember to "lighten" up while lighting the way. It is embracing the balance, not falling prey to the either/or, the need to see the divinity in all people and work to uplift all children of the Earth, and the Earth as well, and to be a Guardian of the wonder, hopes and dreams and memories in each one of us. Respect for Mother Earth and thus the terribly endangered environment is bound up in feminism and responsibilities to the community. As a *people* we need to be willing to listen to each other and celebrate our differences and similarities. No one should be shut down or shamed into silence—male/female, black/white, Muslim/Christian, Gay/Straight—all are one in the Goddess and all voices have significance and meaning. We need to strive to be, as Appiah says, "citizens of the world" and embrace cosmopolitanism, or a conviction in the "oneness of humanity" (xi-xxi). Proper "service" and guardianship is to acknowledge the relationship with the divine in each other, to serve; not dominate, to trust; not sow mistrust, to love not promote hatred. The magic spiral and circle of the Goddess includes us all. The circle is broken, but never closed. We have only just begun the journey as Guardians of her legacy—together.

NOTES

1. Women have been making the journey toward "self-realization" by watching Hero Quest narratives in film, television, or other writings throughout history that have featured male heroes. Women have internalized these narratives, but these are stories told by men for

men. For balance, women and girls do need to learn how to tap into the masculine/animus in themselves, but not to the detriment of the feminine. Women need to follow the path of the heroine, and read, write and create stories that feature feminine issues and concerns if they want to reclaim the part of the "self" that has been replaced with the face of the Father.

2. I am greatly indebted to the women who have forced the path and created their own Heroine Journey models before me—specifically Valerie Estelle Frankel, Maureen Murdock, and Victoria Schmidt. After consideration and study, I have put forward my own interpretation of the Heroine Journey (based on both mythic and screenplay structures). While many of the stages I include are similar to other models, there are slight, but significant, variations.

3. In the case of Moana, Maui has stolen the heart of the Goddess and it needs to be reclaimed, in *The Hunger Games*, Katniss' freedom has been stolen by a repressive Father figure, in *Frozen*, Elsa's creative power have been locked away and in *Maleficent*, Maleficent's wings were chopped off by a jealous King. In each case something "core" in their lives—their very being—has been taken or hidden away. The heroine and our culture both suffer the consequences of imbalance when the feminine embodied in the Goddess is denied.

4. Jack Frost's talent is on par with Elsa in *Frozen* (2013). Both these protagonists have "magical" frost and ice abilities that are considered a "curse" by others. It's interesting both these characters would appear on the screen within one year of each other.

Works Cited

Appiah, Kwame Anthony. *Cosmopolitanism: Ethics in a World of Strangers.* W.W. Norton, 2006.
Buber, Martin. *I and Thou.* Charles Scribner's Sons: 1970.
Campbell, Joseph. *Goddesses: Mysteries of the Feminine Divine,* edited by Safron Rossi. New World Library, 2013.
_____. *The Hero with a Thousand Faces.* MJF Books, 1949.
Canale, Ann. "Barbara Ehrenreich: Dancing in the Streets: A History of Collective Joy." *Journal of Global and International Studies,* vol. 1, no. 2, April 2010. https://www.lindenwood.edu/files/resources/187–189.pdf. Accessed 11 Jan. 2019.
Cartier, Marie, and Annjenette LaBoeuf. "Goddesses and Witchcraft." Whittier College, 17 Jan. 2019. Lecture.
Cochrane, Kira. "The Fourth Wave of Feminism: Meet the Rebel Women." *The Guardian,* 10 December 2013, https://www.theguardian.com/world/2013/dec/10/fourth-wave-feminism-rebel-women. Accessed 10 Jan. 2019.
Daly, Mary. *Beyond God the Father.* Beacon Press, 1973.
Frankel, Valerie Estelle. *Buffy and the Heroine's Journey: Vampire Slayer and Feminine Chosen One.* McFarland, 2012.
_____. *From Girl to Goddess: The Heroine's Journey Through Myth and Legend.* McFarland, 2010.
Haidt, Jonathan. *The Happiness Hypothesis: Finding Modern Truth in Ancient Wisdom.* Basic Books, 2006.
Holland, Norman N. *Laughing: A Psychology of Humor.* Cornell University Press, 1982.
Joseph Campbell and the Power of Myth with Bill Moyers, PBS, Mystic Fire Video, 2001.
Lindsay-Abaire, David. *Rise of the Guardians.* screening script, *IMSDB,* 6 September 12. https://www.imsdb.com/scripts/Rise-of-the-Guardians.html. Accessed 10 Jan. 2019.
Manuel-Paris, Raina. "The Flowering of the Feminine Divine," *Mythblast,* vol. 2, no. 30, 18 September 2018, www.JFC.org.
Murdock, Maureen. *The Heroine's Journey.* Shambhala Publications, Inc., 1990.
Rise of the Guardians. Directed by Peter Ramsey. Dreamworks, 2012.
Schmidt, Victoria Lynn. *45 Master Characters: Mythic Models for Creating Original Characters.* Writer's Digest Books, 2001.
Walker, Barbara. "Vagina Dentata," *Antropologia Critica,* http://antcritica.tripod.com/id36.html. Accessed 10 Jan. 2019.
Vogler, Christopher. *The Writer's Journey: Mythic Structure for Writers.* Michael Wiese Productions, 2007.

SECTION IV

SUPERHEROES

Stings Like a Wasp

Janet van Dyne, Hope van Dyne and the Feminist Superheroine in the Ant-Man *Films*

DON TRESCA

When Stan Lee and Jack Kirby introduced the world to Janet van Dyne, also known as The Wasp, in *Tales to Astonish* #44 in 1963, they had no idea that they were introducing a character into the popular culture that would dramatically impact female comic book characters' portrayal. After all, they had initially created her as little more than window-dressing, something to make her male partner, Hank Pym, the Ant-Man, look better. Her characterization in her early Marvel comics was that of a ditzy, man-obsessed party girl who cared more about fashion and romance than saving the world from maniacal supervillains. Over time (and various tribulations), Janet evolved from that one-dimensional portrayal to a fully capable and strong crime fighter, easily on par with her male counterparts. Now, in the modern era, Janet van Dyne is championed amongst feminists as a landmark character and has passed on her name and legacy to a new character, one created exclusively for the Marvel Cinematic Universe, her daughter, Hope van Dyne, in the films *Ant-Man* and *Ant-Man and the Wasp*. This essay examines both of these diverse characters and the way the power and strength of Janet gradually morphed into Hope, a fiercely independent and strong female character who serves as the ultimate culmination of The Wasp's strong feminist story arc.

The character of Janet van Dyne in the 1960s is vastly different from the character most comics (and film) fans know today. She was introduced in Stan Lee's *Tales to Astonish* #44 as a young debutante and daughter of a wealthy scientist from New Jersey. When her father is killed as a result of a lab experiment that results in the release of an interdimensional alien, she joins forces with another scientist, Hank Pym, to avenge his death. Pym provides Janet with a suit that gives her a variety of super-powers, including the ability to shrink, fly, and fire energy blasts from the gauntlets. She dubs herself The Wasp and partners with Hank, who goes by the name of Ant-Man, to defeat the alien. Once she has had her revenge, however, the focus of her character moves away from the adventurous life of a superheroine and becomes more in line with the traditional (for that time period) pursuit of romance. Janet develops an intense crush on Hank, declaring, "If he thinks I became the Wasp because I like to chase criminals, he's maaad!!! He may go for all that adventure jazz, but I go for big, wonderful, dreamy him." Hank, for his part, is frozen with self-doubt and personal insecurities and refuses to acquiesce to her demands for a romantic partnership, instead opting to refer to her simply as his crime-fighting partner.

Later, in 1963, Janet and Hank team up with Iron Man and Thor to defeat the Hulk who is rampaging across the western United States. When the group learns that the Hulk has been manipulated by Loki, they join forces to defeat the Asgardian deity and decide to remain together as a team to defeat enemies that are too strong for them to defeat separately. While Janet is the one who names the superhero team The Avengers, she continues to be a vain and flighty character throughout the early years of *The Avengers* comic book, more obsessed with clothes and fashionable accessories than crime-fighting. Her obsessive pursuit of Hank as a romantic partner becomes almost stalking. While, at the time, her antics were seen as humorous and cute, in retrospect, they seem demeaning and chauvinistic. Despite his constant denials of an attraction, Hank seems to relish the attention Janet showers on him and the fact that a beautiful woman pursues him constantly. However, for his part, he uses Janet's affections to belittle her and keep her under his control, talking down to her and ordering her around. Janet gladly abides by her orders because she believes it a woman's place to follow the man's commands. When she does show signs of independence and resistance (such as when she flirts with Thor to get Hank's attention or threatens to smash up his lab equipment if he doesn't take her on a proper vacation), he becomes angry at her and denies her even the most basic levels of attention, even going so far as to deny her the ability to accompany the Avengers on missions even though she is just as much a founding member of the team as he is.

Hank's constant undermining of Janet's attempts to exert herself as a valued member of the team gradually begins to evolve her personality. By the 1970s, she goes from basing her existence on Hank to openly calling him out in his attempts to control her. She insists on being more offensive in her capabilities and forces Hank to develop the Wasp's Sting, the laser blaster gauntlets she uses in battle. She also begins to assert herself intellectually, studying to be a scientist by watching Hank while he works in his laboratory.

Strangely, this more assertive personality also works to make Hank more agreeable to a romantic partnership with her, eventually leading to his marriage proposal. However, Janet's stronger personality is mirrored in Hank's more aggressive personality emerging, leading to the development of his Yellowjacket persona. He becomes much more angry and violent when fighting supervillains with the Avengers and much less cerebral, spending less and less time in the laboratory.

After Hank and Janet marry, things only get worse for the couple. His extreme aggression and violence in battle get him censured by the other Avengers and eventually ousted from the team. In *The Avengers* #213 (1981) by Jim Shooter, in a desperate attempt to win himself back into the team's good graces, he creates a robot villain that only he can defeat, which he believes will impress his former teammates. Janet learns of the plan and tries to talk him out of it, leading him to backhand her across the face and sending her crashing to the ground. This single incident forever changed the dynamic of both heroes in the comics. Janet becomes more forceful as a result, finally deciding to take control of her own destiny. She realizes that she need not remain with Hank to be a fulfilled individual (a radical shift from her personality of the 1960s in which she was totally defined by her relationship with Hank), and she makes an immediate play for leadership of The Avengers, which her teammates concede to her, leading to the longest reign of leadership of any Avengers member, save Captain America.

As the twenty-first century era of Marvel Comics moved into the realm of film with the Marvel Cinematic Universe (MCU), much of the backstory of many of the major characters and teams changed as they made the transition. Many Marvel Comics fans bristled at the removal of Ant-Man and the Wasp from their roles as founding members, with the film version of *The Avengers* choosing instead to substitute them for admittedly important (though non-founding) members of the team, such as Captain America, Hawkeye, and Black Widow (with this last taking Wasp's original place as solo female member). When the film *Ant-Man* was released in 2015, the decision was made to retire Hank Pym's Ant-Man (Michael Douglas) to the role of mentor, preferring instead to promote his successor Scott Lang (Paul Rudd) to costumed superhero. Scott was first introduced in David Michelinie's *The Avengers* #181 (1979) as an electrical engineer who had turned to a life of crime to help support his family. After a stint in prison, he became determined to reform and got a job with Stark International installing a new security system in Avengers Mansion. Soon thereafter, however, his daughter Cassie became seriously ill, and the only doctor capable of curing her was being held hostage by the corrupt tech genius Darren Cross. In a bid to rescue the doctor and save his child, Scott broke into Hank Pym's home and stole the Ant-Man suit and canisters of Pym Particles, the shrinking gas Hank used to become Ant-Man. Scott defeated Cross, and his daughter's life was saved. He turned himself in to Hank to face justice, but Hank instead decided to let Scott keep the stolen goods as long as he used them to do good. In subsequent years, Scott became a member of various superhero teams, including the Avengers, the Defenders, the Fantastic Four, and the Guardians of the Galaxy.

In a similar manner, the film *Ant-Man* does not focus on Janet van Dyne, Hank's wife, as The Wasp. Janet's fate is discussed in the film as her having died on a mission with Hank to destroy a missile heading toward the United States. In order to stop the missile and save lives, she shrank down to the point where she could destroy the weapon's systems from within, but, by doing so, continued to shrink until she reached the Quantum Realm, an subatomic landscape from which return is seemingly impossible. Instead of Janet, the film introduces the audience to Hank and Janet's daughter, Hope van Dyne (Evangeline Lilly), who has become somewhat estranged from her father as a result of her mother's "death." The film's characterization of Hope is slightly problematic. Despite being shown throughout the film as smart and capable, Hope is primarily motivated by anger. She is angry at her father for lying to her about the truth of her mother's death and at seemingly been seen by him as too weak and unworthy to become the central hero and angry at Scott for winning her birthright simply by virtue of being a man in the right place at the right time (Dickens 7). "He is a criminal. I'm your daughter," she pleads, stressing her logical status as heir. Still, he refuses. Hope's anger also stems from the fact that, despite her training and intelligence, she finds herself being manipulated and used as a pawn by both her father (who is using her to infiltrate his former company to prevent his former protégé Darren Cross from duplicating the formula for the Pym Particles) and Cross himself (who is using her, he believes, to psychologically torture her father by having her work for him). Her father even frames her role as being the distraction, insisting, "We need you close to Cross, otherwise this mission cannot work." More surprising is that the film allows her to be angry (even to the point of punching Scott repeatedly during training) and presents her anger as perfectly justified. The audience is encouraged to take her side as Hank obliviously has her assist him in training Scott on how to fight and properly use the Ant-Man technology despite her, undoubtedly correct, assertion that she is better suited to wear the suit. "I know the facility inside and out, I know how Cross thinks. I know this mission better than anybody here," she reasons, only to be turned down. Despite this sidelining, she never allows her anger to overwhelm her ability to function and focus on the mission to stop Darren Cross from achieving his goal of replicating the shrinking technology (Givens 9).

Scott tells her Hank chose him for a clear reason: "It proves that he loves you. Hope. Look at me. I'm expendable, that's why I'm here. You must've realized that by now. I mean, that's why I'm in the suit and you're not." Hank's reasoning that he must keep Hope away from the technology because he could not bear to lose her as he did her mother seems a reasonable justification for his actions, but many viewers interpreted his reluctance and his promotion of Scott as an excuse to valorize yet another male hero over a possible female one (Brown, *Modern Superhero* 56). Some critics were even blunter in their evaluation of Hope's treatment, with Esther Bergdahl stating the film "frustratingly goes out of its way to ensure that Hope van Dyne is not the hero of the story … [instead it] draws a circuitous and convoluted narrative path to guarantee it is Lang that takes the mantle instead" (8). Although Scott does eventually prove his valor and become a worthy recipient of the Ant-Man legacy, this does not diminish the fact that Hope was far more qualified to wear the Ant-Man suit, a concept that comes to fruition in their sequel, *Ant-Man and the Wasp* (2018).

The groundwork for *Ant-Man and the Wasp* is actually established in the post-credits sequence of *Ant-Man* where Hank, realizing his error in holding Hope back despite his misgivings, presents Hope with her own Wasp suit to help her become the hero she was born to be. Further, at the start of the second film, the audience learns that, with Hank's assistance, Hope has actually become that hero, using her intelligence to engage in black market deals to assemble the technology to free Janet (Michelle Pfeiffer) from the Quantum Realm. She also wields her power and fight training to bust up criminals that threaten to disrupt their work (Stahler 5). Meanwhile, Scott is under house arrest for his part in the insurrection of *Captain America: Civil War*. Because of that, it is Hope's first real action that sets the tone for the approach the film will take toward her character. Breaking Scott out of his confinement to enlist his help in saving her mother, Hope engages in a behavior rarely seen in heroines in superhero films: the "reciprocal-rescue." This action challenges action film's (and, by extension, superhero film's) most hackneyed plot—the rescue of the "damsel-in-distress" (Walderzak 151). In typical films of this type, the primary female character's main purpose seems to be as bait for the hero to rescue, often as part of the villain's overall plan. We see this in characters like Lois Lane (in the various *Superman* films) and Mary Jane Watson and Gwen Stacy (in the *Spider-Man* films). In this film and other films in the MCU, such as *Iron Man 3* (with Pepper Potts rescuing Tony Stark during the house destruction scene) and *Captain America: Civil War* (with Black Widow assisting Captain America and Winter Soldier to escape in the airport sequence), these female characters' empowerment increases significantly. They are moving from the "helpless, hysterical figure" of the stereotypical "damsel-in-distress" to a character "equipped with agency that enables her meaningful partnership with the hero" (Walderzak 151).

Ant-Man and the Wasp even chooses to strengthen this dynamic further when Hope rescues Scott in much direr circumstances when he falls unconscious and nearly drowns after increasing his size to an unbearable amount.

Hope's increased agency is also suggested through her physical appearance. In the first film, Hope displays a short, severe straight haircut and, most often, business attire. In the second film, she is dressed much more casually in loose fitting clothing with her hair worn longer and in a messy ponytail. In her essay on Hope's fashion sense in the film, Angie Han states that this change is intentional to situate her as a capable superhero, rather than as simply the female love interest:

> [Hope's ponytail is] not particularly sexy or stylish or even polished. She has the fly-aways and dumps of someone who barely even glimpsed in the mirror before yanking it up…. But this 'do isn't about prettiness, it's about pragmatism. It's there to let us know that this lady is more concerned right now with getting the job done than she is with looking cute. It's there to make her seem no-nonsense and relatable at the same time. It's a marked contrast from the untouchable Anna Wintour bob she sported in the first film, when we only saw her from Scott's perspective as a cool, mysterious figure. More crucially, it's a detail that lets us know *Ant-Man and the Wasp* itself cares more about presenting Hope as a capable superhero than as sexy eye candy. She's still attractive, of course … but her prettiness is framed as incidental…. That sloppy pony is a subtle way of positioning Hope as a bonafide lead in the film, rather than just another supporting character [11–14].

Hope's unkempt and casual look also equates her more with the frequently gritty and messy looks of strong male superheroes, such as Thor, Winter Soldier, and Aquaman whose long hair is allowed to look sweaty and greasy in the midst of battle. Meanwhile, female characters like Wonder Woman, Gamora, and Black Widow always look as if they have stepped out of a beauty salon even after engaging in an epic battle (Han 9).

Likewise, the film also goes through great strides in not only placing Hope as a superhero on a level with Scott: it actually demonstrates the ways in which she is a superior superhero. Hope's Wasp suit grants her powers far beyond those of Scott's Ant-Man suit. She is more advanced in both movement (with wings that grant her the ability to fly) and offensive capabilities (with wrist blasters). The film even jokes about the discrepancy with Scott asking Hank, "So I take it you didn't have that tech available for me?" to which Hank responds, "No, I did." This dialogue, while funny, also suggests a disturbing undercurrent: that Hank, despite his faith in his daughter's natural intelligence and abilities, believes she needs something more to bring her into par with the male hero. This concept addresses a concern Jeffrey A. Brown mentions in his book *Dangerous Curves: Action Heroines, Gender, Fetishism, and Popular Culture,* that of the action heroine's story and creation retaining very specific elements of male control. Brown specifically details the important interplay between the action heroine and the father or father figure:

> The sometimes supportive, sometimes troubled connection the modern heroine has with her father and with authority is a crucial ingredient for considering how these women are situated in relation to patriarchy.... Implicit in this discussion of action heroines ... as indoctrinated into the realm of paternal law, is the notion that these characters are made over by some masculine force.... On many levels the action heroine is constructed by men [76–82].

In a similar fashion, Brown also points out that many of the strong and capable female characters in popular culture (with Hope included) were created by male creators. This means that, despite the advances in the development of these characters, they are very much under male control. Brown further equates this to the control men in the entertainment industry hold over women:

> Male producers and directors in particular have long been associated with ... using their power to turn struggling actresses into stars to curry sexual favors. Titillating scandals of this nature have been a mainstay in Hollywood from Fatty Arbuckle and Charlie Chaplin to Roman Polanski and Woody Allen and beyond.... Taking into account the long history of this particular unequal gender relationship in Hollywood raises certain questions about the male-constructed action heroine. At her core, is she just another image of the fetishized woman made for the consumption of men? [*Dangerous Curves* 88].

Brown is not alone in his assessment of the strong and empowered action heroine (of which the Wasp is a prime example) seemingly needing to be maintained under male control. Simantini Dey questioned, because of the film's primary focus on Ant-Man, whether the film's characterization of Hope is "just a case of marketplace feminism where companies/organizations sell their products (in this case, films) by using feminist values, language, and activism without actually embracing feminism" (14). As she adds, "The obvious empowerment of these characters stealthily hides the facts, that at the end of the day, when the earth needs saving in any Marvel film, it's always the men who get to do the job while the women only get to tail them" (14). Similarly, in her essay on the film *Elektra* and its view of the strong and capable superheroine, Miriam Kent still points out that the use of "slender, delicately feminine, white superheroines speaks to a need for media portrayals to provide images of empowered, tough women, while remaining well within the confines of conventional, easily recognizable categories of gender" (167). In the end, says Richard J. Gray III in his essay in *The 21st Century Superhero*, the male creators of these superheroine fantasy figures understand is that they must acquiesce to the desires of the "male gaze" in the development and perception of these characters (79) in order to allow the audience to feel "a sense of control, a command over the world of the ... story" (Childers and Hentzi 174).

As it relates to the trajectory of Hope's story through both films, this level of control also seemingly necessitated adherence to a traditionally unfeminist plot device—the romantic devotion of the heroine for the hero. Although both films work to keep the romantic story of Scott and Hope in the far background of the story, the heroine's strength and independence are seemingly marred by her joy of being tied to a man (Walderzak 150). The Wasp can be seen as a character that embodies "embedded feminism" (Douglas 8). Her feminism is seen as redundant as she has the personal capabilities to be the equal of any man. However, despite her success and seemingly unlimited life choices, such things become ancillary to her romantic role in the end (Walderzak 152). A primary example of this superficiality in Hope's character comes in *Ant-Man* when she finds herself appreciatively checking out Scott's body when he removes his shirt to inspect an injury thus exposing his muscular torso. Such a scene establishes, in an indirect manner, that Hope's admiration for Scott's hypermasculine body seems to overwhelm her own sense of feminine power, making her unable to resist her female desires (Brown, *Modern Superhero* 46).

The other Wasp in the film, Janet van Dyne, is a little more problematic within the post #metoo era. Anita Sarkeesian posted a stinging condemnation of *Ant-Man and the Wasp*, arguing that the film is nothing more than a movie about a damsel-in-distress. She argued that the entire plot revolves around Hope, Scott, and Hank attempting to rescue the helpless Janet van Dyne who is trapped within the Quantum Realm. For this reason, the film should be seen as a false feminist narrative. C.S. Johnson's analysis of Sarkeesian's tweet challenges this notion, stating that her "overall assessment of the film is unaware at best, intellectually dishonest at worst, and misleading for sure" (20). Johnson argues that Janet van Dyne is not a helpless damsel; she is a fallen hero who gave her life to stop a missile from hitting the United States and triggering an international conflict and that the quest to save her is not about rescuing a damsel-in-distress but is instead about reuniting a family with friends assisting in the outcome. It is also noteworthy that Janet exhibits almost unheard of mental strength by being able to withstand the experience of living in the Quantum Realm for nearly 30 years (despite Scott's claim to Hope that the Realm would "rip your mind apart") and assists with the rescue herself, providing Hank and Hope with the proper coordinates to focus on while calibrating their machine. Joining them through the "antenna" she has planted in Scott's mind, she explains, "I need to fix the algorithm. Trust me, after 30 years down here…. I've thought about it a lot." As she adds comfortingly, "You two have done such great work. You just need a little … nudge." Her use of Scott's body to assist her is a rather clever reversal of the traditional male-female dynamic, which often sees the woman's body invaded and used by the man. Scott offers no objection during or after, suggesting his willingness to facilitate Janet's rescue. If there is any character within the narrative that could be said to be suffering from the traumatic effects of a physical invasion, it would be the antagonist Ghost (Hannah John-Kamen), whose body was manipulated beyond her control. Now she flickers in an out of reality, wracked by constant pain. These experiments were forced on her by the government agency S.H.I.E.L.D., an act that could be seen as a "state-sanctioned institution of patriarchal control" (Brown, *Dangerous Curves* 76). It is telling that Janet, the woman Ghost has been planning to murder throughout the course of the film, is the one who sees the tortured soul trapped inside her and seeks to help her, acting without a second thought (Century 9). She pauses from reuniting with her family to approach Ghost and say, "Your pain … I can feel it." Ghost moans that it always hurts, and Janet responds, "I'm sorry. I think I can help you." The music swells. With a glowing touch that suggests her subatomic understanding but also maternal compassion, she repairs the young woman's cells. Breathing with her and clutching her face emphasizes this as a moment of empathy and comfort.

Meanwhile, the relationship between Hank Pym and Janet van Dyne could also be seen as deeply problematic. As discussed earlier, in the comics, Hank and Janet's relationship was marred with manipulation, violence, and heartbreak. Hank's history as a violent wife beater and Janet's history as a scheming woman who would stop at nothing to land her man would likely be seen as archaic at best and demeaning at worst, leading to highly unsympathetic responses to both characters. Their unhealthy power play throughout their relationship and marriage has been considered one of the major reasons most comic book fans view their relationship as incredibly upsetting to read (Century 4). The toxicity in the pages of *The Avengers* was so strong that it took well over twenty years for the couple to reconcile. Nonetheless, some comic book fans still believe the character of Hank Pym is beyond redemption and should have been killed off in the comics as an act of restitution for trauma he caused both to the fictional characters in the Marvel universe and to the readers themselves (Flanagan 6).

However, there is no sign of such strife between the couple in the film version of their relationship. Both films instead depict a beautiful and tragic love story. Moreover, they have a true and equal modern partnership. In the film, Janet takes incredible risks to reunite with her family (including Hank), spouting off quantum physics equations and providing detailed step-by-step instructions on how to calibrate his machine to find her in the Quantum Realm. They are portrayed as the ultimate power couple. Hank, if anything, is in awe of her and her abilities, an emotion he never displays for any other character, not even Hope (Century 3–4).

In her essay on Hank Pym, Meg Downey even suggested that his entire character arc in the two films has been an attempt to redeem him in the eyes of long-time comics fans (Downey 14–15). While there is no mention in either film about his history as a domestic abuser, the films do not shy away from his somewhat disturbing backstory, revealing in his opening scene in *Ant-Man* his penchant for violence by having him headslam Martin Donovan into a desk for making a snide comment about Janet. In *Ant-Man and the Wasp*, his past connection with several of his science colleagues at S.H.I.E.L.D., including Bill Foster and Elias Starr (Ghost's father) indicates that his relationship with them was antagonistic at best. The film even goes so far as to indirectly suggest that Hank was responsible for Ghost's creation, making her motivations (if not her actions) as entirely justified as Hope's anger in the previous film. However, by removing the domestic abuse angle from the character, he is made much more palatable to an audience that is bombarded daily with stories of abuse and sexual assault against women both in the home and the workplace, stories that have given rise to the #metoo movement and the current fourth wave of feminist thought.

With the success of films like *Wonder Woman* and *Ant-Man and the Wasp* and the rise in popularity of female-led comic book shows on television such as *Agent Carter, Supergirl,* and *Jessica Jones,* even detractors who once denigrated female-led superhero films as box office poison now acknowledge the market may be there if the films are of good quality. Marvel President Kevin Feige has championed female superhero movies in the past, claiming that the failure of past films like *Supergirl* (1984), *Catwoman* (2004), and *Elektra* (2005) had more to do with the poor quality of the films than the subject matter of the films themselves. This renewed interest is sparking a new renaissance of female superhero films in the MCU, led by the 2019 release of *Captain Marvel* and a proposed solo *Black Widow* film. Clearly the power of Hope and Janet van Dyne's appearances in *Ant-Man and the Wasp* has set a new standard for female characterization within the MCU. With any luck, the next generation of superhero films will continue to improve upon these strides and show the world just how powerful a woman can be.

WORKS CITED

Ant-Man. Directed by Peyton Reed. Marvel Entertainment, 2015.

Ant-Man and the Wasp. Directed by Peyton Reed. Marvel Entertainment, 2018.

Bergdahl, Esther. "*Ant-Man* Is Less Feminist in 2015 Than It Was in 1963." *Mic,* 16 July 2018. https://mic.com/articles/122293/ant-man-the-wasp-marvel-sexism-feminism. Web.

Brown, Jeffrey A. *Dangerous Curves: Action Heroines, Gender, Fetishism, and Popular Culture.* University Press of Mississippi, 2011.

_____. *The Modern Superhero in Film and Television: Popular Genre and American Culture.* Routledge, 2017.

Century, Sara. "Why Janet Van Dyne and Hank Pym Deserve a Prequel." *SyFyWire,* 26 July 2018. https://www.syfy.com/syfywire/why-janet-van-dyne-and-hank-pym-deserve-a-prequel. Web.

Childers, Joseph, and Gary Hentzi, eds. *The Columbia Dictionary of Modern Literary and Cultural Criticism.* Columbia University Press, 1995.

Dey, Simantini. "*Ant-Man and the Wasp*: Marvel's Wishy-Washy Feminism Is Just a Gimmick to Make Box-Office Hits." *News18*, 18 July 2018. https:// www.news18.com/news/buzz/ant-man-and-the-wasp-marvels-wishy-washy-feminism-is-just-a-gimmick-to-make-box-office-hits-1815249.html. Web.

Dickens, Donna. "Hope Shines for *Ant-Man* and the Future of Marvel Women." *Uproxx*, 20 July 2015. https://uproxx.com/hitfix/hope-shines-for-ant-man-and-the-future-of-marvel-women. Web.

Douglas, Susan J. *The Rise of Enlightened Sexism: How Pop Culture Took Us from Girl Power to Girls Gone Wild.* St. Martin's Griffin, 2010.

Downey, Meg. "How the Marvel Movies Cleaned Up Hank Pym's Controversial Past." *Polygon*, 10 July 2018. https://www.polygon.com/2018/7/10/17534246/hank-pym-ant-man-wasp-comics-backstory. Web.

Flanagan, Josh. "The Hank Pym Issue." *iFanboy*, 17 February 2012. http:// ifanboy.com/articles/whats-wrong-with-you-the-hank-pym-issue. Web.

Givens, Hannah. "A Controversial Theory About Woman in the Marvel Cinematic Universe, or 'I Love Hope Van Dyne.'" *Hannah Reads Books*, 11 September 2015. https://hannahgivens.wordpress.com/2015/09/11/a-controversial-theory-about-women-in-the-marvel-cinematic-universe-or-i-love-hope-van-dyne. Web.

Gray, Richard J., II. "Vivacious Vixens and Scintillating Super-Hotties: Deconstructing the Superheroine." *The 21st Century Superhero: Essays of Gender, Genre, and Globalization in Film,* edited by Richard J. Gray II and Betty Kaklamanidou. McFarland, 2011, pp. 75–93.

Han, Angie. "Hope's Ponytail in *Ant-Man and the Wasp* Is Everything." *Mashable*, 9 July 2018. https://mashable.com/2018/07/09/ant-man-and-the-wasp-hair. Web.

Johnson, C.S. "Twitter Reveals Intersectionality's Problems with Facts." *Hollywood in Toto*, 19 July 2018. https://www.hollywoodintoto.com/twitter-intersectionality-ant-man. Web.

Lee, Stan, and H.E. Huntley, writers, and Jack Kirby, artist. *Tales to Astonish* #44. Marvel, 1959.

Lee, Stan, writer, and Jack Kirby, artist. *Avengers* #1. Marvel, 1963.

Kent, Miriam. "*Elektra*: Critical Reception, Postfeminism, and the Marvel Superheroine on Screen." *Marvel Comics Into Films: Essays on Adaptations Since the 1940s,* edited by Matthew J. McEniry, Robert Moses Peaslee, and Robert G. Weiner. McFarland, 2016, pp. 165–176.

Michelinie, David, writer, and John Byrne, artist. *The Avengers* #181. Marvel, 1979.

Sarkeesian, Anita. "It Took Me a Few Days to Realize This but #AntManandtheWasp is a Movie About a Damsel in Distress. THE ENTIRE MAIN PLOT IS ABOUT SAVING a DAMSEL IN DISTRESS!" *Twitter*, 10 Jul 2018, 1:32 p.m. https://twitter.com/anitasarkeesian/status/1016782136001458176?lang=en.

Shooter, Jim, writer, and Bob Hall, artist. *The Avengers* #213. Marvel, 1981.

Stahler, Kelsea. "*Ant-Man and the Wasp* Is Only Sorta Feminist but Here's Why That's Actually Huge." *Bustle*, 3 July 2018. https://www.bustle.com/p/ant-man-the-wasp-is-only-sorta-feminist-but-heres-why-thats-actually-huge-9667414.

Walderzak, Joseph. "Damsels in Transgress: The Empowerment of the Damsel in the Marvel Cinematic Universe." *Marvel Comics Into Films: Essays on Adaptations Since the 1940s,* edited by Matthew J. McEniry, Robert Moses Peaslee, and Robert G. Weiner. McFarland, 2016, pp. 150–164.

Riding the Waves of Feminism in *Wonder Woman*

A Shock Heard 'Round the World

CAROL ZITZER-COMFORT
and JOSÉ I. RODRÍGUEZ

The 2017 blockbuster film *Wonder Woman* is the "highest-grossing live-action female-directed film in the world," and the film is making history in more ways (Stefansky). As *Wonder Woman* director Patty Jenkins tells *Washington Post's* Comic Riffs, "My mom was a second-wave feminist, and I heard a lot about it and thought a lot about it…" (Cavna). Jenkins' feminist thinking is evident in her praxis throughout the film, and thus, *Wonder Woman* is an instantiation of third and fourth wave feminist imperatives via non-normative gender portrayals, in addition to novel notions of female identity and agency, which are fertile grounds for intersectional inquiry in a growing DC Universe.

The opening scene of *Wonder Woman* is one of earth that invites a view of the planet from outerspace. We are invited to see "Mother Earth," Gaia, the divine feminine. As we break through the atmosphere in London and see the city landscape, we see Diana, zeroing in on her superhero strut for the first time. We hear Diana narrating her multidimensional experiences in the world of man. Then time changes, and we see Diana as a young, rebellious girl, running away from her tutor in order to watch the Amazon women train for battle. Diana longs to be one of the training warriors; however, her mother forbids it, which only makes Diana want it more. Diana's mother tells her that war is not something to be longed for, and tells her the story of the Amazon women, how the women came to be in the world of man, and how Zeus called on them to infuse the world of men with compassion, which had been

184

corrupted by the god Ares who promoted war and hatred. The peace that the Amazons brought to the world was not long-lived because men enslaved them. Diana's mother, Hippolyta, led a revolt to set the Amazons free. This battle transcended the earthly plain and included the gods, pitting Zeus and Ares against each other, as Diana's mother tells us. With his dying breath, Zeus created a safe haven, the Amazonian island (Themyscira), and the Amazons have been secure ever since.

After sharing this narrative, Diana and her mother visit the "god killer," the only weapon that can slay a god (a sword). Diana is transfixed by the sword, and her wish to be a warrior is solidified in this pivotal scene. The young Diana will not abide by her mother's orders to forgo training as an Amazonian warrior. Diana seeks the assistance of the most powerful general on the island, Antiope, to fulfill what Diana knows to be her destiny. With Antiope's guidance, Diana becomes a warrior princess, defeating her acclaimed teacher, with the unexpected power of her wonder-wielding bracelets. In this moment, Diana proves to all that she is the one who can defeat Ares, and her journey into the world of man begins as she plunges herself into the depths of the sea to save her future love, her island, and her new-found world, with an angle of telling that Patty Jenkins orchestrates to navigate the waves of feminism.

Third wave feminism emerged as a response to unresolved issues in previous eras (Snyder). Prominent attributes of third wave feminism include: (1) an emphasis of multiple perspectives (validating diverse voices), (2) multivocality over synthesis of feminist goals (feminism can mean different things to different people), and (3) a refusal to police boundaries of the feminist political (Snyder). In these ways, third wave feminism promotes freedom over choices and one's body, an invitation for the expression of eclectic personal experiences, and a critique of dominant narratives that impede social progress (Garlen and Sandlin). Fourth wave feminism, which is superseding third wave, has evolving definitions linking the movement with theories of intersectionality and "what social critics call *neoliberalism*: a culture that idealizes individual effort, high productivity, good performance, constant improvement, and merit-based achievement" (Ruti, *Feminist Film Theory* 10). Emerging definitions of fourth wave feminism also include the use of social media to reach diverse communities across the globe.

Wonder Woman invites viewers to understand and identify with feminist angles of telling based on what Sonja Foss and Cindy Griffin define as "invitational rhetoric," which promotes progressive social change by subverting hegemonic narratives in that "its purpose is to offer an invitation to understanding and its communicative modes are the offering of perspectives and the creation of the external conditions of safety, value and freedom" (Foss and Griffin 2). In the film, Diana creates the conditions of safety by accepting all of the men on her team as unique individuals. She cultivates a space of value by including everyone in the circle of kinship. She facilitates the experience of freedom by fighting to end the war. In unexpected ways, then, *Wonder Woman* is expanding the agentic dimensions of intersectionality in the DC Universe, and showcasing what critic Mari Ruti might characterize as "the ethics of opting out" (*The Ethics of Opting Out*) in Patty Jenkins' rendering of fragile and "defiant subjects" who pursue utopian desires, however tinged with trauma, for the sake of social justice in a world gone wild with war.

Sonja Foss and Cindy Griffin's invitational rhetoric is applicable to understanding the influence of third wave feminist features in artifacts like *Wonder Woman,* while fourth wave feminism invites further investigation of inclusion and agency. Invitational rhetoric, which is grounded in Starhawk's (*Dreaming the Dark*) rhetoric of inherent worth, power and action, is a constitutional framing of feminist ideals. Foss and Griffin introduce invitational rhetoric as an alternative to constitutions of rhetoric as a primarily patriarchal and persuasive activity. In *Wonder Woman,* the invitational, rhetorical frame encourages audiences to view and understand the perspective of the rhetor (Diana), focusing on equality (Diana's sense of equity), immanent value (Diana's sense of inclusion), and self-determination (Diana's sense of agency); therefore, invitational rhetoric, both literally and metaphorically, as a communication mode, invites audience engagement in the creation of new forms of understanding (new forms of viewing the world through alternative and inviting feminist lenses).

By examining *Wonder Woman* through the lenses of third and fourth wave feminism and invitational rhetoric, our commentary illuminates the way that the film encourages viewers to understand and identify with an innovative angle of telling that promotes progressive social change in the body politic by subverting hegemonic narratives about gender in the expanding DC Universe.

Subiro Wahago and Ron Roberts note that "fourth wave feminism is arguably the most inclusive form of the struggle for female emancipation to date. The movement is closely interlinked with social justice activism which takes as a given the proposition that all forms of systemic oppression are connected" (216); thus, fourth wave feminism allows for an expanded view in *Wonder Woman* as the film emphasizes the formerly excluded: most notably, focusing on the female gaze while replacing the male gaze as a dominant angle of telling. In *Wonder Woman,* the "male gaze," which has for so long dominated master narratives that shape film, literature, and culture, is subverted and shattered. Thus, the audience is invited to see female gaze as dominant, allowing *Wonder Woman* to make a revolutionary move away from the patriarchal, imperial gaze. Traditionally, as E. Ann Kaplan notes, "the male gaze and the imperial gaze cannot be separated in western patriarchal culture" (xi). *Wonder Woman* shatters this hegemonic unification of imperial and male gaze with a new world order, which is literally imbued with birthing power (through Patty Jenkins' cinematic angle of telling, creating female gaze) and metaphorically (through Diana's iconic bracelet blast, which launches her journey into the world of men). In this way, the film also subverts the notions of what Mulvey describes as: "the division of labour in narrative films is explicitly gendered. Women most often play the role of spectacle; they are to be looked at, while men are active; they propel the narrative forward and do the looking" (62).

Wonder Woman ignites a subversive and shattering counter-narrative to traditional representations of gender in the superhero genre. The main protagonists in the film, Diana Prince and Steve Trevor, embody third wave depictions of selfhood in that they perform non-normative representations of gender. Even as a young girl, Diana fights for her right to learn the skills she needs as a warrior—skills that will ultimately save not only her life, but the life of the Amazon community. As an adult, Diana represents the value of self-determination through agency. She is extremely dissatisfied with her place on the island and makes a conscious choice to escape under the cover of darkness for the sake of justice. Equally importantly, however, Diana is relatively unhappy with her life of isolation on the island, and she longs for adventure and exploration. In this light, Diana's experience is similar to second wave feminist concerns with the limits of the domestic sphere (or for Diana—the Amazon Island), conditions that Betty Friedan noted in her 1962 book *The Feminine Mystique* in which women longed for more than cooking, cleaning, and being subservient to their husbands. While Diana is not subject to these types of demands, she wants more than the island can offer and longs for diversion. She discovers a unique opportunity for change when she meets Steve on the shores of Themyscira.

As the self-proclaimed "above average" man, Steve embodies a uniquely subversive gender identity for male leads in superhero films. At the beginning of the film, for instance, Diana rescues Steve when his plane crashes off the coast of her Amazonian island as he attempts to evade his German pursuers. This scene subverts so many superhero films in which the woman must be rescued by a man. After rescuing Steve, Diana learns that the world is at war and even her island is in danger. Diana persuades Steve to help her reach the front lines and attempt to stop the conflict. Diana knows, in some way, that this heroic journey is her destiny, casting her as the central hero while Steve is messenger and guide. As Diana and Steve are traveling to London, Steve is embarrassed by Diana's invitation to sleep next to her on the deck of the boat. His awkwardness is not gender normative because "real men" are supposed to want to sleep with women. In these ways, Steve exhibits physical and emotional vulnerabilities that are atypical of men in superhero films, but his masculine identity remains intact without requiring him to perform the role of a hypermasculinized, serial misogynist who must "save" the damsel in perpetual distress. As such, *Wonder Woman* depicts Steve and Diana as reciprocal and eclectic characters in communal relationship with one another, especially in their eventual sexual union, which occurs through mutual agreement and respect later in the film.

Steve and Diana rely on each other for protection through their journey. Steve acts as Diana's guide while they are in London, not because he is innately better suited for the journey to the front lines, but because he is more familiar with the terrain. As they travel, Steve and Diana develop a collaborative relationship to ensure survival; they help each other in reciprocal ways. Initially, Diana saves Steve from drowning as his plane crashes off the shores of her island paradise. In turn, Steve saves Diana from the German soldiers who storm the beach. This interplay of cooperation shows the subordination of male identity, through the inclusion of qualities that are in direct opposition to hegemonic masculinity—the male is not the undisputed hero. Perhaps most importantly, Diana and Steve both exhibit physical prowess, critical thinking skills, and nurturance of one another. Though these character traits are traditionally gendered in rigidly scripted forms on film, *Wonder Woman* renders these features androgynous, and thereby, open to multiple interpretations (polysemous).

The androgyny and multiplicity of Diana's third wave notion of choice and fourth wave notion of embodied agency are demonstrated throughout the film. At first, she makes the decision to leave Themyscira in a radical departure that is typically associated with the heroic journeys of male protagonists. In another rupture, as she makes her way to the front lines, Diana decides to co-create a romantic relationship with Steve, indicating a relational mutuality that is non-normative and fluid. Diana behaves in non-traditional ways because she feels no shame as a result of her choices, demonstrating androgyny and agency. On the basis of this non-shaming attitude, her behavior is indicative of the third wave refusal to conform to boundaries, which previously policed feminine performances of self. This behavior also illustrates a proactive constitution of selfhood, which is indicative of feminist ideals in popular culture. As Ariana Grande decrees in her 2018 YouTube video, with over 666,571,056 views, "God is a woman," and Diana Prince, as Wonder Woman, is a cinematic instantiation of that revolutionary claim.

Diana is never presented as hypersexualized "eye candy" (Flynn); indeed, Steve is the only character who appears nude in the film. He feels the need to cover his genitals and experience embarrassment as a result of the "female gaze," especially after Diana asks, "What is that…?" We, the audience, along with Steve, think that she is asking about his penis, as he looks down in awkward embarrassment. However, then he says, "Oh, this is a watch.... It tells you when to eat, when to sleep…" to which Diana replies, "You let that little thing tell you what to do…?" This commentary by Diana is about the watch explicitly, but about the penis implicitly, indicating that Diana does not suffer from penis envy. Instead, she mocks the phallus. It is little, and "you" (Steve explicitly and society implicitly) should not listen to this little prick. In a direct and subtle critique of toxic masculinity, Diana is dismissing the male organ, indicating that "bodily organs themselves have no meaning; it's the collective mythologies that cultures impose on them that do" (Ruti, *Penis Envy* xiv). From this angle of telling, Diana is in the position of power and feels no shame, guilt, or embarrassment, forging a new, feminist line of sight in the growing universe of superhero films.

Diana demonstrates the move from second wave feminism to third wave to fourth wave feminism in her actions. She is inherently motivated to act against oppressive boundaries, demonstrating the value of personal experience that is central to third wave feminist narratives and the inclusion and intersectionalities inherent in fourth wave feminism. The simultaneity of these standpoints in the film illustrates the multiple-perspective lens, typifying third and fourth wave feminism. For most of the film, Diana does not know that she is the daughter of Zeus, showing her heroic humanity in the simultaneity of her inherent divinity. Diana likewise does not know that she is the "god killer," the only one who can kill Ares, the god of war. In her final confrontation with Ares, her identity as the divine feminine emerges when she witnesses the shattering of her sword—an alleged, secret weapon of choice, which is also a traditionally masculine weapon that proves useless as it has no actual power to kill her foe. This shattering is a shock to her and to the audience because both are invited to identify with the mystery of the moment. What will happen? What now?

Cinematic moments of mystery, a gap of unknowingness before the known is revealed, invite audiences to see that Diana occupies the positionality of a female subject in a distinct manner that challenges dominant narratives of female passivity and opens spaces for social progress for real women (Starhawk, *Truth or Dare*). *Wonder Woman* reveals that Diana is incredibly strong in every way (physically, mentally, emotionally), assertive, and capable of protecting herself and others; all the while showing a depth of empathy for human suffering. Diana is not "othered" in this film—none of the women are. Women are portrayed as strong, as real. For instance, Caitlin Flynn notes in her review, "Wonder Woman's (Gal Gadot) thigh jiggled when she made a superhero landing," exemplifying the importance of a superhero movie that's directed by a woman in which women's bodies are not necessarily unrealistically thin, perfect, and curve-less. Indeed, Patty Jenkins' Diana is powerful, overcomes oppressive boundaries, and challenges domination without abandoning her female identity because she does not rely on male gaze for validation, does not rely on a male lover to define her. Instead, Diana partners collaboratively with Steve, a spy who ultimately does not survive the horrors of war, illustrating another sharp departure from the modus operandi of gender relations in superhero films—the love interest dies in the visceral brutality of "the real" (Ruti *The Singularity of Being* 9). In this way, *Wonder Woman* typifies the embodied activism, with all accompanying trauma, that is central to the core definition of fourth wave feminism.

In a pivotal scene, Diana rushes into No Man's Land and starts taking fire. As a woman, she enters a space no man can occupy and then takes fire, thereby turning the tide in a decisive battle against oppression (the Germans). This act is profoundly agentic. As Rollo May, in his critically acclaimed tome, *The Courage to Create*, puts it, "We are called upon to do something new, to confront a no man's land, to push into a forest where there are no well-worn paths and from which no one has returned to guide us" (12). As a creative agent, Diana traverses the terrain of tyranny on what Cherríe Moraga and Gloria Anzaldúa, in their classic text, might characterize as "This bridge called" her (Diana's) back (xv). Diana enters a borderland, a liminal space, a bridge between two worlds, a space of possibility, where the divine feminine reclaims sacred ground, as if for the first time, giving birth to the dawning of a new day, a new world order. This scene works as a metaphor for what happens when courageous women go into "no man's land" and take fire (such as the accusers of Weinstein, Cosby, and Nassar). These women are opening a pathway for other women because, at least in some cases of sexual assault, powerful men are being held accountable. One woman takes fire, so other women can help turn the tide in a battle for social justice resulting most recently in the #MeToo movement. Harvey Weinstein lost his company. Bill Cosby and Larry Nassar were convicted. These are contemporary examples of "a turning of the tide" in the struggle for social justice, and *Wonder Woman* is an instantiation of these fourth wave tenets, especially the feature of embodied activism.

As an embodied activist, Diana is inherently inclusive as she moves in the world. Consistent with fourth wave feminism and its emphasis on intersectionality, especially the intersections of race, class, gender, and ability, we see these inclusive manifestations in *Wonder Woman* when Diana includes Chief, a member of the Blackfoot tribe, Sameer, an Arabic spy, and Charlie, a soldier with PTSD who feels as if he should not accompany them into battle. In *Wonder Woman*, these men are not discarded, but welcomed into what Father Greg Boyle (from Homeboy Industries) characterizes as the "circle of kinship" where no one is outside, reflecting common humanity identity politics. In this sacred, social space, in the unfolding moments of authentic humanity, empathy is a mode of being that informs doing. In these instances of genuine solidarity, the audience discovers diversity and inclusion as modes of other-oriented selfhood that inform other-oriented agency.

Wonder Woman shows us that difference can be transcended by focusing on common humanity through empathy. She doesn't discard the sniper because of his PTSD. As Charlie questions his ability to go with them into battle, and whether he would be a hindrance, Diana asks, "But who will sing to us?" emphasizing his ability rather than focusing on his disability. She welcomes him into her circle of kinship, offering a move away from exclusion and toward inclusion, which is emblematic of fourth wave feminism at its best.

The Chief introduces himself to Diana, using a traditional Blackfoot salutation, presenting himself as "Napi" (Dyce). Like Diana, he's anything but ordinary. Chief's unique identity is evident in his name because "Napi" refers to Old Man in the Blackfoot tradition, a trickster god who is known as "the world's creator" (Dyce). Chief joins alliances with Diana and Steve with other World War I allies. He explains to Steve and Diana that his people had been wiped out by Steve's, thus adding a plea for tolerance and acknowledgment of America's moral culpability and demonstrating that "survival… is not a matter of mere existence, but the holistic and embodied manifestation of a people constituted in and by place" (Kelly and Black 3).

Sameer, played by Saïd Taghmaoui, is also an outsider. He became a spy because he could not find acting work due to racial discrimination. While Sameer initially joined the group expecting money, which Steve promised him, he became dedicated to the mission upon witnessing Diana's depth of empathy and profound agency in the midst of war. He, too, is emblematic of fourth wave feminism's emphasis on diversity, inclusion, and acceptance.

The cinematic praxis, in *Wonder Woman*, much like Anzaldúa's scholarly activism, "calls for expanded awareness (conocimento) and develops an ethics of interconnectivity, which she [Anzaldúa] describes as the act of reaching out through the wounds—wounds that can be physical, psychic, cultural, and/or spiritual—to connect with others" (xxiii). Diana is the embodiment of radical acceptance, illustrating the profound value of empathy in moments of living. Her presence creates a space, not too far from the heart, where suffering surrenders to solace in a cinematic centering that proclaims wholeness in the midst of brokenness. Thus, the fractures of contemporary selfhood become burdens to bear in a battle for being (ontology) that informs doing (agency) in a world gone wild inventing the insignificance of the human heart. As if for the first time, Diana deems humanity worthy by noticing that which is most broken, most discarded, most insignificant and forges a path of light on a journey tinged with trauma. In this way, trauma is transmuted as companion on a path of perpetual recovery where coming home to worthiness occurs one day at a time. Ultimately, this invitation into wholeness is Diana's greatest gift to the world.

Narratives such as *Wonder Woman* are a particularly important genre for feminist analysis because of their mass appeal across the globe as an ongoing part of the DC brand. Its effective gender subversions invite the audience to understand and perceive gender in novel forms that are open to diverse interpretations, and thereby, open to alternative social as well as political performances of self. Furthermore, it is useful to examine artifacts that embody third wave and fourth wave axioms within the framework of invitational rhetoric, providing a lens for viewing that is beyond the confines of simple, patriarchal persuasion. In this way, the potential is clear for *Wonder Woman* to be influential and empowering through invitational praxis. The film invites audiences to view the world from a third wave and fourth wave standpoint, while allowing other interpretations to coexist in the multigeneity of meaning. The DC Universe, where *Wonder Woman* has a cinematic home, is a strong cultural force that shapes constructions of social reality and the body politic. Thus, *Wonder Woman* is an impactful birthing point for the cultivation of revolutionary understandings of gender identity and intersectionality.

WORKS CITED

Anzaldúa, Gloria E. "Re-envisioning Coyolxauhqui, Decolonizing Reality." *Light in the Dark (Luz En Lo Oscuro): Rewriting Identity, Spirituality, Reality.* Ed. Analouise Keating. Duke University Press, 2015, pp. x–xxxvii.

Boyle, Gregory. *Barking to the Choir: The Power of Radical Kinship.* Simon and Shuster, 2017.

Cavna, Michael. "How *Wonder Woman* Director Patty Jenkins Cracked the Superhero-movie Glass Ceiling." *The Washington Post*, 31 May 2017. www.washingtonpost.com/news/comic-riffs/wp/2017/05/31/how-wonder-woman-director-patty-jenkins-cracked-the-superhero-movie-glass-ceiling/?utm_term=.1b275b239478. Accessed 17 July 2017.

Dyce, Andrew. "Wonder Woman's Secret Native American God Explained." *Screenrant*, 26 June 2017. www.screenrant.com/wonder-woman-movie-napi-native-american-god/. Accessed 25 October 2018.

Flynn, Caitlin. "Wonder Woman's (Gal Gadot) Thigh Jiggled When She Made a Superhero Landing." *Refinery29*, 8 June 2017. www.refinery29.com/2017/06/158291/wonder-woman-thigh-jiggle-male-gaze. Accessed 10 June 2017.

Foss, Sonja K., and Cindy L. Griffin. "Beyond Persuasion: A Proposal for an Invitational Rhetoric." *Communications Monographs*, vol. 62, no. 1, 1995, pp. 2–18.

Friedan, Betty. "The Feminine Mystique." 1963. Reprint. DeU, 1983.

Garlen, Julie C., and Jennifer A. Sandlin. "Happily (N)ever After: The Cruel Optimism of Disney's Romantic Ideal." *Feminist Media Studies*, vol. 17 no. 1, 2017, pp. 1–15.

God Is a Woman. Directed by Dave Meyers. Freenjoy, 2018.

Kaplan, E. Ann. *Looking for the Other: Feminism, Film, and the Imperial Gaze.* Routledge Press, 1997.

Kelly, R. Casey, and Black, E. Jason. *Decolonizing Native American Rhetoric: Communicating Self-Determination.* Peter Lang, 2018.

May, Rollo. *The Courage to Create.* Norton, 1994.

Moraga, Cherríe. "Catching Fire: Preface to the Fourth Edition." *This Bridge Called My Back*, edited by Cherríe Moraga and Gloria Anzaldúa, 4th Edition. State University of New York Press, 2015, pp. xv–xxvi.

Mulvey, Laura. "Visual Pleasure and Narrative Cinema." *Film Theory and Criticism: Introductory Readings*, edited by Leo Braudy and Marshall Cohen. Oxford University Press, 1999, pp. 833–44.

Ruti, Mari. *The Ethics of Opting Out: Queer Theory's Defiant Subjects.* Columbia University Press, 2017.
_____. *Feminist Film Theory and Pretty Woman.* Bloomsbury Academic Press, 2016.
_____. *Penis Envy and Other Bad Feelings: The Emotional Costs of Everyday Life.* Columbia University Press, 2018.
_____. *The Singularity of Being: Lacan and the Immortal Within.* Fordham University Press, 2012.
Snyder, R. Claire. "What Is Third-Wave Feminism? a New Directions Essay." *Signs* vol. 34, no. 1, pp. 175–96. doi:10.1086/588436. 2008.
Starhawk. *Dreaming the Dark: Magic, Sex and Politics* (rev. ed.) Beacon, 1988.
_____. *Truth or Dare: Encounters with Power, Authority, and Mystery.* Harper and Row, 1987.
Stefansky, Emma. "Wonder Woman Is the Highest-Grossing Live-Action Female Directed Film in the World." *Vanity Fair*, 25 June 2017. www.vanityfair.com/hollywood/2017/06/wonder-woman-highest-worldwide-gross-female-director. Accessed 27 July 2017.
Wahogo, Subira, and Ron Roberts. "Fourth Wave Feminism: Protests and Prospects." *The Journal of Critical Psychology, Counselling and Psychotherapy.* vol. 12, no. 4, 2012, pp. 216–220.
Wonder Woman. Directed by Patty Jenkins. DC Entertainment, 2017.

Deconstructing the Wonder

*Liberal Versus Conservative Thought
in Patty Jenkins's* Wonder Woman

CHRISTIAN JIMENEZ

Patty Jenkins's work on *Wonder Woman* (2017) has been received as both a pro-feminist and anti-feminist text. While Jenkins has been careful to not self-identify as a feminist, she has often situated herself as a female director working within the studio system of Hollywood (Martins 117). In some cases, however, Jenkins has been careful to distance herself from her gender saying that she "can't take on history of 50 percent of all people because [she's] a woman" (Martins 117). Still, simultaneously, she explains she walked away from the offer to direct *Thor: Dark World* because she considered that would be a "big disservice to women" (Martins 117).

Several reasons mark her out for analysis. For one, she is in rare company in directing films with budgets exceeding $100 million dollars—being only the second woman as of 2017 to direct a $100-plus million-dollar film. Secondly, *Wonder Woman* was not just successful as a woman's film but broke several records within the comic book genre, action genre, and women-led genre.[1] She remains the only woman to have her film earn more than $100 million in its first weekend (Martins 118). Its record has yet to be exceeded even nearly two years after its release. Third, Jenkins has the rare distinction of having directed both Oscar-nominated as well as big-budget superhero films; additionally, she is only woman to direct a DC female character making her film debut. While there have been some directors with similar pedigree, no male director—yet—has the distinction of being Oscar-nominated and simultaneously a director of Marvel or DC projects.

Wonder Woman deliberately tries to mark a point between conservative and liberal forms of feminism as a text. It is a middling film, overall, as a genre film within superhero mythologies but also within the war genre, specifically. However, in marketing, Jenkins presented the film and herself as well as her lead star as much more liberal and feminist than the actual film is. In essence, on the one hand, the film is much less feminist and political than the Golden Age character created by William Moulton Marston. On the other hand, the film is relatively more liberal than most films even within the superhero genre as well as mainstream Hollywood film culture as a whole. All in all, *Wonder Woman* is mildly feminist ... but much more feminist than most films being produced.

Wonder Woman succeeded by being received as a moderate feminist mythology. In of itself there is nothing amiss here. Simply its existence is a remarkable fact. However, when measured against representations that could have occurred and even much stronger, more agentic representations of *Wonder Woman* (even when written by men), the film should be seen as (accurately) a negotiated position between two extremes. One extreme is typified by the arthouse/studio work of Christopher Nolan and his *Batman* trilogy which sometimes endorses reactionary political positions, while the other is more strenuously, self-consciously feminist works like *Ladybird* (2017) by Greta Gerwig or Rebecca Miller's *Maggie's Plan* (2015) where characters and plot are thoroughly about how women think and feel. *Wonder Woman* has a female-centered plot, but its action and wit are meant to be enjoyed by even a conservative male audience.

Women and Myth: From Genderless to Gendered Politics

While feminist analyses have often highlighted how restricted women have been in gaining access to the creative arts, in fact, women, then, have for centuries been creators of myth, even female myths. Often these pro-female myths are distorted through patriarchic revisions such as the positive mother-daughter relationship in the Demeter-Persephone myth turned into a myth of victimization by rape (Seiler). When myths have been produced by women more recently, they have been naively situated in a space where pro-female politics is often suppressed. Mary Shelley's *Frankenstein* (1818) draws on the Prometheus myth about the dangers of humanity tampering with science. The theme here is universal and not gendered.

It was only within the twentieth century that authors like Charlotte Gilman, Margaret Atwood, and Ursula K. Le Guin presented female-centric myths where gender politics was explicitly part of the narrative. To be sure, the space here is restrictive, as only a handful of non-white female writers like Alice Walker and Octavia Butler were able to enter, but myth as a genre had female artists.

Liberal feminism, paradoxically, wants the liberal state to recognize woman as a person entitled to a certain bundle of rights and responsibilities (Okin). Still, while the state should recognize woman as woman, this recognition is to be limited only to a few key areas. Conservative feminism simply goes further in wanting more restrictions on women as a class. However, the motivations for such restrictions are not always reactionary. For instance, while women's colleges exist and continue to exist, it is no longer possible that women's colleges as such disallow men to enter as students. Still, in the past, it was understood women's colleges existed solely for women and to raise a certain kind of conservative woman.

For conservative feminists, women should be equal yet be equal only within a certain separate domain. Advocates of these positions include Midge Decter and Ayn Rand, with the latter famously arguing that a woman should be not be elected president. Conservative and liberal feminists debate often how large and/or small these domains should be, but both endorse this dualistic vision of rights. While *Wonder Woman* has a message of tolerance, it is tolerance for being merciful to someone loyal to the liberal state.

Still, *Wonder Woman* is a derived source, so let us briefly define how adaptations are approached and then analyze the film. Geoffrey Wagner in classifying adaptations offered a three-tiered model. Adapted works are either analogy, transposition, or commentary. An analogy will differ substantially from its source material when being put into another medium or work. A transposition tries to be as faithful as possible to the source work and depart only minimally. A commentary, however, only takes elements of an original work and uses those parts to "comment" on a certain theme (Wagner). Hence as Jack Zipes notes in Peter Jackson's *Lord of the Rings* trilogy, the quest-narrative strengthens the original work's anti-war theme by emphasizing how women are victimized by war. The "commentary" that war is for the profit of evil and greedy men is shown through casting of female leads and giving them more agency and more narrative power than J.R.R. Tolkien intended.

Wonder Woman is hard to judge at two levels. For one, it vacillates between analogy and commentary. Secondly, unlike Jackson, Jenkins makes the film more conservative than the source material. The feminist intent of Marston is diluted to make Diana's message a universal one of love and mercy; the larger politics of how the wars in World War II were guided by fascist masculinity is simply elided. In essence, *Wonder Woman* as film is a liberal footnote to Wonder Woman as myth whereas Jackson presented a more liberal version of the Tolkien myth.

The work might be considered transposition, but many signs suggest Jenkins clearly did not want to transpose the Marston version of Wonder Woman. Marston explicitly noted repeatedly that his version of Wonder Woman was not just meant to be a brave heroine but one with a distinct political message. Marston explained the reason for making Wonder Woman sexually attractive in a letter to comic historian and cartoonist Coulton Waugh:

> Frankly, Wonder Woman is psychological propaganda for the new type of woman who should, I believe, rule the world.... I have given Wonder Woman this dominant force but have kept her loving, tender, maternal, and feminine in every other way.... Her magic lasso, which compels anyone bound to it to obey Wonder Woman ... represents woman's love charm and allure by which she compels men and women to do her bidding [Miles 114–115].

Wonder Woman as a comic book heroine was created several years prior to World War II. But once the war began, Marston framed Wonder Woman in opposition to the Hitler view that women's world is defined and limited to "her husband" (Ullrich 272). As Marston explained: "Women's strong qualities [are] ... despised because of their weakness. The obvious remedy is to create a feminine character with all the strength of Superman plus ... the allure of a ... beautiful woman" (Campbell 8). The subversion goes beyond merely contrasting femininity to masculinity.

Superman as character is partly derived from Nietzsche mythic *Ubermensch*, a being that overcomes the values of his time and recreates the world through violence and force. To Marston, Wonder Woman is even stronger than the Overman and hence her power is not in dominating but cooperating with others. The Hitler view that only mass violence could resolve political issues and was an exclusive male domain was thus contested on its own ground. A woman could be even more powerful than the fascist masculine ideal.

Instead of World War II, *Wonder Woman* is set in World War I. The original feminism versus fascism frame is thus no longer present. However, the villains do represent and symbolize male authority and aggression run amok. Another missing element is Diana's anti-militarism. Whereas Wonder Woman in the comic books uses great violence, she is not a part of a formal military organization and though the Amazons are presented as a race of warrior women, they do not enjoy warfare for its own sake. However, Jenkins as she has explicitly admitted is an "army brat" and daughter of a male pilot who served in Vietnam (Martins 117). Jenkins has, tellingly, never dissociated herself from her father or his service in Vietnam. This theme of militarism is present in Gadot as well who served in the Israeli Defense Forces (IDF). Service in the military in Israel is compulsory but Gadot herself did not distance herself from her service—even the 2006 intervention into Lebanon killing hundreds, mainly civilians (Graham). She has framed her military experience as a positive one. "You give your freedom away. You learn discipline and respect" (Sherman 18).

In neither case has Jenkins nor Gadot hidden their backgrounds as soldiers or daughters of soldiers. Hence Diana as a violent but, ultimately, radical pacifist is also absent in the film.

To be sure, these might be minor points even potentially sexist. Adam Driver, the star of the new *Star Wars* trilogy, who plays the villainous Kylo Ren, was a marine before becoming an actor. Many Hollywood directors from Robert Altman to Oliver Stone were war veterans and they often used their war experiences as the basis of their films. Still, several key distinctions are needed. For one, both Jenkins and Gadot *emphasized* their past within the military; in contrast, marketing for Star Wars *de-emphasized* Drivers' military career. Another is that while many Hollywood directors identify with the military and have served within it, some have been notable critics as is clear in the case of Stone criticizing military policies in *Salvador* (1986), *Platoon* (1986), and *Born on the Fourth of July* (1990). In contrast, the image of the military is fairly positive in *Wonder Woman* on the Allied side (U.S., UK, etc.). German militarism is criticized and framed as barbaric; in contrast, the American military and British military are only selectively criticized.

Militarism with Emotion: The Female Gaze Goes to War

Wonder Woman begins with a pro–American and pro-military view where the feminist values of Marston are strategically contained and only partially applied. *Wonder Woman* boasts not just Gadot but several key women in the narrative like British suffragist Etta (Lucy Davis) and Diana's mother Hippolyta (Connie Nielson). At the same time, the narrative has many roles for men, making sure men never feel excluded wholly from the narrative. Female beauty and power are valorized but war itself is not.

Jenkins, then, is situating *Wonder Woman* away from many war films. However, *Wonder Woman* shares many of the biases in the war-film genre. Let us use Stanley Kubrick's *Full Metal Jacket* as a contrastive case. Michael Klein in analyzing Stanley Kubrick's *Full Metal Jacket* notes that the film has contradictory messages. The U.S. military is shown to be brutal, fascistic, racist, and sexist. However, while Kubrick does clearly condemn parts of the indoctrination recruits undergo, the Kubrick film adopts a partially sympathetic view of how heroism is shown by U.S. military men (Jimenez). While the training of U.S. soldiers is shown to be brutal and imperialistic, Kubrick is not necessarily condemning such training as much as showing its awful necessity to survive warfare. The fact that *the majority* of those who suffered directly and indirectly from U.S. power were Vietnamese women, often in the form of rape, is deliberately suppressed. The genocide/gendercide committed by the U.S. military is slyly covered up (Jimenez).

In sharp contrast, at the beginning of the film, Diana sees how the Amazonian adult women train and are ready for combat, and she as a small girl imitates their movements. Though Jenkins does not denigrate Diana in the way Whedon does in the *Justice League* film, she does play down her goddess-status. Diana is made into a warrior woman who simply happens to have extraordinary strength. She is deliberately misled by her mother to think she has no brother.

Steve Trevor, an American pilot, lands on the island and tells Diana about the world war raging. Outraged, Diana leaves in defiance of her mother. In 1918 England, Diana as played by Gadot is put into a generic story (fish-out-of-water) to attract a mass audience. She has several comical and action episodes before she and Steve gather a multiracial and multicultural band of warriors to finish a secret spy mission.

Feminist critics were largely dismissive because *Wonder Woman* was turned into a sexually attractive body for the viewing audience. To be sure, there are many shots of Gadot's body in a sexually alluring manner as well as the Amazonians; these are embedded in the story. In contrast, when Chris Pines takes off his shirt, the shot seems to be a prime example of the female gaze.

Laura Mulvey in her essay on the male gaze assumed male power would structure scenes and imagery to favor how men viewed women in a subordinate fashion. Confirmation of the argument is easy to find in some cases. In Whedon's *Justice League*, the costumes of the Amazonian women were made more sexual and exposed more of their bodies than did *Wonder Woman* (Mitimore). Mulvey is drawing on the psychoanalytic tradition and assumes a binary notion of gender. While Jenkins does not contest too strongly the binary understanding of how the gaze operates, the scenes with Pine undressing show the gaze is not a monotonic power relationship. Although limited, female spectators can sometimes be allowed to gain entry and control how men are seen and represented.

Marston's version of Diana has her sexual attraction being strong enough that men want to reject violence. Jenkins does not take that direction. Instead as Freeman correctly notes, she frames Wonder Woman as a post–9/11 heroine and moves her story to World War I in a way that "can still be directly related to the attacks of 9/11 by offering a different tactic than retaliating with more violence" (Freeman 42).

Male violence—especially against women and children—is deliberately de-glorified. In his films, Kubrick adopts a stance of ironic detachment in presenting warfare and male violence (Webster 85). In contrast, Jenkins uses Wonder Woman as mythic figure to provide a message of attachment. Whereas Pine's Steve Trevor insists Wonder Woman ignore her feelings in order to complete their secret mission, Diana is unwilling to let her emotions be suppressed.

After, Trevor convinces her to disguise herself in wartime London and they gather a team together. The team, as is now a common cliché, is a multicultural multiracial band of comrades as in Spielberg's *Saving Private Ryan* and Stone's *Platoon*. The team finally composed, they set off on a secret mission. However, Diana is shocked at the atrocities she sees with people suffering. Diana is frustrated at being held back. Trevor tries to abstract himself from the evil being done to humans—notably, the camera frames the victims as mainly women and children. Trevor's concern is that the team "make our next position by sunset." Diana is stunned and asks: "How can you say that?"

> STEVE: This is No Man's Land! … No man can cross it, all right? This battalion has … barely gain[ed] an inch [in a year] … This is not something you can cross. …
> WW: So what? So we do nothing?
> STEVE: No, we are doing something. … We can't save everyone in this war. This is not what we came here to do.
> WW: No … but it's what I'm going to do.

It is at this point that Diana discards her disguise and reveals herself and enters the No Man's Land. Unlike a male soldier or spy, Diana as a woman is unwilling to shut off her feelings of empathy with those suffering. She must act, even if the reaction is not wise.

While Wonder Woman is able to make some headway, it is only by the team helping her that she passes the No Man's Land. Jenkins, then, is making a feminist argument but it is extremely moderate. Diana's logic is good, but even if she is as right as she is powerful, she needs to be strategic. If the men she worked with did help in firing weapons to give her some respite, then she might have been badly injured. As Panic argues: "What makes Wonder Woman such a powerful artifact is her connection to the viewers. Jenkins uses…. Diana as an artifact…. The use of love as Diana's core value makes her even more relatable and graspable to different generations of viewers" (11). What makes *Wonder Woman* challenging to the fascist bias in superheroes is how strongly love—and mercy—are at the core of title character (Miles 117). Whereas a Batman or Wolverine would save the civilians, they would also probably execute the Germans—and enjoy doing so. Wonder Woman does kill some German soldiers in the No Man's sequence. But she does not enjoy the use of violence. Her main concern is saving the women and children caught in the crossfire.

While critics almost universally applauded the power and energy of the scene, they seemed to miss the subtext that is not just a woman who stops the German soldiers but a woman leading men into battle. If the hero's journey in *Full Metal Jacket* and *Platoon* is about the glorification of one, individual, solitary great man, usually white and young, gaining knowledge and power, *Wonder Woman* is about a collectivity becoming self-conscious. Still,

Urick and Sprinkle in an essay on *Wonder Woman* point to dialogue to verify that Diana is not acting like the masculine hero taking all credit for himself. She says to her team: "We did this" (Urick and Sprinkle 5). She means that they as a team saved the civilians in no man's land.

Just as Joker and Chris must become disenchanted with their romantic notions of war, so, too, Wonder Woman has to awake from her naïve belief of why World War I began. Wonder Woman presumes Ares (David Thewliss) is behind World War I. However, she discovers that men are indeed responsible for the mass violence and killing Ares will not affect mankind's self-destructive tendencies. After being unmasked, Ares offers a woman for Diana to kill. The target is not sexism of course. Still Jenkins is making a critique of how film normalizes male violence.

It is interesting, too, that the final scenes of *Full Metal Jacket* and *Wonder Woman* parallel. A female antagonist is offered as a sacrificial lamb as the American soldiers fight a female Vietnamese sniper. After successfully killing a few men, the soldiers corner the sniper and proceed to kill her and symbolically become heroes. Scholars debate to what degree Kubrick is glorifying male violence but the visual symbolism is explicit. A peace sign is on Joker's jacket, which is present for most of the film before he kills the woman. After he kills the woman, the peace button is gone. Whether Joker has fully accepted the fascism of the U.S. military is unclear, but he has clearly moved beyond ironic detachment and agrees that some of the fascist masculinity in the U.S. military may be a necessary evil to survive war.

However, Wonder Woman does not make any such concession to male violence or fascism. Diana refuses Ares' offer of alliance and confronts Doctor Poison (Elena Anaya) but Diana does not kill her. This might be a substantial subversion of the genre. Instead Diana kills Ares yet rejects his nihilism. Still, she refuses to give up hope. She accepts Steve's sacrifice and the narrative flashes to the future with Diana looking at a photograph of her war-time comrades. In Kubrick, the woman as symbol and person is sacrificed. The hero's journey demands the feminine side (which the U.S. military demonizes as weak) has to be killed for hero's journey to be complete. As Luis M. Garcia-Mainar puts it: "In killing the most feminine aspects of the men's personalities … the male gains access to the woman precisely by killing the woman in himself" (qtd. in Webster 125).

However, Jenkins moves in two counter directions. First, she is not being as beholden to trying to legitimize a masculine myth as Kubrick does glorifying Nietzsche's Overman in *2001: A Space Odyssey* and thus distances herself from most Hollywood films where this is normal (Webster 44–45). Diana has a heroic journey, but several elements are missing. Diana has no mentor looking over her—no Obi Wan-Kenobi or even a female equivalent.[2] She also is not setting out to redeem society. Originally, this was her goal, but the end of her heroic journey is realizing the *impossibility* of redemption of humanity. Still, unlike Joker, Wonder Woman does not integrate herself into a larger militaristic collective unit.

Wonder Woman does not become cynical or jaded and adopt a form of nihilism like Batman, Wolverine, or Rorschach in *Watchmen*. Evil is fought by these male heroes for often selfish reasons; they adopt a survival-of-the-fittest ethos and choose to help innocent people by choice not duty. In contrast, Diana like an Arthurian knight reaffirms she does have an obligation to help others and will never fight simply to please herself or her subjective whims—as shown by her acceptance of Steve's sacrifice.

On the one hand, there is a bland anti-war message, but Jenkins as Freeman situates her film within the consensus of 9/11 cinema where terrorism is wrong and a violent response is justified. To be sure, Jenkins is careful not to invoke George Bush, Barack Obama, or the war on terror directly or implicitly. By cleverly situating the film a century ago, the subtext can be legitimately said to be non-existent as the 9/11 attacks did not happen. Hence any insinuation that the American military is impure is avoided.

Nevertheless, where *Wonder Woman* differs is that the character is not just violent but also has a message of love. Some might point to Buffy Summers, created by Joss Whedon, as a precursor to Diana. Nonetheless, several key differences crop up. While even canonical heroes like Marvel's Captain Mar-Vel and DC's Superman have died in the comics as characters, Buffy has died *three times* in her television series. Wonder Woman, by contrast, has never died either as a comic book character or in film. Buffy is powerful, but her power levels are far below Diana's. Moreover, the anti-war fairytale message is mixed with Buffy's willingness to endanger innocent lives to stop an enemy whether Glory, the First, or Adam and sacrifice even fellow Slayers like Faith and the "potentials." In contrast, Diana never forces anyone to give up their life. Steve's sacrifice is wholly voluntary.

Further, if mercy is a key virtue in *Wonder Woman*, Buffy is willing to exceed several ethical norms to exact revenge. In an extremely controversial storyline, a rogue slayer, Faith, whom Buffy successfully defeats and renders comatose, is able to revive herself and seek revenge. She hunts down Buffy, switches bodies with her, and humiliates her sexually. Buffy manages to reverse the body-switch. Faith flees to Los Angeles and attempts to kill Buffy's ex-lover/vampire Angel but, ultimately, wants Angel to kill her. Angel refuses and seeks to rehabilitate her. Buffy intervenes and mocks Angel's naïveté saying: "she tried to kill you." He acknowledges "that's true."

> BUFFY: So you decided to punish her with a severe cuddling.
> ANGEL: Is that why you're here? To punish her?
> BUFFY: I was worried about you ["Sanctuary"].[3]

The storyline is controversial because Buffy seems to be acting extremely out of character. Normally, humans including Faith are off-limits. However, Buffy lies to Angel. As she admits off-handedly in the conclusion of the episode she did come to LA to kill Faith, revealing that her earlier claim that she only wanted Faith imprisoned was a lie.

> BUFFY: ... Do you have any—idea what it was like for me to see you with her? ...
> ANGEL: Buffy, this wasn't about you! ...
> BUFFY: I came here because you were in danger.
> ANGEL: I'm in danger every day. ... You were looking for vengeance.
> BUFFY: *I have a right to it* ["Sanctuary," emphasis added].

The concluding dialogue rejects mercy as even a plausible option. Buffy has the right to kill anyone even a woman if that person sexually humiliates her.

In sharp contrast, Wonder Woman rejects full-heartedly even the supposition Diana because of her power has the right to murder humans. Only under extreme circumstances would she do that. Offered a parallel opportunity to exact vengeance, Diana refuses and spares Doctor Poison. If Angel had not intervened, Buffy would as she promises have killed Faith without hesitation. This theme of mercy is thus strong exceptional in *Wonder Woman* but lacking in many male-driven superhero films and even television shows like *Buffy*, starring pro-female heroines.

Vengeance is not Diana's goal as much as empathy. Making mercy a female trait, Jenkins is subverting how Zack Snyder tried to orchestrate the new origins of Superman and Batman in his films *Man of Steel* and *Batman v Superman*. In Snyder's vision, Superman as Clark Kent and Kal-El learns who he is from his two fathers, Jor-El and Jonathan Kent.

While Superman's human mother, Martha (Diane Lane), plays some role, it is Jonathan Kent who helps shape Superman. Superman becomes a man in *Man of Steel* through his father, Jonathan (Kevin Costner), teaching him certain values. When Superman as a teenager saves a school bus that falls into a pit of water, his father questions him.

While Superman did something virtuous, doing so risked exposing his identity and thus crippling how he might help others in the future. The beginning scenes of *Man of Steel* show him selflessly helping others but notably as an anonymous Christ-like figure. In another flashback to his teenage years, Superman sees a tornado approach. Jonathan rushes to help others. Superman is set to use super-speed to save his father, but Jonathan raises his hand and signals for him to let him die so that his identity remains secret. Superman is haunted by obeying his father and *Batman v Superman* has him imagine his human father as a ghost speaking to him.

Several things are noticeable through these framing devices. One is the assumption by Snyder that the rituals to become an American male are appropriately bloody and Christian. To gain access to such power means some sacrifice, usually involving death, is needed. Joss Whedon's version of Superman in *Justice League* (2017) as mythic being is only superficially lighter than the Snyder version—the film begins with him joking with several children about super powers, hope, and hippopotamuses. However, after this, Steppenwolf, a denizen of a hellish planet, has come to Earth to harness the power of several boxes.

Using Para-demonic troops, Steppenwolf terrorizes Earth until Batman gathers heroes including Diana and resurrects Superman to defeat Steppenwolf. However, in the climactic battle, Batman is willing to sacrifice himself. Batman is stopped but the assumption in *MOS, BVS,* and *Justice League* despite different directors is that the male sacrificing his body to the larger good is just assumed to be virtuous and legitimate (Klein; Webster). No alternative vision is allowed in these films. *Wonder Woman* does offer a slight alternative where sacrifice is allowed (but only if it is voluntary) and the end is not to continue to glorify male violence but feminine mercy and forgiveness.

Conclusion

Jenkins's *Wonder Woman* is a commentary on female mythology and the war genre in film. While Jenkins does give into many key clichés of the genre, she resists the standard stance seen in *Full Metal Jacket* or many other war films where the hero embraces death and sacrifice as ultimate good. In contrast, in *Wonder Woman* the highest goal of the hero is love and love is given to even one's enemies. This message puts Wonder Woman as myth and icon at odds with not just fascist-like heroes like Rorschach but even feminist heroines like Buffy.

However, this praise for Jenkins has to be tempered with the reality that the film is dedicated to her soldier-father. While warfare in the abstract is condemned harshly in *Wonder Woman* it also situated in a supposedly apolitical past. Jenkins is careful to condemn masculine violence in a broad way but slyly does not comment on Vietnam or Iraq or Israel's military dominance in the Middle East. Hence the pro–American nationalist subtext of *Wonder Woman* co-exists uneasily with the liberal message of mercy before vengeance. The two can meld but only if this moderate liberal stance is taken as the only stance possible and thus opposes feminist philosophers who question it (Okin).

However, this verdict about the film's conservatism should be qualified as the analysis has focused solely on one film and Jenkins is as of this writing is finishing her work on *Wonder Woman: 1984*. It will be necessary to compare and contrast Wonder Woman as a text to the sequel to see if Jenkins's moderate condemnation of male violence coupled with subtle praise of military prowess by America and her allies is a one-time ideological affair or part of a more disturbing pattern to try to militarize feminism. In *Wonder Woman*, to her credit, Jenkins does try to popularize mercy over vengeance as a cinematically powerful motif. The slight move away from the fascist male hero as the normal standard for heroism in *Wonder Woman* is worth noting and applauding but it is not a full-throated rejection of fascism or imperialism as much as an easy middling point between pacifism and complete cultural conformity to statist violence.

NOTES

1. As of this writing *Aquaman* (2018) has exceeded *Wonder Woman*'s profitability as a superhero film. But when *Wonder Woman* is classified as a female-directed film, it remains an unprecedented success.
2. It might be argued Robin Wright as Antiope fulfills that role in the film. However, the actual scenes between her and Wonder Woman are rather short. It might be that cut scenes make this relationship deeper.
3. While Tim Minear is credited as writer of the script, it is well-known Joss Whedon wrote all of Buffy's dialogue for this episode.

WORKS CITED

Batman v Superman. Directed by Zack Snyder, performances by Henry Cavill, Gal Gadot, and Ben Affleck, Warner Bros, 2015.
Campbell, Lori. "Introduction." *A Quest of Her Own: Essays on the Female Hero in Modern Fantasy*, edited by Lori Campbell. McFarland, 2014, pp. 4–14. Print.
Cocca, Carolyn. *Superwomen: Gender, Power, and Representation*. Bloomsbury, 2016. Print.
Freeman, Katherine. "The Feminist Superheroine: A Critical Evaluation of Patty Jenkins' *Wonder Woman*." MA Thesis, Sam Houston State University, May 2018. Print.
Graham, Ruth. "Why So Many People Care That Wonder Woman Is Israeli," *Slate*, 1 June 2017. www.slate.com/blogs/xx_factor/2017/06/01/why_so_many_people_care_that_wonder_woman_is_israeli.html. *Accessed 10 October 2018.* Web.
Jimenez, Christian. "Filming the Unspeakable? Patriarchy and Cinematic Resistance in Depicting the Vietnamese and Native American Holocausts." Unpublished Conference Paper. New Brunswick, Rutgers, February 19, 2014.
Justice League. Directed by Joss Whedon/Zack Snyder, performances by Henry Cavill, Gal Gadot, and Ben Affleck, Warner Bros, 2017. Film.
Klein, Michael. "Historical Memory, Film, and the Vietnam Era." *From Hanoi to Hollywood: Vietnam in American Film*, edited by Linda Dittmar and Gene Michaud. Rutgers University Press, 1990, pp. 19–40. Print.
Man of Steel. Directed by Joss Whedon/Zack Snyder, performances by Henry Cavill, Michael Shannon, Russell Crowe, and Kevin Costner. Warner Bros, 2013.
Martins, Ana. "Jenkins, Patty (1971-)." *Hollywood Heroines: The Most Influential Women in Film History*, edited by Laura L.S. Bauer. ABC-CLIO, 2018, pp. 116–117. Print.
Miles, Johnny. *Superheroes and Their Ancient Jewish Parallels: A Comparative Study*. McFarland, 2018. Print.
Mitimore, Jon. "Feminists Are Furious with How *Justice League* Changed the Amazonian Costumes. There's Just One Problem." *Intellectual Takeout*, 16 November 2017, www.intellectualtakeout.org/article/feminists-arefurious-how-justice-league-changed-amazonian-costumes-theres-just-oneproblem. Accessed 10 October 2018. Web.
Okin, Susan Moller. *Justice, Gender, and the Family*. Basic Books, 1989. Print.
Panic-Cidic, Natali. "Relations in Media—*Construction of Identity in Patty Jenkins' Wonder Woman (2017)*." Heinrich Heine Universitat Dusseldorf, 2017. Print.

Pender, Patricia. "'I'm Buffy and you're…. history': The Postmodern Politics of Buffy the Vampire Slayer." *Fighting the Forces: What's at Stake in Buffy the Vampire Slayer*, edited by Rhonda Wilcox and David Lavery. Rowman and Littlefield, 2002, pp. 35–44. Print.

"Sanctuary." *Angel: The Series*, WB Network. 2 May 2000. Television.

Seiler, Rachel E. "Re-Imagining the Myth of Demeter and Persephone: Exploration of the Constructs of Marriage and Nuclear Family." Presented at the Third North American Conference on Spirituality and Social Work. Unpublished Conference Paper. 2008. Print.

Sherman, Jill. *Gal Gadot: Soldier, Model, Wonder Woman*. Lerner, 2018. Print.

Sunderraman, Shruti. "How Justice League Panders to Male Gaze with Overt Sexualisation of Wonder Woman." *The Ladies Finger*, 21 November 2017, www.firstpost.com/entertainment/how-justice-league-panders-to-male-gaze-with-overt-sexualisation-of-wonder-woman-4220451.html. Accessed 10 October 2018.

Ullrich, Volker. *Hitler, Ascent: 1889–1939*. Translated by Jefferson Chase. Viking, 2017.

Urick, Michael, and Therese Sprinkle. "Teaching Leadership: Using *Wonder Woman* to Highlight the Importance of Gender Diversity." *Management Teaching Review* vol. 0, no. 0, 2018, pp. 1–9. Print.

Wagner, Geoffrey. *The Novel and the Cinema*. Farleigh Dickinson University Press, 1975. Print.

Webster, Patrick. *Love and Death in Kubrick*. McFarland, 2011. Print.

Wonder Woman. Directed by Patty Jenkins, performances by Gal Gadot, Robin Wright, and Chris Pine, Warner Bros, 2017.

Zipes, Jack. "Beyond Disney in the Twenty-First Century: Changing Aspects of Fairy Tale Films in the American Film Industry." *Fairy Tale Films Beyond Disney: International Perspectives*, edited by Jack Zipes, Pauline Greenhill, and Kendra Magnus-Johnston. Routledge, 2016, pp. 278–294. Print.

Black Panther and *Wonder Woman*

A Study in Feminist Representation

SHOSHANA KESSOCK

Director Patty Jenkins did a phenomenal job telling Diana's story on the big screen. However, there has always been a part of the Wonder Woman story that rubbed me the wrong way. As a little girl, when I saw misogyny growing up in the world around me, I longed for a place where I could escape, a society of women who were not only strong but intelligent, thoughtful, creative, and loving. Themyscira truly was Paradise Island, where a woman could be everything she ever imagined, without the influence of patriarchy on her growth.

Still, now, as a grown woman, I can see a fundamental flaw in this idea. Though the thought of a world without men is seductive when faced with the dangers of toxic masculinity on all society, removing one's self from "man's world" to only focus on a woman-based culture devoid of men is to ignore a larger part of society. Toxic masculinity, in fact, affects men in a "man's world" just as painfully as it does women, if only in other ways. To ignore those effects and abandon the rest of the world to its own devices is to truly ignore the promise of feminism's positive impact on the world. By separating themselves from men, the Amazons evolved into a utopian society to the detriment of the rest of the world. Their influence could have changed history if only they'd emerged from their hiding sooner.

After thinking this, I saw an image pop up online asking why more white women weren't speaking up about the feminism in *Black Panther* when so many are touting *Wonder Woman* as such a feminist film. Indeed, *Black Panther* is a *more feminist* film than *Wonder Woman*. And I'm going to show you how.

Feminism as an Integrated Force

Though Wakanda is an isolationist society much like Themyscira in regard to the rest of the world (a subject for much debate elsewhere and addressed directly in the *Black Panther* film), it is also a well-balanced, nearly utopian society, growing technologically and societally with every passing generation while still holding onto its ancient traditions. Still, unlike other societies, Wakanda does not focus on patriarchal ideology, despite its male-dominated leadership Instead, Wakanda has fully integrated the idea of women as equals, creating a society where women are not only respected but accepted without surprise when in positions of power, from at the Tribal Council to within the king's family.

An early scene with Princess Shuri (Letitia Wright) emphasizes this egalitarian perspective and her potential for even more. During her brother's ascension ceremony, she appears to begin to question T'Challa's claim to the throne and T'Challa (Chadwick Boseman) responds with a mix of incredulity and fear. She quickly reveals she was kidding, adding in a moment that undercuts the serious coronation, "This corset is really uncomfortable, so can we all wrap this up and go home?" Still, comic book fans realize that in the arc The Deadlier of the Species, Shuri actually gets the throne. Reginald Hudlin, the writer of the series from 2005 to 2009, said he first created Shuri because, "I wanted girls who read the book to feel as empowered as boys. So, I wanted her to be smart and tough and brave and everything you think of as a Black Panther, so that eventually she would be a Black Panther as well" (Tillet). Critic Salamishah Tillet explains:

> [Writer director Ryan] Coogler expands Hudlin's vision by giving us a Shuri who grows up without being limited by white supremacy and the male gaze. Not circumscribed by the shadow of slavery and colonialism, we are able to witness Shuri come of age—alongside boys and surrounded by men—with the utmost sense of safety, visibility and autonomy. And in this era of #MeToo, as women—ranging from Hollywood actresses to hotel workers all over the country—demand equal pay, equal protection and workplaces, classrooms, and homes free of sexual violence and harassment, the gender equality of Wakanda feels both utopian and urgent.

There are powerful examples of this integration all across the film. Shuri is the princess of Wakanda and yet, as a super genius, serves as the driving force behind Wakanda's technological evolution. Her supersuit gives Black Panther much of his power, and her augmented car—with her at the wheel—is even better. She invented the vibranium-transporting trains with their sonic stabilizers but also takes a moment to offer her brother the "sneakers" she has made. Her actress told *Vogue*: "I hope it can spark someone to say, 'I'm not a superhero, but I can be a scientist or build the next spaceship, like Shuri'" (Hickey). Walt Hickey writes in his essay, "*Black Panther* Is Groundbreaking, But It's Shuri Who Could Change the World" that she's the funniest character onscreen and yet offers much more:

> The volume of evidence shows that when audiences see on-screen representations of themselves, particularly aspirational ones, that experience can fundamentally change how they perceive their own place in the world. Black people have been historically underrepresented on screen, and black women in strong roles even more so. Shuri provides a science-y role model for black women, a group distinctly underrepresented in STEM fields.

Similarly, Okoye (Danae Gurira) is the leader of the Dora Milaje, a fighting force of women drawn from every tribe of Wakanda to be its most dangerous protectors. As the bodyguards of the royal family, the Dora Milaje are never questioned as warriors but instead accepted not only as equals but as superiors in combat. Even King T'Challa knows he is meant to be deferential in many ways to Okoye, who has more experience as a warrior and general than he does. Let me say that a little louder: *never once does the king of the sovereign, advanced nation of Wakanda speak down to or diminish the power of the women warriors and creators all around him.* He humbly recognizes women as equals, worthy of respect as a matter of common course.

> One especially striking scene occurs when Nakia [Lupita Nyong'o] and Okoye chase the villain Ulysses Klaue on the streets of South Korea in order to retrieve stolen vibranium, Wakanda's unique mineral with energy-manipulating qualities. Without hesitation, they, in haute couture dresses and stiletto heels, run out of the Seoul nightclub without T'Challa. "He'll catch up," a defiant Nakia says, providing a glimpse into another theme running throughout the movie: it is clear that T'Challa as King and Black Panther cannot live without these women; however, we are left wondering why they are not in charge in the first place [Tillet].

Okoye and her warriors stand out for their choices and independence even as they transcend their origin. In fact, the film makes an interesting adjustment to the story of the Dora Milaje that sets it apart from the comic book version. In the comics, the Dora Milaje are indeed chosen to become elite warriors to protect T'Challa and the royal family. However, they are also meant to be taken from every tribe so eventually T'Challa will choose a bride from one of their ranks. This idea was stripped from the film, a choice that mirrors a more progressive ideology being embraced by the film's creators. The Dora Milaje were always badasses, but they've now become more than just badass prospective consorts as they were originally written. What is more, Okoye has a male lover and gets a plot arc when she chooses Wakanda over him, and yet stops his charging rhinoceros with their relationship (as it already feels affection for her), rather than force of arms. Gurira said of her character, "What I thought was really interesting was the idea of when someone has the responsibility of the longevity and the thriving of a nation on their shoulders…. The idea of protecting the leadership of this nation, the sovereignty of this nation, even if you don't like what's happening" (Thomas).

Never is T'Challa's acceptance of the influence of women more apparent than in his relationship with his ultimate spy, Nakia. Nakia left Wakanda to embed herself in other societies for the purpose of saving people (especially women) endangered in the turbulent outside world, flying directly in the face of Wakandan tradition and T'Challa's own interests. Before the film's beginning, T'Challa sought out Nakia as a love interest and yet respected her choice to leave, even when he disagreed. When he finds her once again at the beginning of the film, he is struck nearly dumb at the sight of her, a king lost for a moment in the sight of the woman he obviously still cares about, much to Okoye's snarky delight. Still, with every interaction between Nakia and T'Challa, we see a man not only besotted with the spymistress, but a man who does not treat her as a sexual or romantic object. Instead, he values her experience, her opinion, and her power, accepting her choices without real complaint and listening to her advice so much she influences his entire foreign policy. She insists, "Wakanda is strong enough to help others and protect ourselves at the same time," and by the film's end, he has come around to her thinking. This theme of inclusion is central to T'Challa's own arc, reaching outside his kingdom through his women's influence. "*Black Panther* is about a highly advanced African kingdom, yes, but its core theme is Pan-Africanism, a belief that no matter how seemingly distant black people's lives and struggles are from each other, we are in a sense 'cousins' who bear a responsibility to help one another escape oppression" (Serwer). From Queen Ramonda (played by the unbelievable Angela Bassett) to every one of the Dora Milaje, from Okoye and Nakia and Shuri and the councilwomen who serve as representatives of their tribes, the powerful leading women of the *Black Panther* film are not presented to the audience as exceptions to the rule in Wakanda. Instead, they stand as examples of how Wakanda has evolved as a society which allows women to flourish to their full potential equal to men in all ways, with no question or compromise. In Wakanda, women and men live lives of nearly unvarying potential with no need to withdraw or hide. But beyond their own integration and acceptance in society, the women of Wakanda seem to have brought a very important influence as well on the men around them.

The Divestiture of Toxic Masculinity *in* Black Panther

When watching *Wonder Woman*, the message of Diana's journey into "man's world" is hammered home over and over. As representative and in fact the idealization of all the Amazons' beliefs, Diana (Gal Gadot) is acting as an ambassador from her world of women's idyllic perfection to the patriarchal outside world. She is, as she states, becoming "a bridge to the world of men" so as to bring the Amazon's message of peace and understanding to a world ripped apart by strife. She wants to present the idea of feminine equality to the rest of the world, where it has been so long repressed, suppressed or destroyed in so many cultures. She is the exceptional woman, out to influence the men around her with her clarion call of justice, truth, and love. While this is a beautiful idea, a truly feminist ideology in many ways, it rings a little hollow when one looks at Diana as the exceptional outsider.

Diana enters the world outside an innocent, ready to bring her ideas to someone else's culture without any idea of their real history, their issues, or the ingrained ideas she'll be facing. "One of the great things that came with [Director] Patty [Jenkins] was this great use of Diana's naiveté from living such a sheltered life on Themyscira," producer Charles Roven notes. "So even though she ends up [...] becoming a fighter, she's still pretty sheltered because she's never been off the island. So she's got no life experience really" (Chitwood). She believes she can change men's minds just by bringing them a better way from the outside of their society, from a clearly "superior" place. Roven adds, "Her mother was a hero, her aunt was a hero, and she felt it was the destiny of herself and the other Amazons to be heroic, and so she wanted to fulfill that destiny from the very beginning, from the time that she was a little girl. That was always there, how she was gonna go about doing it" (Chitwood). In a strange way, she is a cultural tourist, if a well-meaning one, presenting her feminism into a world which is in many ways unprepared for a radical cultural shift and unwilling to change so quickly just because they're told about "superior" feminist ideology from an outsider. It's for that reason Diana struggles so hard to influence "man's world"—she is not a part of it, but an alien influence presenting a new form of thinking to a world with thousands of years of ingrained thinking to undo.

It's no wonder then that the men around Diana remain, in large part, still entrenched in their toxic masculine ideas. Though Wonder Woman earns the respect of many of her male colleagues both in the comics and in the recent film, her ideas are still considered foreign to most men around her. In fact, most do not divest themselves of their ideology to embrace a way of living outside the influence of toxic masculinity. They instead bend to Diana's ideas only when they are the most needed, flexing back to their ingrained patriarchal thinking often right after she's not around. Steve Trevor is an example, as in the film he spends the entire time attempting to influence Diana to his way of thinking instead of the other way around. At the front, he tells her over and over, "There is nothing you can do about it, Diana" and

"This is No Man's Land! Diana! Means no man can cross it, all right? ... This is not something you can cross" until she rebels in spectacular fashion and runs across No Man's Land, costume gleaming. Following this, and failing to learn a lesson, Steve forbids her from infiltrating German High Command and then dismisses her belief that Ares is among them. With all this, he's using his patriarchal thinking to drag her halfway across Europe and blocking her action with what is clearly his male privilege—a male privilege which is obviously lacking in Wakanda.

From the very beginning of the *Black Panther* film, a strange vibe appears in Chadwick Boseman's portrayal of King T'Challa. While T'Challa is the royal leader of his country and therefore, presumably, the representation of the pinnacle of its masculine representation in the narrative, he doesn't exude many of the typical traits of a film's leading male character. T'Challa is both powerful and sensitive, thoughtful and respectful. He is from the beginning willing to not only express his emotions in front of others but especially to and in front of women, who surround him as his closest family and advisors. T'Challa never disrespects or tries to strong-arm the women around him, even when he disagrees with their choices, but praises and welcomes their input, agreeing to disagree and offering support where he can.

T'Challa also has powerful emotional connections to the men around him, including Zuri the priest and especially his father, the late King T'Chaka. When he is put into the trance during his test to assume the throne, he speaks to his father and falls crying against his side, showing a level of emotion often considered anathema to a male protagonist. He doesn't brood but instead shows his inner conflicts over his right to be king with quiet consideration and a willingness to take criticism and advice without anger or retaliation. He, to be plain, showcases all the hallmarks of a male protagonist stripped of the signposts of toxic masculinity influence, as do the other male characters in Wakanda.

> Unlike Tony Stark, Thor, Bruce Banner, Peter Quill, Steven Strange, or many of the other male heroes the MCU has introduced thus far, T'Challa is shown to be a man who is neither afraid nor embarrassed to not only have emotions, but also to display them. Whether greeting his mother or his good friend W'Kabi (Daniel Kaluuya), he does not shy away from physical or verbal displays of affection. When emotionally charged interactions with the people he cares for do occur, he does not feel compelled to undercut these moments through the use of sarcasm or witty barbs, a strategy so common among the MCU's other heroes that it has practically become a calling card of the MCU brand. When he requires saving from a woman, there is neither undue hesitation in asking for help nor accepting it, whether that be from his fearsome bodyguard Okoye (Danai Gurira) or Shuri, because he knows better than to believe there is any shame in it, or that requiring a woman's help makes him any less of a man [Wardlow].

With T'Challa as the pinnacle example of Wakanda and the other male characters expressing similar emotional signs during the film, we can then surmise T'Challa is not the exception to the rule but instead a typical example of how Wakanda has evolved as a more emotionally open society, stripped of toxic masculine influences. That, matched with the equal treatment of women, suggests that the cultural acceptance of those women have helped Wakanda evolve as a place where patriarchal influences did not rise up to quash men's emotional expression and their chances to grow outside of westernized masculine archetypes. "He is generally shown to have a large number of meaningful relationships with women—all based on mutual respect, trust, and admiration—that is far beyond anything audiences have seen from any MCU superhero before him. More than once, T'Challa is shown to be in situations where he is outnumbered by women, and at no point does he make any sort of quip about it or give any indication of discomfort, because it is clear that it is, for him, a perfectly normal, everyday situation," Ciara Wardlow notes in "How T'Challa Avoids Toxic Masculinity." Wakandan men are not bound by the western idea of what it is to be a "man" but have grown instead with the comfortable acceptance of what western culture might see as "feminine" behavior. It is the influence of Wakandan women as equals that have brought a truly feminist idea forward: the defeat of toxic masculinity not only for the damage it does to women but the damage it brings to men as well.

Never is the Wakandan ideal of the sensitive, more "feminized" man so contrasted as when looking at the villain Killmonger (Michael B. Jordan). Left out in the outside world to grow up in a dangerous life, Killmonger does not have the influence of Wakanda's more sensitive society to smooth down his rough edges. He does not live in a place where his rage over his father's death might have been cooled or at least channeled in a different way. Instead, Killmonger represents the harsh, toxic masculinity of the outside world, where his somewhat thoughtful (and even partially correct) ideas about the unfairness of Wakanda's isolationist policies are twisted into hateful, angry actions. "You want to see us become just like the people you hate so much," T'Challa tells Killmonger during their climactic battle. "I learn from my enemies," Killmonger retorts. "You have become them," T'Challa responds.

Like Magneto, another comic-book character who is a creation of historical trauma— the Holocaust instead of the Middle Passage—Killmonger's goal is world domination. "The sun will never set on the Wakandan empire," Killmonger declares, echoing an old saying about the British Empire, to drive the point home as clearly as possible. He sees no future beyond his own reign; he burns the magic herbs Wakandan monarchs use to gain their powers because he does not even intend to have an heir [Serwer].

Killmonger shows all the brash hallmarks of a man trapping his pain away in rage, using violence to solve his problems rather than embracing his emotions to give way to catharsis and resolution. His disconnection to women is also apparent in the film, as he is followed by a woman of color who barely has any speaking lines or so much as a name (I had to look it up, it's Linda). In every scene, this woman is treated as the token girlfriend/henchwoman, and then killed by Killmonger when Ulysses Klaue uses her as a hostage. She is the ultimate expression of Killmonger's embroilment in the toxic masculine culture. Even Killmonger's influence on others brings patriarchal influence and damage to Wakandan culture, as he twists Okoye's beloved W'Kabi away from his loyalty to T'Challa and turns his entire tribe against the throne with promises of revenge and violence.

Still, even in Killmonger's scenes, we see a spark of that Wakandan emotional connection, when he goes into the trance and speaks once more to his father. Killmonger's father N'Jobu clearly expresses the same emotional complexity and sensitivity showcased by other Wakandan men when he tries to connect to his son, but despairs at the rage and closed-off pain he sees in the man his son has become. He says, "I gave you a key hoping that you might see it someday. Yes. The sunsets there are the most beautiful in the world. But I fear you still may not be welcome....They will say you are lost." Killmonger rejects his father's worry and, indeed, his entire philosophy, even as the film emphasizes how his vision is terribly limited. "When T'Challa goes to the spirit world, he sees his ancestors. When Killmonger goes, in one of the most moving scenes in the film, he sees only his father; the rest of his ancestors have been lost to The Void. He is alone in a way T'Challa can never comprehend. So like his father N'Jobu, Killmonger is radicalized" (Serwer) It's only through T'Challa's attempts to reconcile with Killmonger that we see a little of the emotional sensitivity of Wakanda rubbing off on the furious villain. Still, the outside world has trapped Killmonger so badly into the patriarchal cycle that, even in his end when T'Challa offers him peace and solace in his final moments, he is unable to be anything but angry in his own sorrow.

If we step away from speaking about men again for a minute, we can look at the women of Wakanda in the *Black Panther* film for what they are: exceptional without being exceptional at all.

The Non-Exceptional Exceptional Woman

As stated above, Wonder Woman is the exceptional woman in a world of men, the ambassador and outsider who shirks her own society's xenophobic tendencies to save the outside world from itself. She is the one in a thousand, one in a million, the beautiful and infinitely powerful immortal goddess on earth who brings her special brand of love and ass-kicking to both the battlefield and her personal relationships. When one reads her comics and watches the film, the narrative makes one thing clear: there is no one truly like Diana, and she is the ultimate of her kind. Further, when we look at her sister Amazons, they all are expressed with similar, if less powerful, expressions of the same archetype of idealized feminism and utopian female ideology. Together, they are an often-uniform face of the Exceptional Feminist, set apart and ready to impress with their evolved ideas.

By contrast, the powerful women of Wakanda are not only exceptional in their power but nuanced in their presentation in the narrative. Their equality and power are not packed into a single package of ass-kicking and peace and love, but instead, each woman is her own nuanced expression of a fully realized woman.

Where Shuri is brash and feisty and in many ways a typical teenager, her mother is regal and loving, the complicated mother figure transitioning from a queen into the queen mother she has become. Though Okoye and Nakia are both ass-kicking women who take to the streets at T'Challa's side, both are very different women with their own thoughts, ideals, skill sets, and struggles. Okoye spends the film trying to decide where her loyalties lie, to the throne or to what is right, while Nakia follows her heart no matter the danger to her position in Wakandan society. This clash allows the women to speak together understandingly and decide the country's fate together: "Their conversation plays like an AP Bechdel Test; even as Wakanda falls, these two women are able to engage in passionate, intelligent debate that involves men but is actually about the women themselves, and actually speaks not only to who they are, but what they want their country to be" (Thomas).

After Killmonger has taken over, Nakia says, "You are the greatest warrior Wakanda has. Help me overthrow him before he becomes too strong,"

"Overthrow?" Okoye replies. "I'm not a spy who can come and go as they so please. I am loyal to that throne, no matter who sits upon it." Nakia insists she isn't doing this for the man she loves. "Then you serve your country," Okoye says.

Nakia answers, "No, I *save* my country" and steals the fruit that is Wakanda's legacy and can anoint one more king who will respect Wakandan tradition. With this, she ensures her society's future. Each woman lives her own stories as complex as any male protagonist, weaving narratives around that of T'Challa and his conflict with Killmonger and yet transcending their war. "It is nothing short of revolutionary that these two female characters get to state their beliefs, fight for their beliefs, and hold those beliefs throughout the film, without question and without hesitation. Okoye and Nakia not only provide a model for political discourse and disagreement, but also a model for cinematic representation. These women are crucial to the structure of the film and to how the film's central ideas play out" (Thomas).

In *Black Panther,* the women of Wakanda are complicated and different from one another, telling the story of the different archetypes women can represent, while in fact evolving those archetypes beyond to represent the complexity of real women. They are not the tropes we so usually accept from the Girlfriend, the Woman Warrior, the Mother, or the Sister. They are women all their own, and they are brilliant.

In Conclusion

While Wonder Woman brings us a kind of exceptionalist feminism, *Black Panther* brings us a vision of what a truly gender-equal society can accomplish, breaking down the barriers of gender stereotypes to present opportunity for anyone to be anything they wish in their full complexity and freedom of choice.

Thankfully, the world of comics and film has room for both kinds of feminist representation. In fact, it'd be inspiring to see multiple complex versions of feminist representation flood media so we could have more women-empowering films and television and books along with countless conversations and essays to foster more discussion.

In the meantime, *Black Panther* presents us with a more hopeful vision of feminism, a world where men and women can embrace what they wish without persecution or protestation. We could all use a little more of that kind of feminist representation in our lives.

WORKS CITED

Black Panther. Directed by Ryan Coogler, Disney, 2018.
Chitwood, Adam. "*Wonder Woman* Producer Charles Roven on the Many Writers That Tried to Tackle the Script." *Collider,* 1 June 2017. http://collider.com/wonder-woman-script-changes-writers-charles-roven.
Hickey, Walt. "*Black Panther* Is Groundbreaking, but It's Shuri Who Could Change the World." *FiveThirtyEight,* 16 February 2018. https://fivethirtyeight.com/features/black-panther-is-groundbreaking-but-its-shuri-who-could-change-the-world.
Serwer, Andy. "The Tragedy of Erik Killmonger." *The Atlantic,* 21 February 2018. https://www.theatlantic.com/entertainment/archive/2018/02/black-panther-erik-killmonger/553805.
Thomas, R. Eric. "The Most Important Debate in *Black Panther* Is, Unsurprisingly, Between Two Women." *Elle,* 26 February 2018. https://www.elle.com/culture/movies-tv/a18370982/black-panther-okoye-nakia-debate.
Tillet, Salamishah. "*Black Panther:* Why Not Queen Shuri? (Guest Column)." *Hollywood Reporter,* 19 February 2018. https://www.hollywoodreporter.com/heat-vision/black-panther-why-not-queen-shuri-guest-column-1086012.
Wardlow, Ciara. "*Black Panther:* How T'Challa Avoids Toxic Masculinity." *Hollywood Reporter,* 19 February 2018. https://www.hollywoodreporter.com/heat-vision/black-panther-how-tchalla-avoids-toxic-masculinity-1085741.
Wonder Woman. Directed by Patty Jenkins. DC Entertainment, 2017.

About the Contributors

Lisann **Anders** is a research and teaching assistant and Ph.D. candidate at the University of Zurich, Switzerland. She holds an MA in screenwriting from the National University of Galway, Ireland, and an MA in English literature and linguistics from the University of Zurich. Her main field of research is the imagination of violence in the city space of American postmodern fiction.

Aamir **Aziz** has a Ph.D. in English literature from the LUCAS Institute, Leiden University, The Netherlands. He is an assistant professor of English literature at the University of the Punjab, Lahore, Pakistan. His research has appeared in *New Theatre Quarterly* (2016), *American Book Review* (2017), *English Studies* (2018), and *The Journal of South Texas English Studies* (2018).

Nisarga **Bhattacharjee** is a lecturer at Seth Anandram Jaipuria College (Day) and at Acharya Prafulla Chadnra College in West Bengal, India. He has a master's degree and M. Phil. in English from the University of Calcutta. He is the author of several journal articles and books, including "Modernism, Personal Myths and the Condition for Poetry" and "Heaney's Spiritual Archaeology and the Poetic Promise of Political Memory."

Alexis **Brooks de Vita**, Ph.D., analyzes African, diaspora, women's, and supernatural literatures, games and film. She is the author of *Mythatypes: Signatures and Signs of African/Diaspora and Black Goddesses*, the translation *Dante's Inferno: A Wanderer in Hell*, and several novels. She is also a contributing editor of *Tales in Firelight and Shadow* and *Love and Darker Passions*.

Ananya **Chatterjee** is a lecturer of English at JIS University, Agarpara, India. She is a Ph.D. research scholar at Techno India University, Kolkata. She has contributed research articles to several books and journals, including "Death Matrix, Thanatopolitics and Gendered Expressions of 'Death' in J.M. Synge's *Riders to the Sea*" and "Heaney's Spiritual Archaeology and the Poetic Promise of Political Memory."

Valerie Estelle **Frankel** is the author of more than 60 books on popular culture. Many of her McFarland books focus on women's roles in fiction, from her heroine's journey guides *From Girl to Goddess* and *Buffy and the Heroine's Journey* to books like *Superheroines and the Epic Journey* and *Women in Doctor Who*. She teaches at

Mission College and San Jose City College and speaks often at conferences. You can explore her research at www.vefrankel.com.

Farwa **Javed** is a final-year MPhil scholar in the Department of English at Forman Christian College in Lahore, Punjab, Pakistan. Her research interests include, but are not limited to, modern English and American drama and fiction, modern critical theory and praxis, and gender studies.

Christian **Jimenez** is an independent scholar who has published several essays on race, gender, mass media, and the superhero genre, including "Cynical Tolerance: Gender, Race, and Fraternal Fears in *Sons of Anarchy*," and "Strategies of Containment: Sexual Liberation and Repression in the Sci-Fi Genre." He is working on several projects on Stanley Kubrick, M. Night Shyamalan, and diversity in science fiction.

Shoshana **Kessock** is a writer and game designer. Her work has been included in multiple game design academic journals such as the *Knudpunkt Journal,* and she has contributed blog posts to sites like *Tor.com, Geek Initiative,* and *The Mary Sue,* as well as academic articles deconstructing media for progressive representation. She is the CEO of the independent game design company, Phoenix Outlaw Productions, and is a narrative lead at Meow Wolf.

Patti **McCarthy** is an assistant professor of film at Whittier College. She holds a Ph.D. (critical studies) and an M.F.A. (film production) from USC. Prior to teaching and developing the film studies program at the University of the Pacific, she worked as Head of Development at Rastar Productions at Sony Pictures Entertainment and was involved in the production of many major motion pictures, including: *Random Hearts* (Harrison Ford) and *The Curious Case of Benjamin Button* (Brad Pitt). She is working on two books related to the heroine's journey.

Fernando Gabriel **Pagnoni Berns** is a Ph.D. student and a professor at the Universidad de Buenos Aires (UBA). He teaches courses on international horror film and has published essays in *Divine Horror*, edited by Cynthia Miller, *To See the Saw Movies*, edited by John Wallis, *Critical Insights: Alfred Hitchcock*, edited by Douglas Cunningham, *Reading Richard Matheson*, edited by Cheyenne Mathews, and *Time-Travel Television*, edited by Sherry Ginn, among others.

Tim **Posada** is the chair of Journalism and New Media at Saddleback College. His writings have appeared in *The Journal of Popular Culture*, an edited collection on Batman fandom, another on the ethics of special effects, and a forthcoming piece in a volume on mass hysteria from Cornell University Press. He holds a Ph.D. in cultural studies from Claremont Graduate University.

Martin **Ricksand** is a Ph.D. student in media and communications at the University of Wolverhampton, with a background in film and literary studies. He has written articles about philosophy and ideology in movies by Woody Allen and Lars von Trier for the Scandinavian philosophical journal *Theofilos*. His dissertation examines questions pertaining to the concept of truth in fiction.

José I. Rodríguez, Ph.D., is a professor of communication studies at Long Beach State University. His work has been published in *Text & Performance Quarterly, Western Journal of Black Studies,* and *Communication Education.* He has received research awards from the National Communication Association and the International Communication Association. He tweets (with an intuitive grasp of the obvious) @JRodriguez_Ph.D.

Canela Ailén **Rodriguez Fontao** holds a degree in arts at the Universidad de Buenos Aires (UBA), Argentina. She has published a chapter in *Deconstructing Dads,* edited by Laura Tropp and Janice Kelly, *Romancing the Zombie,* edited by Jessica K. Richards and Ashley Szanter, *Clint Eastwood's Cinema of Trauma,* edited by Charles R. Hamilton and Allen H. Redmon, and *Uncovering Stranger Things,* edited by Kevin J. Wetmore, Jr., among others.

Paula **Talero Álvarez** holds a Ph.D. in media, art, and text from Virginia Commonwealth University, Richmond. Her research problematizes how representation operates in our current cultural circuit, and encompasses film and cultural studies, gender and sexuality studies, and critical media and communication. She is working as a communication and outreach specialist for the Spanish National Research Council in Barcelona, Spain, where she promotes scientific culture.

Don **Tresca** has a master's degree in English from California State University, Sacramento, where he specialized in 20th-century American literature and film studies. He has published essays on a wide variety of pop culture subjects, including the works of Joss Whedon, J.K. Rowling, Stephen King, and Clint Eastwood.

Melissa **Wehler**, Ph.D., serves as the Dean of Humanities and Sciences at Central Penn College, Summerdale, Pennsylvania. Her publications include essays in the edited collections *Exploring Downton Abbey* (2018), *Jessica Jones, Scared Hero* (2018), *A Quest of Her Own* (2014), *Transnational Gothic* (2013), and *Demons of the Body and Mind* (2010). Her forthcoming publications include a coedited volume on *Supergirl.*

Mariana S. **Zárate** has an MA from the Universidad de Buenos Aires (UBA). She has published in *Racism & Gothic,* edited by Universitas Press, *Bullying in Popular Culture,* edited by Abigail G. Scheg, *Projecting the World,* edited by Russell Meeuf, *Uncovering Stranger Things,* edited by Kevin J. Wetmore, Jr., and *The Handmaid's Tale and Philosophy,* edited by Rachel Greene.

Carol **Zitzer-Comfort**, Ph.D., is an associate professor of English at Long Beach State. Her areas of interest include reading and composition, cognitive development, American Indian literature, disability studies, and English education. She has published several journal articles and a book chapter on Williams syndrome, authored a textbook for basic writing, coedited *Through the Eye of the Deer,* and presented at several conferences. She is available via email at carol.comfort@csulb.edu.

Index

224   Index